CHILDREN · OF · THE · GODS

The Complete Myths and Legends of Ancient Greece

KENNETH · McLEISH

CHILDREN OF·THE·GODS

THE · COMPLETE · MYTHS · AND · LEGENDS
OF · ANCIENT · GREECE

Illustrated by

ELISABETH · FRINK

LONGMAN

FOR ANDREW McLEISH

LONGMAN GROUP LIMITED
Longman House, Burnt Mill, Harlow, Essex CM20 2JE, England
and Associated Companies throughout the world

Map and diagrams by Bob Chapman

First published 1983
Second impression 1984
ISBN 0 582 39115 6

Set in 11/13 Linotron Palatino

Printed in Great Britain by Butler & Tanner, Frome

CONTENTS

v

CONTENTS

INTRODUCTION

The Stories

The English word *myth* comes from the Greek word *mythos*. Its first meaning is 'story' – and that explains the purpose of most of the myths in this book. They are folk-stories, made up and told just for the fun of it. In earliest Greek times, several thousand years ago, people lived in scattered villages. Few could read; there was hardly any writing, and there were certainly no books. Story-telling was a main form of entertainment, sometimes among small groups of people, sometimes by professional entertainers (or 'bards') who earned their living by telling stories to large numbers of people at a time.

In later Greek times, when more people could read and write, many of the old folk-stories were collected and written down. Two famous collections (made, perhaps by a writer we call Homer, in about 800 B.C.) were the *Iliad* (telling part of the story of the Trojan War: see chapter 17) and the *Odyssey* (telling Odysseus' adventures: see chapter 18). All Greek schoolchildren learned parts of the *Iliad* and *Odyssey* by heart – and for those of the people who still could not read, they were recited at festivals, or told by bards, just as Greek myths had always been.

The Supernatural

But myths, to the Greeks, were always far more than simple stories. Another meaning of the word *mythos* is 'explanation' – and many myths were made up to give reasons for sights or happenings not otherwise easy to explain. Nowadays we have scientific explanations of such 'natural' events as thunderstorms, earthquakes and tidal waves; the early Greeks thought of them as 'supernatural', and explained them by inventing myths about the gods. Many people also believed that every tree, river, road or field had its guardian spirit. Often, they thought, these spirits appeared to mortals and enjoyed adventures with them – and some myths are stories of adventures just like these. The myths helped to explain the supernatural in ways ordinary mortals could understand.

Later (from about the 7th century B.C.), when books, poems and plays began to be written, writers often took the myths as their starting-point. Everyone knew the basic happenings in a myth; this meant that a writer could adapt it to suit his or her own point of view without making it too hard for the audience to follow. Once, myths had explained how whole villages or districts thought about the supernatural; now they were used to help single individuals put forward new explanations of matters which everybody knew.

Later still, long after Greek civilisation was overcome by the Romans, the old myths lived on. They were still used as the basis for new writing: first by Roman authors (eg Ovid and Virgil), then by later writers in the Middle Ages, the Renaissance and right up to our own time. (Shakespeare, for example, based plays and poems on mythological stories, in exactly the same way as ancient Greek writers like Aeschylus and Euripides had done.) Artists, too, painted pictures and carved sculptures based on Greek myths (the story of Laokoön, page 178, was one favourite): the old folk-myths were as well-known then as stories from the Bible.

This Book

In schools and colleges nowadays, few people still study ancient Greek. But Greek myths live on: many people still enjoy both them and the poems, plays and stories based on them. The first purpose of this book is to give a clear account of each main myth, told straight through without interruption, as all good stories ought to be. Then, for readers who want to use this book for *reference* (to help explain Greek names or references in other books), we have put shorter myths, alternative versions and all kinds of other material in a separate section at the end of the main text. (A * in the text means there is more information in this section. A † at the end of some chapters refers to one of the family charts grouped together separately.) On pages 273–276 are some suggestions for further reading, a first sampling of the marvellous uses later writers have made of myth.

NOTE: Kenneth McLeish's versions of the myths of Prometheus (Chapter 3) and Persephone (Chapter 7) appeared, in a slightly different form, in the myth-collection *Gods and Men* (edited by John Bailey, OUP 1981). We are grateful to the Oxford University Press for permission to reprint them here.

How to pronounce the names

S ome of the best-known names are spelled in their familiar way even if this is far from the original Greek (Oedipus not Oidipous, for example): the index gives the most important Greek or Roman equivalents. So far as Greek forms of names are concerned, two general rules to guide pronunciation are: (1) always pronounce -e at the end of a word as a separate syllable (eg Penelope has four syllables, not three); (2) stress the syllable next before the last (eg Hippo-dam-EI-a). Otherwise, consonants, and the vowels a, e, i, o and u have the same sounds as in English; diphthongs are generally pronounced as follows:

ai (and *ae*) as in English *aisle* (or the 'i' in *fight*)	
au	as in English *fraud*
ei	as in English *eight*
oi	as in English *voice*
eu	as in English *feud*
ou	as in English *soup*

(*ao* is not a diphthong but two separate sounds: Menelaos, for example, is correctly pronounced Me-ne-LA-os.)

Map of main places mentioned in the stories

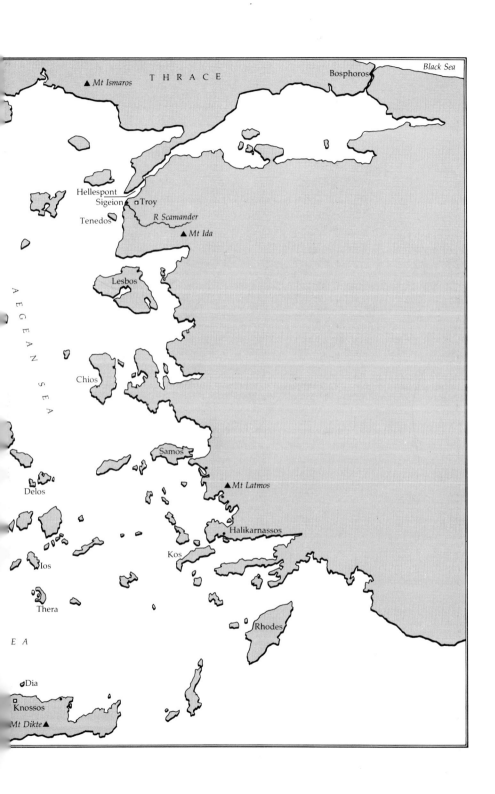

Black Sea

T H R A C E

▲ Mt Ismaros

Bosphoros

Hellespont
Sigeion □ Troy

Tenedos   R Scamander

▲ Mt Ida

Lesbos

A
E
G
E
A
N

S
E
A

Chios

Samos

▲ Mt Latmos

Delos

Halikarnassos

Kos

Ios

Thera

Rhodes

E A

◁Dia

□ Knossos

Mt Dikte▲

1

THE · COMING · OF
THE · GODS

How Earth and Sky began

To begin with, there were no shapes. Nothing existed; there were no forms of things. All the elements and atoms that would one day make matter swirled and seethed in endless, meaningless movement. If a mortal had existed and been able to watch the dance of the elements, it would have seemed as beautiful as dust dancing in a sunshaft. But there was no dust, no sun, no mortal: only the endless dance. The name of the swirling elements was Chaos.

From time to time as things seethed and whirled in Chaos, in the dance of the elements, patterns were formed. For a fleeting moment, in one place or another, shapes appeared: circles, ridges, humps and hollows in the elemental flow. Most of them vanished as quickly as a mirage; but some repeated themselves, growing ever stronger and more permanent. The heavy atoms began to make patterns separately from the light atoms; gradually the patterns of each grew fixed and purposeful, until the first shapes of things were formed. The heavy atoms made the shape called Gaia (Earth): a living organism with clefts, folds and hills like gigantic limbs. The light atoms made Ouranos (Sky): quick-moving, always changing, as restless as breath itself.*

Turning and twisting in the swirl of Chaos, Gaia and Ouranos danced a slow dance of love. Sky embraced Earth; Earth opened herself to Sky and grew fertile. Life-giving rain from Sky sought out Earth's cracks and crevices; streams, rivers and oceans formed; the ground produced trees, green plants and flowers, and soon there were birds, animals and insects of every kind. These were the first children of Earth and Sky.

So they floated peacefully in the space made by their own crea-

1

tion. Earth was like a huge flat dish, hillocked and humped by mountain ranges, river-valleys, lakes and seas; Sky soared above like an umbrella of clouds and light. All round, at Earth's circumference, they touched. The touching-point, the horizon, was marked by a fast-flowing river called Ocean; it whirled round in an endless circle and held everything in place. At the eastern edge of Earth the Sun rose each morning to begin its journey across the dome of Sky; each evening it plunged into Ocean at the western edge and began its night's voyage to the east, ready to emerge again next morning. Below Earth lay the Underworld, so far below that a dropped object would take nine days to reach it. The entrances to the Underworld were at the edge of the circle of Ocean; there were also cracks and openings in Earth's floor itself. The shortest distance between Earth and Sky was at Ocean's edge; the dome of Sky at the centre, its highest point, rose above Earth to the height of three great mountains piled on top of one another, Mount Olympos, Mount Pelion and Mount Ossa.

Monsters

As well as rivers, beasts and plants, Gaia and Ouranos had children of other kinds. They made three giant sons, half men half trees: each had fifty heads and a hundred branching arms and hands. Their names were Briareus (Strong), Gyges (Earthson) and Kottos (Son of the Great Mother). They were squat and brutish, with ungainly, top-heavy bodies. They skulked in dark mountain-valleys, baleful as toads.

After the giant sons, Gaia and Ouranos made three Cyclopes (Round-eyes), a mixture of men and rock and fire. Their names were Brontes (Thunder), Steropes (Lightning) and Arges (Dazzle of Light). Their strength was enormous: they could tear up hills bare-handed and stack mountain-peaks as men stack bricks. They were called 'Round-eyes' because they had one eye each, set in the centre of the forehead.

There were other monsters too. Though Gaia and Ouranos were the most important beings to form from Chaos, they were not the only ones. They had a brother, Erebos (Darkness) and a sister, Night – vast, sombre presences spread like stains across the universe. All round them, Night's children roosted: the Fates, Luck, Justice, Warfare, Dreams, Sleep and Death. Some were transparent, hardly visible, no more than ghost-figures flitting in the mind. Others were like monstrous bats; others like tadpoles writhing in a pond.

The Titans

After the Hundred-handed Giants and the Cyclopes, Gaia and Ouranos had twelve more children, the Titans (Honoured Ones).* The six females were Theia (Divine), Rhea (Earth), Themis (Right), Mnemosyne (Memory), Phoibe (Bright-shining) and Tethys (Settler). The six males were Okeanos (Swift), Koios (Intelligent), Krios (Ram), Hyperion (Dweller-on-high), Iapetos (Racer) and Kronos (Crow). Like their parents Earth and Sky, the Titans were living beings but had no fixed shape. Sometimes they took on human form; sometimes they patterned themselves after water, rocks or fire; sometimes they abandoned shape altogether and spread their essence invisibly across the universe.

Ouranos was a harsh, uncaring father, and his children were rebellious and quarrelsome. In the end he could stand the sight of them no longer. He took the Hundred-handed Giants and the Cyclopes and hurled them down into Tartaros, the distant dark below the Underworld. Then he began prising open the huge body of his consort Gaia and thrusting his other offspring into her deepest clefts and chasms. Earth groaned; rocks splintered; lava boiled red and spat; smoke billowed as the tormented world writhed apart.

As her children cowered in her inmost crevices, Gaia turned to Kronos, her cleverest child, and begged him to fight Sky and end their agony. Deep in Earth's womb, Kronos took a curved metal sickle, toothed like a shark, and sharpened it. Then he hid the blade and waited for his father's next attack.

Roaring and snarling, Sky bore down on Gaia; he was like a flood, a thunderstorm, a dark throat gaping to swallow the land alive. At once Kronos drew his sickle and jumped out of his hiding-place into the teeth of the storm. Hurricanes ripped his flesh; lightning stabbed; acid rain seared his skin. He groped forwards into the howling dark and his hand gripped tight. With his other hand, he brought his sickle round and sliced.

There was an immense sucking hiss, like an indrawn breath of agony. A moment's roaring whirlwind, as if the force of all the universe was gathered into a single scream of shock. A voice began, a whispering roar that grew from silence till it filled the air and pulsed in Kronos' ears. 'As you ... dethrone ... your father ... so your child ... will dethrone you ... As you ... dethrone ... so you will be ... dethroned ...'

The words beat in Kronos' mind like waves against a cliff. He screamed and cringed; his brain fluttered. 'Dethrone ... dethroned ... Dethrone ... dethroned ...' He thought his skull would split.

Then, abruptly, silence. Calm; peace; the storm had gone. Sky was serene and blue overhead; Earth lay placid at his fleet. All anger was spent; it was as if no violence had ever been.

Then, in his left hand, Kronos felt the weight of the thing he had sliced from Ouranos. It was his father's penis. It lay in his hand, bleeding. Kronos held it up in triumph, and crimson blood-drops spattered brown Earth; then he threw it far into the sea, to make the teeming waters fertile for evermore.

So Ouranos was punished and the Titans were set free. They stumbled out from the clefts of Earth and the sunlight warmed them. Sky and Earth, the first beings, had completed their creation. From now on they took no active part in making; they became the background, the fertile soil and the air and rain of life. A new time, the time of Kronos, began. He became ruler of the universe, with his sister Rhea as queen. The other Titans, too, had places to fill and roles to play. Only the Cyclopes and the Hundred-handed Giants had nothing. Kronos left them imprisoned in Tartaros, monsters hidden out of mind and out of sight.

Meanwhile, from the red drops of Sky's blood which fell on Earth, their very last children had been born. There were twenty-four Giants, tall as cliffs, with wild hair and dragons'-tails for feet. They shared their mother's earthy nature and muttered in sympathy for their Giant brothers imprisoned in the Underworld. There were three Erinnyes, the Furies, who took their form and nature from the brooding storm-clouds of their father Sky. And Aphrodite (Foam-born), the immortal goddess of beauty and of love, was created from the foam made by Ouranos' penis when it fell into the sea.

The birth of the gods

For a long time the Titans lived happily and at peace. Each had his or her own territory and place in the scheme of things. The universe was as placid as a warm, calm sea, and the Titans and their children basked in it. The Titans were huge, contented powers untroubled by any kind of thought, ambition or memory.

As they always had, they could change their shapes at will: to think a thing was to become it. It was their delight to frolic across the seas and continents of the world, to take wing and soar in the vastness of space, now meteorites, now planets, now dazzling lights or shadows tumbling in the void.

Only Kronos their king was anxious. From time to time the words of his father Ouranos gathered like storm-clouds in his memory. 'As you dethrone your father, so your child will dethrone you.' The words throbbed and beat – and the more he thought about their meaning, the more he himself changed shape and became his own guilt for Ouranos and fear for his own future. A concentration of agony filled him, pulsating and billowing till he thought his brain must burst.

The pain began, each time, with the start of his consort Rhea's pregnancy. At first it was small and far away, like a distant light; but as the baby grew inside Rhea's womb his terror grew and the light moved nearer. It grew ever faster and brighter, until at last, as the newborn child was placed in his arms, he became a single, searing explosion of torment and fury. In the midst of it, like a helpless leaf, the newborn baby bobbed, floated and was sucked out of sight. At once Kronos' pain receded, his rage was calmed – and the child had disappeared, swallowed whole to end its father's agony.

So, one by one, Kronos' children were born and eaten: Hestia (Hearth and Home), Demeter (Corn Queen), Hera (Protectress), Hades (Invisible) and Poseidon (Drink-giver).

The children's mother, Rhea, knew nothing of Kronos' inner pain and fear: she saw only mindless cruelty. As her next pregnancy progressed and she saw Kronos growing ever more irritable, she determined that this child at least would survive to enjoy the light of day. She bore her third son, Zeus (Shining Sky), at midnight, in the shadowless darkness of Wolf-mountain in Arcadia; at once she had him carried away to Crete and hidden in the Diktean Cave, deep in a forest on a lonely mountain-side.

5

Rhea wrapped a stone in baby-clothes and took it to Kronos. Blurry-eyed, agonised from the blackness inside his skull, he snatched the 'child' and gulped it down. At once, as it always did, the pain vanished. He smiled – and Rhea smiled.

In Crete, in the mountain woods beside the Diktean Cave, the child Zeus was looked after by two mountain-nymphs, Adrasteia and Io. His cradle, plaited from strips of gold, hung on a tree-branch. (That way, if Kronos ever heard of his son's existence, Rhea could say truthfully that he was hidden neither on land nor in sky nor sea.) In the cave-mouth was a curtain of bees, who provided wild honey for Zeus' nourishment. For milk he sucked the teats of Amaltheia,* half nymph half she-goat; side by side with Amaltheia's own baby Pan, he fed and slept and grew. He was guarded by warrior-spirits called Curetes (Shaven Ones);* whenever the baby cried they howled and danced, clattering their spears against their shields to keep his wailing from Kronos' ears.

So Zeus grew up, safe from his father's rage. At last, when he was fully grown, it was time to punish his father and claim his inheritance. He went for advice to Metis (Cunning). She was a Titan, a daughter of Air and Earth, and took Rhea's side in the matter of Kronos and the children. She lived in a far corner of the world, beside the swirl of Ocean. She was hard to find and harder to talk to, for she disliked taking recognisable shape and preferred to hover invisibly in empty air. As Zeus watched she took on different shapes before his eyes, finally settling as a creature part owl, part fox, part snake.

'Speak, Zeus,' she said at last. 'What do you want?'

'My throne, and Kronos' punishment.'

'Go to him. Your mother Rhea will persuade him to make you his cup-bearer. Give him a drink of nectar, mixed with these herbs.'

No more than that, and she was gone. Where she had been, a tuft of grey herbs grew beside a stone. Zeus gathered them and went to Kronos' palace on Mount Othrys. His mother Rhea knew him at once; but Kronos suspected nothing – had he not swallowed all his children as they were born?

For Titans, eating and drinking were new ideas. Animals and birds took food and drink, but the Titans fed on light and air and needed no other nourishment. Kronos, therefore, thought that swallowing a drink would be a delightful new game to try. He watched with interest as Zeus filled a goblet with nectar (a mixture of grape juice, water and honey), sprinkled grey herbs on top, and handed him the goblet. Kronos raised it to his lips and drank.

At once he was engulfed with the agony that had accompanied all his children's births. But this time, instead of coming gradually from a long distance, it swooped on him instantly and complete, an explosion of torment beyond endurance. He writhed and vomited – and as he vomited, up from his gullet came first the stone Rhea had given him in place of Zeus, then his five children, unharmed and whole. His two sons, Hades and Poseidon, and his three daughters, Demeter, Hestia and Hera, were all reborn as full-grown, immortal gods.

The throne of Zeus

For forty seasons of the world, civil war rumbled round the universe. On one side were the male Titans: huge, slow-thinking and powerful, the dinosaur bones and sinews of creation. Their leader was Atlas,* their citadel Kronos' palace on Mount Othrys. On the other side were Zeus, Poseidon, Hades and their followers: less powerful but quicker-thinking, faster and more organised. Their citadel was on the peaks of Mount Olympos in Greece. Brute strength fought strategy; brawn locked with brains.

Because the combatants were immortal, they suffered no casualties. The war-victim was the world itself. What had once been placid and beautiful became a ragged no-man's-land. The air was torn by storms; sunlight gave way to searing rain; clouds flinched from the fighters' rage. On earth the battle left broken wreckage of ice and stone, splintered mountain-peaks, chasms and cracks like wounds bubbling white-hot rock. Plants, trees, animals, birds and insects shrank into crevices or were blotted out.

At last Gaia, mother Earth herself, tired of the pointless struggle and whispered to Zeus a way to finish it. Leaving his brothers to distract the Titans, he made his way down to the Underworld, and deeper still to the empty halls of Tartaros. In later ages, in the time of mortal people, these eerie caverns would be thronged with the souls of the dead; but now they were gaunt and empty, filled only with booms and echoes from the battle overhead.

Deep in the vaults of Tartaros were the prison cells where Zeus' father Kronos had locked the Cyclopes and their brothers the Hun-

7

dred-handed Giants. All through the reign of the Titans they had lain there, brooding on revenge. They were guarded by Kampe, a she-monster gnarled and bent with age. Her power had long begun to fade; her limbs shook with senility and grey wisps of hair straggled on a bony skull. But there was still an ember of aggression, a memory of her purpose, inside her crazed old mind. When she heard Zeus' footstep she hissed, turned sightless eyes on him and crooked her talons.

But her strength no sooner flickered than it was spent: she crumbled before him into a pile of dusty bones and rotting cloth. Zeus took her keys and began to unchain the prisoners, stepping warily across their sprawled limbs and brainless, gulping heads. Their minds were as sluggish as their limbs were cramped; blinking, licking their lips, they stood and watched him, pathetic hulks from a forgotten age.

At first it seemed that they would make useless allies. Their strength had wasted away and left nothing but sour resentment. But Zeus gave them nectar to drink, and it brought strength back to them as sap brings life to trees. They stretched, they straightened, they seemed to flower and grow. They felt their power; they remembered Kronos, the cause of their anger; their eyes flashed fury and they roared their rage.

At once the blacksmith Cyclopes found fire and set to work. They fashioned three weapons: for Hades a helmet of darkness, for Poseidon a three-pronged trident and for Zeus himself thunder, captured and stored in a thunderbolt. Zeus took the weapons and soared to Mount Olympos; the Cyclopes and Hundred-handed Giants stayed hidden in Tartaros till he gave them the signal to attack.

Without hesitation Zeus, Poseidon and Hades put their plan to work. First Hades, invisible in his helmet of darkness, crept into Kronos' citadel Mount Othrys and stole his weapons; then Poseidon appeared before Kronos and threatened him with his trident; while Kronos' attention was distracted, Zeus hurled the thunderbolt and stunned him to the ground. Then Zeus gave the signal and the Hundred-handed Giants streamed up from Tartaros, began tearing up boulders and jagged rocks and hurling them at the Titans. As the Titans retreated from this unexpected attack, Zeus' foster-brother Pan (who had grown up with him in Crete) gave an enormous shout that sent panic echoing round the universe. The Titans turned tail; the gods had won.

8

One by one the defeated Titans were rounded up and taken to Zeus' citadel on Mount Olympos. He showed mercy only to those such as Metis and Prometheus who had taken his side in the war.* The others were locked away in Tartaros, guarded by the Hundred-handed Giants. Atlas, their war-leader, was made to stand for all eternity on the edge of Africa, supporting on his shoulders the arching, crushing weight of the sky.

So the dawn age of the Titans came to an end and the long daylight of the Olympian gods began.*†

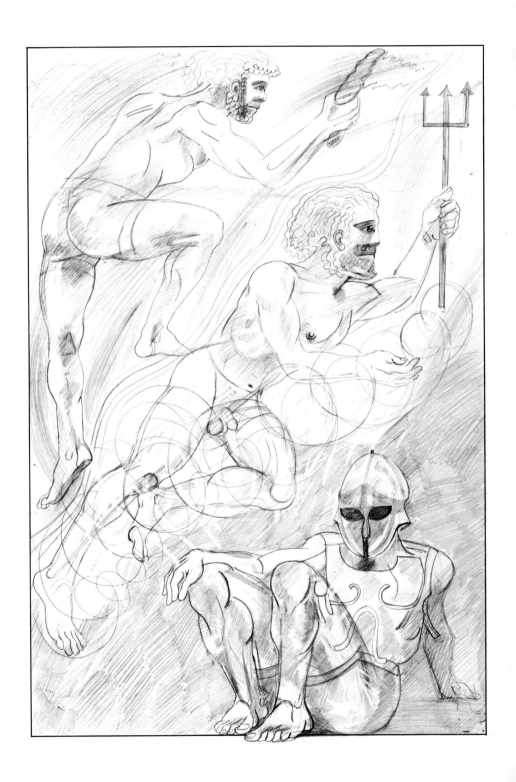

2
RULERS · OF · OLYMPOS

Zeus and Hera

Although the gods' victory ended the war in the universe, it brought no peace to Olympos itself. Two of Kronos' six children, Hestia and Demeter, were gentle and unambitious, content to accept whatever came their way. But each of the others, Zeus, Poseidon, Hades and Hera, wanted the royal power he or she had helped to win.

The three male gods met to decide the issue. There was no sense in fighting. The universe was already in tatters from the war with the Titans, and in any case each brother still had his own powerful weapon: Hades his helmet of darkness, Poseidon his trident and Zeus an unending supply of thunderbolts. In the end they decided to cast lots for kingdoms. They shook three differently-coloured pebbles in a helmet and spilled them out. The lots gave Zeus the sky, Poseidon the sea and Hades the Underworld. The earth was left as common territory, to be enjoyed by all.

So the three brothers were satisfied. Poseidon built himself a palace under the sea near Aigai in Greece, Hades set up court in the echoing halls of the Underworld, and Zeus made his palace on Mount Olympos. In their own kingdoms their power was absolute: no other god could interfere or challenge their authority. Demeter and Hestia settled peacably on earth. Demeter took charge of the harvest and all growing things, and Hestia looked after hearth and home.

Only Hera appeared to be forgotten. Furious, she set up home on Mount Thornax. It was a desolate, comfortless place of mist and rain. No one else lived there – and those who took the trouble to visit her were turned sharply away, unheard.

11

But Zeus found a way to win her round. He decided to make her his queen and consort in the court of Heaven. The problem was, how was he to persuade her? Her anger was like a throbbing wound: she sat sullenly on Mount Thornax and saw no one.

One day, while she was out walking alone on the mountain-side after a rain-storm, Hera heard a despairing, two-note cry in the undergrowth. Huddled among the bracken was a small, bedraggled cuckoo, feebly fluttering and trying to preen its feathers dry. Filled with pity, Hera picked it up and laid it against her bosom, in the folds of her dress, to warm it back to life.

At once, in the blink of an eye, the cuckoo disappeared and in its place was her brother Zeus. Before she could break free he held her, kissed her and persuaded her to become his queen.

Zeus and Hera spent their wedding night on the island of Samos. To gods it was a single night; to mortals it would have been three hundred years. Then they set up court on Mount Olympos, and for a time there was contentment in the universe. (Mount Thornax was renamed Cuckoo Mountain, and the cuckoo became a cheat till the end of time, forever lying in the nests of other birds.)

Zeus and Hera had children: Ares and his twin sister Eris, Hephaistos, Eileithuia and Hebe. But Zeus was a restless lover, not content with a single wife. He slept with Maia, Atlas' daughter, and their child was Hermes. He took the form of a quail and slept with Leto, daughter of the Titans Koios and Phoibe; there were two children, Apollo and his sister Artemis. Zeus slept with Themis, creator and guardian of the turning year, and was the father of the Seasons; with Mnemosyne (Memory) he was the father of the Muses.

Zeus' most astonishing fatherhood came when he slept with Metis, the Titan who had helped him in the war against Kronos. Before Metis' child was born, Mother Earth prophesied that if she had a boy-child he would dethrone his father, just as Zeus had dethroned Kronos and Kronos Ouranos. To prevent this, Zeus swallowed Metis alive. Shortly afterwards, he began to suffer from an appalling headache. He paced up and down beside Lake Tritonis in Libya, roaring and grinding his teeth with pain; the sky groaned in sympathy with its master's agony; no one knew the headache's cause or cure. At last Zeus asked Hermes to help him. Hermes called to Hephaistos to bring a hammer and a wedge. Hephaistos placed the wedge on Zeus' forehead and struck a single, careful blow – and in the instant before the wound healed up (for the wounds of the gods are short-lived and trifling) Metis' child, the goddess Athene, was born, springing out fully grown and fully armed from her father's head.*

Zeus' constant love-affairs were not at all to Hera's liking. She also remembered how he had tricked her on Cuckoo Mountain; and above all she was jealous of his power. He ruled by thunderbolts: he alone knew how to wield them, and every other god was afraid of them. Zeus made the laws, fixed the stars' courses in the sky and the order of the seasons, and proclaimed the future in omens and oracles. He was all-knowing, all-powerful and arrogant; the only times Hera could master him were when she borrowed Aphrodite's girdle of desire (a belt that made the wearer irresistible) and charmed him into making love.

The revolt of the gods

Hera began plotting with the other gods to overthrow Zeus and end his tyranny. They knew that they must catch him unawares, before he had time to snatch up a thunderbolt. So they crept up on him when he was sleeping, and tied him to his bed. Zeus woke with a start and found himself helpless. The ropes were leather; they were tied in a hundred knots; he could not move. He raged to the gods to release him or die. But they were immortal – and in any case his thunderbolts were out of reach. They laughed in his face and went off, discussing who should sit first on the royal throne.

Discussion turned to argument. Storm-clouds billowed; the earth shook with the echoes of their rage. Terrified of another civil war, the ocean-nymph Thetis went down to Tartaros to fetch Briareus, leader of the Hundred-handed Giants. Blinking in the sunlight, Briareus scrambled across the plains of Greece and up the steep slopes of Olympos. He untied the leather knots, using all hundred hands at once, and Zeus was free.

Zeus appeared before the gods, who were still squabbling in the council chamber. His thunderbolt was in his hand; anger flashed like lightning in his eyes. He snatched Hera and strung her up on the roof of the sky by golden chains round each wrist. To make her torment more excruciating, he hung an anvil, a heavy block of iron, on each of her ankles. Then he took his thunderbolt and stood on guard beside her.

Hera dangled, screaming to the other gods to overpower Zeus

13

and rescue her. But they were afraid of the thunderbolt. They stood in a helpless, shamefaced group.

'Bow down!' said Zeus. 'Bow down and swear loyalty!'

The gods looked furtively at one another. Who would refuse? Who would stand up to Zeus? None of them. One by one they knelt, clasped Zeus' knee in one hand and his beard in the other, and swore loyalty. Hera was last. Zeus cut loose the anvils and freed her wrists; tearful and trembling she knelt and swore the oath.

After that, there was no more rebellion in Olympos. Zeus ruled, and the other gods accepted his authority. He punished Poseidon and Apollo, the chief rebels, by making them servants, for a time, to a mortal man (he was King Laomedon, and their task was to build him a city: Troy). But for gods this punishment, though humiliating, was light, short and soon forgotten.

At first Zeus hardly changed his ways: he was unbending and arrogant, just as before. But the longer he remained king the more he grew in wisdom, until he was ruler of the universe by right as well as by force of arms. Even so, Hera never approved of his love-affairs, and the married life of the king and queen of heaven was often sharp and quarrelsome.

3
THE · MAKING · OF HUMANKIND

Claypeople

In their new kingdom, the gods were settled and secure. Their universe was bounded by the deep darkness of space, and by the sun's brightness glinting and glowing from the waters of the earth and from the marble palaces of Mount Olympos. They lived in royal ease, galloping their chariots down wide star-highways or taking their places at banquets and councils on polished thrones in marble halls.

The earth was their pleasure-garden. It offered orchards, rippling meadows, placid lakes – or snowfields, glacial peaks, seas snarling at jagged peaks. Its animals were their servants and their pets; its fruits and elements were their delight.

One of earth's elements for which there seemed no use was clay. It was flabby and sterile: too limp for building (and not needed when stone and wood were plentiful), too waterlogged to nourish growing plants.

It was Prometheus (Forethought) who discovered what to do with it. He was a Titan, the son of Iapetos and Themis. His half-brother Atlas had led the Titans in their war against the gods; but Prometheus had supported the gods, and so escaped banishment to Tartaros. He had held Zeus' aching head for Hephaistos to split open and release Athene, and as a reward she had taught him every art and science, from geography, mathematics and medicine to mining and metalwork.

Prometheus used Earth's clay to make images, little statues of the gods.* They were the first fine art, the first copies of reality made for no other reason than to give delight. They were also the origin of humankind:* for Athene was so charmed with Prometheus' model

15

figures that she breathed on them and brought them to life. Like tiny, naked doll-gods they tottered at Prometheus' feet, unsteady as foals, squealing like kittens fumbling for their mother.

Prometheus was delighted with his new creatures, and determined to teach them language, cultivation, seafaring – in fact, to share with them all the knowledge of the gods. This plan did not appeal to Zeus. The storm of his anger roared across the universe, darkening the stars. It whirled like a hurricane round Prometheus' head, till even the Titan flinched.

But there was nothing to be done. Human beings were made and could not be unmade. At last Zeus crashed his sceptre on the marble floor and said, 'Very well! Your people may live. But they must live like beasts in the fields, innocent and free, without understanding, guilt or memory. They must be denied knowledge.'

'Even knowledge of the gods?'

'No. They must know us and fear us. They must worship us and sacrifice the best of their flocks and herds to us. See to it!'

Prometheus went down into the world. He watched his humans scurrying about, busy as ants, and pitied them. They were so clever, so dexterous, so godlike – why must they know nothing but pain and fear?

From Olympos, Zeus was watching. He saw the toiling mortals and Prometheus like a hillside above them. He saw the pity in Prometheus' heart. It was time to act. He sent for Hephaistos, craftsman of the gods, and ordered him to make a clay doll in the shape of Aphrodite. When it was finished, Athene breathed into it the breath of life, just as she had with Prometheus' dolls. Pandora (All-gifts), the first woman, was created. The Graces gave her beauty; Peitho (Persuasion) gave her charm; the Seasons garlanded her with flowers, and last of all Hermes taught her lies and treachery. Zeus hid her away in the recesses of Olympos until he had need of her.

Meanwhile, on earth, Prometheus took a magnificent bull, the finest and most perfect animal in the world, and slaughtered it. He skinned it and divided the meat. He gathered the bones and fat and wrapped them carefully in the beautiful, creamy-brown hide. He stuffed the lean red meat into the foul-smelling bag of the stomach. Then he shouldered the bundles and went back to Zeus.

'Choose, lord,' he said. 'One bag for the gods, the other for mortals. Your choice will fix the way of sacrifice forever.'

Zeus looked at the bundles, the smooth unblemished sack of hide and the oozing bag of guts. 'Let the gods' portion be . . . this one,' he said, pointing to the hide. But when Prometheus opened it and showed a pile of bones wrapped in yellow fat, his fury shook Olympos. 'So be it!' he shouted. 'Let the gods' portion be bones and fat! As for mortals, from this moment onwards let them eat their meat raw. They are forbidden fire!'

Prometheus bowed his head. For every advantage gained by mortals, there was an equal penalty. And Zeus had not finished with humankind. He fetched Pandora, beautiful and treacherous, and sent her as a gift – not to any mortal or to Prometheus, but to Prometheus' slow-witted brother Epimetheus (Afterthought). Prometheus had warned Epimetheus to trust no gifts from Zeus; but Pandora soon charmed his heart and he accepted her. As a wedding gift she brought with her a small, sealed jar. Like inquisitive forest creatures, mortals gathered shyly round, their eyes bright with curiosity but without understanding.

Pandora fumbled with the seal, and at last broke it and opened the jar. At once, from inside, a low buzzing began and grew into a cloud of insects that flew up and blanketed the sun. They were the Spites, Zeus' gift to humankind: Old Age, Disease, Delusion, Passion, Wickedness, Despair . . . Biting and stinging, they pursued the herd of mortals across the world. In the dropped jar, stuck to the stopper like a shrivelled seed, Hope lay unnoticed. Even when Zeus sends evil, he still allows the possibility of good.

Fire-thief

So man came to the earth, and woman too; and with them came every kind of plague, mischief and disaster. Prometheus' people were hardly equipped to survive; their creator was forbidden to teach them necessary skills – and now Zeus, although he could not personally destroy what another god had made, arranged things so that the world's seasons would do his work for him.

Winter came . . . and with it came humankind's first snow. It whispered across fields and forests, settling on the branches like a soft, white death. It slipped soundlessly into cracks between the rocks, and choked the gullies where sheep huddled and died. In lakes and the sea snowflakes disappeared and died. There was no sound.

In caves, under trees, men and women cowered for warmth. They were naked, their skin putty-coloured and pitted with cold. They looked at the falling snow with gentle eyes: without intelligence, they saw no link between the white drifts and the chill that dulled their bones. Like sheep they huddled and watched, and died.

From up above, where the gods feasted in the palace halls of Olympos, warmed by iron fire-baskets glowing on the polished floors, Prometheus looked down and pitied them. If once they understood, if once the spark of knowledge glowed, their minds would become fertile with the secrets of nature, the secrets of the gods. Wrapping his shadow-cloak about him, he stood up and slipped away. No one noticed: sweating, laughing, joking, the gods continued their feast.

Wrapped in his cloak, soaring like a night-bird, Prometheus passed from the home of the gods to the earth below. He made his way deep inside, to the caverns of Sicily. Here, in the searing heat below the earth's crust, were the blacksmiths' forges where the Cyclopes sweated and toiled, shaping earth's iron bones into thunderbolts for Zeus. Fires flickered and roared; hammers thudded and anvils rang; waste rock, white-hot, flowed out through vent-holes on the surface, the volcanoes of Sicily.

Unseen, Prometheus knelt by a stream of glowing fire. From his belt he took a stalk of the green fennel-plant and split it open. The inside was hollow and damp: it would keep a glowing coal alive. Quickly he took a coal, slipped it inside the stalk and drew back into the shadows.

Fire! Prometheus' last gift to mortals. The fire of intelligence, to save them from death and teach them the secrets of the gods. When Zeus next looked out over the earth (a morning later, to the gods; to mortals, a dozen generations), the world had changed. From every part of it pencils of smoke rose up from the wink and glint of cooking-fires. Men and women hurried about, eager and purposeful. They wore clothes of animal-skin and woven cloth; they had learned farming, sailing, a thousand crafts and skills; they were busy with markets, parliaments, fishing, hunting and harvesting. And above all, they had learned speech: a hum of voices, a bee-swarm of languages, rose up and drowned the wind's rustle, the murmur of the sea.

Zeus' anger was a lightning-storm, a blare of thunder. The sky darkened; the earth shook; the gods shrank back in fear. And for Prometheus, Fire-thief, there was no escape. There was the hiss of a

thunderbolt, a flare of light, an eruption of pain. Black, greasy smoke; a stench of charred flesh; silence.

There was worse to come. Might and Force, the gods' slaves, gathered up the rags of Prometheus' body. Hermes led them and Hephaistos limped beside them with chains of unbreakable steel. They took Prometheus to Mount Caucasus, a jagged tooth of rock in thin, cold air. Might and Force stretched him on tiptoe and held his arms high while Hephaistos chained him to the rock.

Their job done, the gods went back to Olympos. Prometheus was left alone. He could see and hear nothing. His charred flesh stuck to the rock; his muscles locked with cramp; his wrists and ankles were ripped ragged by the chains. Then, in the echoing dark, he heard wings whirr. A black shape loomed over him. There was a searing pain as a curved beak tore into his ribs, stripping its way past bone and sinew till it found his liver.

The vulture of Zeus. All day it gorged on his flesh. At night it rested, and his wounds healed ready for the next day's pain. Prometheus, Fire-thief, was locked in an eternity of suffering. He knew before he stole that this would be his punishment. He knew it and chose it. To save his creation, he chose to destroy himself.*

Mother's bones

For an age of the world, while Prometheus suffered on Mount Caucasus, his creation prospered. Prosperity bred confidence; confidence bred pride; pride bred arrogance, until some mortals snapped their fingers and mocked the gods.

Among the most arrogant of all were Lykaon's fifty sons, the princes of Arcadia. Long ago their father had angered Zeus by offering him human sacrifice, and Zeus had punished him by turning him into a wolf. Now the sons repeated their father's crime. When Zeus visited their palace, disguised as a mortal traveller, they served him a stew made from the innards of their own brother Nuktimos. Zeus was so revolted that he not only changed them into a pack of wolves on the spot, but also sent a great flood to wash the world clean of humanity forever.

At first, when the rain began, people mistook it for a summer shower. They splashed through the puddles, laughing and shaking the drops from their eyes. It was freak weather; it would soon pass. But instead of easing, the rain grew heavier. Day after day, cold winds gusted in and whipped the drops to torrents. Puddles turned to ponds, ponds to lakes, lakes to seas. Rivers burst their banks and flooded the countryside; crops were ruined, animals drowned, houses and villages engulfed.

As the waters rose, the people of the earth crowded for safety on to higher and higher ground. Now they remembered the gods: re-membered and cursed them. Prometheus' creatures were as they had been before he gave them fire: they knew nothing and understood nothing; they huddled together against the storm and died. Finally, Zeus gave his brother Poseidon the word to open the floodgates of the sea. A wall of water roared across the world and swallowed it. People and animals were swept away like toys; houses splintered; for a time there was crashing and shrieking – but not for long.

Only two people knew what to do: Deucalion King of Phthia and his wife Pyrrha. Deucalion was Prometheus' own son, and had vi-sited his father in his agony on Mount Caucasus. There Prometheus had warned him of the flood and told him to build a boat, place in it food and fire and prepare to ride out the flood. Now, as the tidal wave filled every cranny of the world till there was nothing to be seen but smooth, calm water, Deucalion's boat bobbed safely on the surface.

Bubbling and gurgling, the water at last began to recede. First mountaintops, then forests appeared, then muddy lowlands steam-ing in the sun. There was no life: as the water slid away it carried with it every trace of living things. The world was as empty, as fresh and clean, as if human beings had never existed.

Deucalion and Pyrrha beached their boat on a hillside, Mount Par-nassos. They stepped out on to the damp turf and stared round in dismay. There were no birds, no insects, no animals. Except for water dripping and gurgling on every side, the world was still.

There was a shrine of Themis nearby, on the bank of the river Kephissos. Its marble columns steamed in the sun; its roof was co-vered with flood-debris: weed and twigs. Deucalion and Pyrrha fell on their knees and begged Zeus to renew the earth, to stock it once more with living things.

Zeus answered their prayer. All round them, the damp woods were suddenly busy with the chirp and rustle of newly-awakened life. And a voice filled the air, whispering to Deucalion and Pyrrha the words of Themis herself: 'Mother's bones ... gather ... throw ... Mother's bones ... mother's ... bones ...'

After a moment's bewilderment, Deucalion and Pyrrha understood. Their real mother was dead and long forgotten. The voice was speaking of Mother Earth, and her bones were stones. Deucalion bent down, picked up a pebble and threw it over his shoulder, holding his breath to see what would happen.

As soon as the pebble touched the ground, it turned into a young man: tall, laughing, strong.

Slowly at first, then faster and faster, Deucalion and Pyrrha began gathering pebbles and throwing them over their shoulders. Deucalion's stones turned into men and Pyrrha's into women.* Prometheus' creation was born again – this time with Zeus' help and full approval.

4
THE · LAST · REVOLTS
AGAINST · THE · GODS

The Earthborn

While the gods' attention was distracted by Prometheus and his new creation, Mother Earth (who was still furious at the way they had long ago treated her children the Titans), awoke the twenty-four Gegeneis (Earthborn) and sent them to attack Olympos. The Earthborn were the giants born from the blood-drops spilt on Mother Earth after Ouranos was mutilated by his son Kronos; they were huge creatures with man-like heads and bodies, manes of writhing snakes and dragons' tails for feet. Because they were made from earth, there was no way of destroying them so long as they remained near their place of birth: if they were killed they simply melted into their native soil, were reborn and sprang up again. For this reason they decided to attack Olympos from their actual birth-place, Phlegra in Thrace; and to give themselves extra protection they began looking for a magic herb called *ephialtion* (pouncer) which heals the wounds of anyone who chews it. While some of the Earthborn searched for ephialtion, others began making a pile of stones in Phlegra: when it was high enough they meant to jump across into Olympos and attack the gods.

This surprise attack might have succeeded. But their fury drove out their common sense, and long before the stone-pile was finished they began pelting Olympos with boulders and treetrunks from the top of it, trying to terrify the gods.

Hastily, the gods held a council of war. They asked Hera to look into the future and tell them how to win the battle. 'Two things are certain,' she said. 'We must find ephialtion before they do, and we must ask for the help of a mortal dressed in a lion-skin. Without him, Olympos is sure to fall.'

25

Athene, goddess of wisdom, knew at once which mortal Hera meant. 'His name is Herakles,' she said. 'His magic arrows never miss. While I find him, the rest of you search for ephialtion. Look carefully, and in the meantime darken the earth to delay the giants.'

Zeus ordered the Sun and Moon to hold back their light. Darkness flowed over the earth. Athene hurried to fetch Herakles, and the other gods groped for ephialtion in all the world's corners and crevices. At last Zeus found it and took it back to Olympos.

While this was going on, the Earthborn had taken advantage of the darkness to finish their pile of stones. When the Sun and Moon began to shine again, the first thing the gods saw was Alkyoneus, leader of the Earthborn, on top of the stone-pile, ready to jump across into Olympos.

The sudden light dazzled Alkyoneus. He stood teetering on the topmost boulder, shielding his eyes. Just at that moment, Athene came back with Herakles. Herakles hastily aimed, and fired an arrow which struck Alkyoneus to the heart and toppled him from the stone-pile. But as soon as the giant's body touched his native earth in Phlegra his strength was restored, and he leapt up snarling as before. Herakles jumped down from Olympos, dragged him by his snaky hair across the border into the next country and clubbed him dead.

Meanwhile the other Earthborn were clambering up the stone-pile and leaping across into Olympos. Mother Earth gave them power almost enough to match the gods': the Olympians could wound them and hold them back, but only Herakles' arrows could finally destroy them. Porphyrion tried to choke Hera in his serpent's coils; he was slowed down by an arrow from Eros and a thunderbolt from Zeus, but it was not till Herakles climbed back from Phlegra and shot him that he finally died. Ephialtes beat Ares to his knees and was about to finish him; he was stopped just in time by an arrow from Apollo in his left eye and one from Herakles in his right.

So the battle raged. Dionysos fought the Earthborn Eurytos; Hekate fought Klytios; Athene fought Pallas; Hephaistos fought Mimas (using a ladle of red-hot iron) — and would have lost if Helios had not dazzled Mimas in the nick of time; the Fates beat back the giants with pestles and mortars from the Olympian kitchens. Each time one of the Earthborn fell, Herakles was there with an arrow to finish him.

At last the Earthborn gave ground, and began scrambling down their stone-pile to safety in Phlegra. But the gods ripped up whole mountains and islands and hurled them after them. Athene crushed

Enkelados with Sicily; Poseidon broke off Nisyros, part of the island of Kos, and used it to smash Polyboutes under the sea and drown him. The Earthborn made a last rally at Trapezos in Arcadia; but away from their native country they were no match for the gods or for Herakles' arrows, and were all finally killed. Their huge bodies were buried deep in Mother Earth, and a volcano was piled above each of them so that they could never rise again.*

Typhon

After the destruction of the Earthborn, Mother Earth slept with Tartaros, and gave birth to the largest and foulest monster in the universe. Its name was Typhon (Smoke/Hurricane), and when its wings and limbs were at full stretch it covered an area equal to the entire land-area of Greece. From its rocky trunk sprouted a hundred dragons' heads; its countless arms and legs were snakes; its wings darkened the sky; its eyes flashed flame, and its mouths spat molten rock.

When this monster began battering itself against Olympos, the gods fled to Egypt, disguised themselves as animals, and cowered till the danger was past. Only Athene stayed; from Olympos she jeered at Zeus (disguised in Egypt as a trembling ram) until she shamed him into flying back to fight. He sent Typhon reeling with a thunderbolt, and ran to finish him with the sickle his father Kronos had used to mutilate Ouranos.

But Typhon, even weakened by a thunderbolt, was more than a match for Zeus. He twined his serpents round him and flew to a cave on Mount Kasios in Syria. There he took the sickle and hacked out the sinews of Zeus' hands and feet. Zeus' immortal flesh soon healed; but without sinews he lay helpless, unable to move. Typhon gave the sinews to a she-monster, Delphyne, to guard, and flew off to deal with the other gods.

In the meantime, however, Athene had persuaded Hermes and Pan to leave Egypt and come and fight. They crept to Delphyne's cave. Pan sent his terrible shout echoing across the countryside, and while Delphyne shrank back in panic, Hermes replaced the sinews in Zeus' limbs. Zeus snatched up his thunderbolts and raged after Typhon.

Typhon had gone to Mount Nysa (where Dionysos had once invented wine) and demanded food and drink. The three Fates were waiting there; they enticed him and flattered him, but instead of giving him immortal food they gave him wine to drink and a fruit called 'for a day' – mortal nourishment which would weaken him and sap his strength. Cheated and satisfied, he flew out across Mount Haimos in Thrace, and the battle with Zeus began.

Even weakened by mortal food, Typhon still had the strength of a thousand gods. His weapons were whole mountains, ripped up and thrown at Zeus. There was no defeating him by force: the only possible weapon was cleverness. So, instead of aiming his thunderbolts at Typhon himself, Zeus aimed them at the hills he hurled. The blast turned the rocks in mid-air; they crashed back on Typhon and battered him to the ground. Jagged splinters tore his flesh; his blood dyed the mountain red and gave it its name (Mount Haimos means Mount Blood); roaring in agony, he picked up his ragged body and fluttered to Sicily.

Now Zeus used strength. He tore up Mount Etna by the roots and flung it at Typhon. The monster was battered by tonne after tonne of rock; hurtling like a meteorite, he plummeted to earth; Mount Etna crashed down on top of him, and its weight pushed him through the earth's crust, through the Underworld, down to the dark chasms of his father Tartaros. There he lay broken and submissive, Zeus' prisoner.*

5
STORIES · OF
THE · GODS

Hermes

Hermes was the son of Zeus and Maia. He was born in a cave on Mount Kyllene in Arcadia, and his nursemaid was the mountain-nymph Kyllene herself.

From the moment of his birth Hermes was full of pranks. He was born at dawn; three hours later he was running about; at noon he slipped out of the cave to explore the world outside. On the path by the cave-mouth he found a discarded tortoise-shell. He stretched three strings (made of plaited grass) across the hollow side; when he plucked them with his fingers they made musical notes. So he invented the lyre – and Maia was so charmed by its music that she forgot to scold Hermes for wandering away.

That evening Hermes wandered even further. He toddled all the way from Kyllene to Pieria at the foot of Mount Olympos (several hundred kilometres, a good walk even for a baby god) and there found a herd of magnificent cattle browsing in a field. They were the gods' cattle, and they were in the charge of Hermes' half-brother Apollo. Hermes gave the guard-dogs a herb which drugged them asleep. Then he chose fifty of the finest cows, covered their hooves with shoes of plaited grass and drove them tails-first as far as Pylos, where he hid them in a cave. He sacrificed the two most perfect, and divided up their meat in honour of the gods. For himself he kept only the hides and seven lengths of cow-gut, to make strings for his newly-invented lyre. With these he toddled back to Kyllene, climbed into his cradle and went to sleep.

Next morning, when Apollo came to inspect the herd, he found fifty cows missing. There were no hoof-tracks: all he found was the blurred print of many shod feet – and the tracks ended at the field's edge, as if an army had marched up to it and then disappeared into thin air. Baffled, Apollo sent the Satyrs (fast-running forest spirits with men's bodies and goats' legs and hooves) bounding all over Greece to look for the cattle.

In fact it was not the Satyrs but chance that showed him where they were hidden. While Hermes was taking the cows to Pylos, he'd met an old farmer on the road, and bribed him to tell no one of the extraordinary sight he'd seen: fifty cows walking backwards, led by a toddling baby. If he'd known the old man's name he'd have spared his breath, for it was Battos (Blabberer). As soon as Apollo asked, Battos eagerly told him everything.

Apollo stormed angrily to Maia's cave on Mount Kyllene. 'Where are those cattle?' he shouted.

'Shh!' Maia said. 'You'll wake the baby. Look how peacefully he's sleeping.'

'He's pretending. Hermes, give back those cattle.'

Hermes sat up. 'What are cattle?' he asked innocently.

But Apollo saw the hides of the two sacrificed cows spread out in a corner of the cave. He bundled them under one arm, picked up wriggling Hermes in the other and went straight to Olympos. He dumped Hermes and the hides before Zeus' throne and started to complain. Halfway through, he noticed a broad smile on Zeus' face. This was because, even while Apollo was accusing him of theft, Hermes had cheekily crawled behind him and stolen his bow and arrows.

Baby or not, Hermes was clearly a master-thief. Zeus ordered him to give back the cattle, and he took Apollo to show him where they were hidden. On the way he played his lyre and sang a cheerful song about Apollo's kindness and good nature. The music fascinated Apollo and he asked Hermes to lend him the lyre and show him how to play.

'Keep it,' said Hermes. 'I can soon invent other toys.'

So Apollo kept the lyre, and became the finest player in Olympos. In return he made Hermes guardian of the gods' cattle in his place, and also gave him persuasiveness, eloquence and a golden shepherd's staff. He taught him how to tell the future by swirling pebbles in a bowl of water and reading the patterns they made. Hermes invented the game of knucklebones (or jacks), and the two gods often used to play.

Later, when Hermes grew up, he became the gods' messenger,

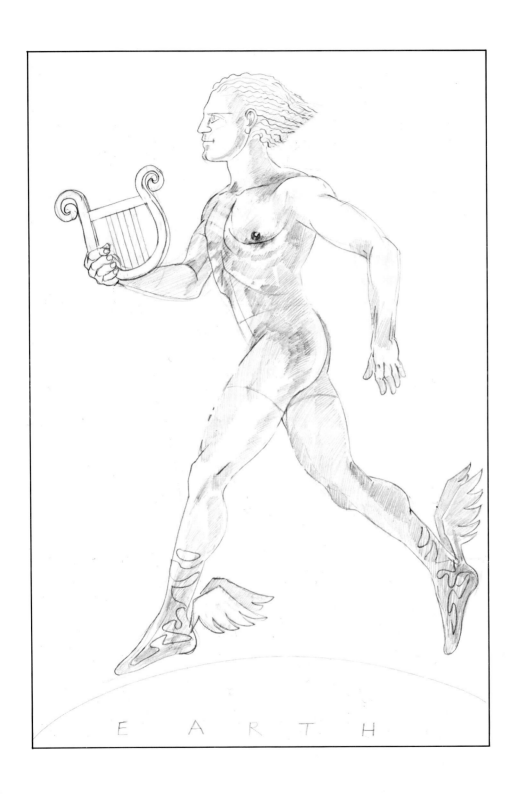

E A R T H

running their errands and flying on winged sandals between Heaven, earth and the Underworld. He also led the souls of the Dead on their journey to Hades' halls. He invented many other things besides the lyre: a shepherd's pipe cut from a hollow reed, musical scales and patterns, astronomy (the study of star-patterns in the sky), boxing, gymnastics and the art of writing. He was an easy-going, high-spirited god, and as well as enjoying his mischief mortals chose him to guard their homes, putting a small Hermes-statue (called a Herm) on a pedestal just outside the door.

Apollo

Apollo was the son of Zeus and Leto. Jealous of his birth, Hera sent a gigantic serpent called Python to hunt Leto to her death across the world. But four-day-old Apollo begged a bow and arrows from Hephaistos, cornered Python in the sacred cave at Delphi and shot him dead. (Later, the Pythian Games were held every four years in Delphi to celebrate this victory.) Next Hera sent the giant Tityos to hunt Leto. Once again Apollo, helped by his sister Artemis, protected her with arrows, and at last Zeus assisted and hurled Tityos down into Tartaros. He pegged him there on the rock floor, covering an area of nine acres; a pair of vultures feasted daily on his liver.

Throughout his youth Apollo was fierce, quickly angered and unforgiving. One of his victims was the satyr Marsyas. Athene had invented the flute, and played a tune on it to entertain the gods. When they saw her red face and puffed-out cheeks they laughed at her, and she threw the flute angrily down to earth, putting a curse on anyone who picked it up and played it. Marsyas found it, and knowing nothing of the curse began to play. His playing delighted all who heard it; they said his music was better than Apollo's; conceited Marsyas agreed. Apollo challenged him to a contest: Marsyas was to play the flute and Apollo the lyre, and the Muses would judge between them. At first, when they played, the Muses judged them equal; but then Apollo proposed that they should play and sing at the same time. This was easy for the god, playing the lyre, but impossible for Marsyas with his flute. Apollo was declared the winner – and at once he savagely punished Marsyas for daring to compete with a god: he skinned him alive and nailed his shaggy skin to a nearby pine-tree.

32

Apollo was equally merciless to girls who refused to sleep with him. One was Kassandra, princess of Troy. He cursed her by giving her true knowledge of the future, and then arranging that no one would believe a word she said. Another was the Sibyl, priestess of Cumae in Italy. He offered her immortality if she slept with him; she refused and asked instead to be allowed to live as many years as she held grains of sand in her hand. Cruelly, he granted her wish – for she had forgotten to ask to remain young and beautiful. She lived a thousand years (one for each grain) and gradually shrivelled until she was a withered husk hung up in a glass bottle. When visitors to Cumae asked her 'Sibyl, what do you want?' a whisper came from the bottle: 'I want to die'.

In the end Apollo's wildness angered even Zeus. Apollo's son Asklepios was a skilful doctor; but he was also ambitious, and when Artemis begged him to bring to life her dead lover Hippolytos, he used his skill to rescue the young man from the world of death. Hades, lord of the Underworld, furious at losing one of his subjects, complained to Zeus – and Zeus dashed Asklepios to the Underworld with a thunderbolt, so replacing soul with soul. Apollo was beside himself with rage at his son's death, and cried 'There will be no more thunderbolts now!' He then shot and killed Zeus' blacksmiths, the Cyclopes. They were immortal and immediately sprang back to life; but Zeus lifted a thunderbolt to banish Apollo forever to Tartaros. Only the pleading of Apollo's mother Leto saved him. He was punished instead by being sent for a year as cowherd to a mortal man, King Admetos of Pherai.*

Apollo served his punishment and learned his lesson. He became one of the calmest and most dignified of all the gods. He spent his time healing disease and making music with the Muses on the mountains at Delphi. His favourite proverbs were 'Know yourself' and 'Moderation in all things', and his oracle at Delphi gave this advice to many enquirers.

Artemis

Artemis was Apollo's sister, the daughter of Zeus and Leto. When Zeus slept with Leto, to prevent Hera finding out he changed both himself and her into quails. Leto therefore bore her child Artemis (on

Ortygia, Quail Island, not far from Delos where Apollo was later born) with as few birth-pains as a mother quail suffers when it lays an egg. Ever afterwards women in childbirth used to pray to Artemis to ease their labour-pains. Artemis was a goddess of the moon and months; one of her cares was the monthly cycle of women; she was a virgin goddess, untouched by god or man, and in her honour her followers promised to keep lifelong virginity as well.

Artemis was a huntress, with a silver bow and arrows made for her by the Cyclopes. Sometimes her prey was human: when sudden death came to a mortal its cause was an arrow from Artemis, punishment for some crime of which the guilty person might not even be aware. But usually her prey was deer and other wild animals. She hunted them either in a golden chariot pulled by two horned hinds, or on foot with her company of nymphs and pack of hunting dogs.

Although Artemis and her nymphs would have nothing to do with men, they were among the most beautiful and graceful of all the immortals, and many men pursued them and tried to make love to them.* This made Artemis shy of being seen by men at all, and merciless with any who came on her unawares. Once Aktaion caught sight of her bathing naked in a river; she threw water in his face to blind him, turned him into a stag and made his own hunting dogs tear him to pieces. On another occasion, on the island of Chios, Orion surprised her in a forest clearing; she conjured from the ground a giant scorpion which stung him dead.**

Artemis was the goddess of children and baby animals. She shielded them from harm until they grew out of helplessness and could fend for themselves. When she came to help at childbirth she carried a pine-torch blazing with the light of life; its warmth and radiance were a symbol of security for the newborn child.

Athene*

After Athene was born fully-grown and fully-armed from Zeus' forehead, Hephaistos (who split open Zeus' temple to release her) fell in love with her and wanted to marry her. But Athene had no time for him or for anyone else: her love was reserved for the land of Attica and particularly for the rocky Acropolis of Athens and the countryside round about.

Poseidon also coveted Attica, and he and Athene argued bitterly and constantly over it until at last Zeus ordered them to stop. 'Hold a contest,' he decreed. 'Whoever gives Attica its greatest blessing will be its lord and protector forever.'

Athene and Poseidon prepared for the contest, and the gods gathered in Attica to judge it. Seeing the countryside parched and dusty, Poseidon decided that the greatest blessing he could give was water. He stood on top of Acropolis Hill, raised his trident and stabbed it down. The rock split apart and a spring of grey-brown water, leaping and glinting in the sun, bubbled out to irrigate the land.*

With the tip of her spear, Athene touched the ground beside the spring. At once her gift to the land appeared: an olive-tree, bright with berries.

For a long time the gods discussed the two gifts. Which was the greater blessing – life-bringing water, or the olive-tree (the life it brought)? At last, by a single vote, they declared Athene the winner. The olive, and the oil made from it, would enrich Attica and spread all over Greece. It would be a staple crop, a source of life and wealth for future generations.

Poseidon was furious. He punished the mortals of Attica by sending a flood to swamp the plain; his anger lasted until all its water had drained away. To punish Athene, he visited Hephaistos (who was still in love with her) and told him that Athene was just as hotly in love with him, but was too shy to admit it. The next time Hephaistos saw her, he said, he should snatch her and make love to her.

Some time afterwards Athene went to Hephaistos' smithy to ask for a spear and some arrows. Before she could speak, Hephaistos leapt on her and tried to embrace her. Amazed and disgusted, she struggled free. In the struggle a drop of Hephaistos' seed fell and fertilised the earth, and a baby was born, godlike to the waist and serpent-tailed below (as are all earth's children).

Not wanting Poseidon to find out about her humiliation, Athene hid the child in a wooden box and gave it to Aglauros, daughter of King Kekrops of Athens, to guard for her. She forbade her, on pain of death, to open the lid. Aglauros kept the box in the house on the Acropolis she shared with her father and her sisters Pandrosos and Herse. The three girls were eaten with curiosity to see what was inside. For a time they held back; but at last, ignoring Athene's warning, they opened the lid and peeped inside. The baby had wriggled round, and instead of a child's face and hands the girls saw a writhing serpent's tail. They ran terrified out of the house, fell over the edge of the Acropolis and were smashed to pieces on the rocks below.*

Athene was flying down from Olympos to Athens, carrying a boulder to add to the fortifications, when a messenger came with news of the three girls' death. The messenger was a white crow, and it cooed its sad news without warning into Athene's ear. She was so startled that she dropped the boulder (it became Mount Lykabettos). She cursed the crow and its descendants forever, turning their feathers black, giving them raucous, ugly voices and forbidding them ever to fly above the Acropolis again. (The crow was thus the first messenger to bring bad news, and the first, though by no means the last, to suffer for it.)

Athene rescued the baby, which was lying on the barren rock. She called him Erichthonios (Earth-born-in-strife) and hid him in a fold of her cloak. Here he grew up, and could often be seen peeping out. (He later became King of Athens; at the end of his reign he passed into the sky and became the constellation Auriga, the Charioteer.)

Athene is the goddess of wisdom (and her pet bird, the symbol both of wisdom and of the city of Athens, is the owl); she is also the goddess of peace-making and of the crafts of peace, especially weaving and spinning. A foolish mortal, Arachne, once challenged her to a contest of weaving. In warning, Athene wove a tapestry showing scenes of mortals who were punished for challenging the gods; but Arachne took no notice – *her* tapestry was full of scandalous pictures of the gods' love-affairs. Athene angrily ripped it to shreds and thrashed Arachne with her own shuttle. Arachne hanged herself; but Athene (always merciful) changed her into a spider, and still her descendants are the most skilful weavers (apart from the gods) in all the world.

Pan

Pan's mother was Amaltheia, the she-goat who nursed baby Zeus. No one knows the name of his father. Some say it was Kronos; some say a ram; some say a rock-spirit disguised as a mountain-goat. (Others say Zeus or Hermes; but as Zeus was Pan's half-brother and Hermes was Zeus' son, this is unlikely.) In form Pan was half human, half goat – and in his nature he was a mixture too, partly easy-going and merry like a human being, partly bad-tempered, greedy and shameless like a goat.

Pan never lived with the other gods on Mount Olympos. He preferred the pastures and wooded hillsides of Arcadia. He was the god of flocks and herds, and had the power of soothing and calming all animals. With humans and gods he had a different skill. He could send out an enormous shout which made hills and sky echo and caused panic in all who heard it; or he could steal up on a traveller in a lonely place and fill him or her with nameless fear.

Pan was a great chaser of nymphs. Some he caught and raped, peopling Arcadia with fauns and all kinds of other half-human creatures. But he was a boaster and a liar, especially when he was drunk: once, for example, he claimed to have made love to every one of Dionysos' Maenads in a single afternoon. Sometimes the gods took pity on the nymphs he chased, and changed their shapes before he caught them. Pitys, for example, was changed into a pine-tree, and Syrinx into a bed of hollow reeds – whereupon Pan cut several of the reeds, bound them together and invented the Pan-pipes, the delight of shepherds ever since.*

Dionysos

Another god who grew, like Apollo, from wildness to self-control was Dionysos. His birth and upbringing were turbulent. His father Zeus slept with a mortal woman, Semele, daughter of King Kadmos of Thebes. When Hera heard of the affair, she was eaten with rage and jealousy. Disguised as Semele's old nurse, she visited her in her room in the royal palace of Thebes.

'How do you know your lover is really Zeus?' she said. 'He looks just like a mortal. He could be some smooth-tongued stranger, passing himself off as Zeus.'

'How can I find out for sure?'

'Next time he visits, ask him to reveal himself in his full majesty as king of the gods. Then you'll know for sure.'

Next time Zeus came to her, Semele begged him to appear in immortal majesty. At first Zeus refused: he knew that no mortal can see a god's true shape and live. But he also knew that the Fates had long ago chosen this death for Semele, and that he must give way. At last, reluctantly, he shed his mortal shape and revealed himself.

To the people of Thebes it seemed as if a meteorite had struck the palace. There was a blur of light, a stab of thunder, then silence. In the heart of the palace, where Semele's room had been, nothing was left but charred rubble and a plume of smoke.

So Semele was destroyed, and Hermes led her soul to Hades. On the way, he rescued her unborn baby and carried him to Zeus. Zeus, lacking a mother's womb, opened his own thigh, placed the baby inside and stitched up the wound. So baby Dionysos grew in safety, and when the time came he was born from Zeus' thigh (and given the nickname 'Twice-born'). Because his second birth was from an immortal, Dionysos was a true god, not a demigod or hero as he would have been as merely a mortal woman's son.*

The child's godliness did not save him from Hera's jealousy. She sent Titans to destroy him, and they snatched him from his cradle, tore him to pieces and made the pieces into stew. Dionysos was only saved by Rhea, who reassembled him and brought him back to life. He was placed in the care of Ino, the sister of his mother Semele, and of her husband King Athamas. To prevent Hera recognising him they dressed him as a girl and kept him with the women. Even so, Hera soon saw through the trick and punished Ino and Athamas by driving them insane. In the nick of time, before Hera could destroy Dionysos again, Zeus rescued him, disguised him as a ram and hid him with the nymphs of Mount Nysa in Boeotia. Here at last Dionysos was able to grow up unharmed.*

At first, it was hard for mortals to recognise the grown-up Dionysos as a god. In his childhood he had been treated as ram and girl as well as youth; even now his shape deceived people, and they saw him sometimes as an animal (usually fawn, goat or bull), sometimes as a beautiful young man, sometimes as a majestic and powerful god. He still had in him a portion of mortality, inherited from his mother, and this often blinded people to his true godliness as son of Zeus. Finally, jealous Hera filled him with wandering madness and sent him roaming across the world. His companions were goat-footed or horse-tailed Satyrs (led by their king Silenos), mountain-nymphs and the wild, dancing women known as Bacchae (revellers) or Maenads (women possessed). They wore fawnskins and each carried a thyrsos, a pine pole twined with ivy and tipped with a pine cone. When they dashed these poles on the ground in their frenzy, streams of fresh milk or wine gushed out; Dionysos' ecstasy filled them with superhuman strength, so that neither sharp weapons nor fire could harm them; their dances reached climax with the ripping to pieces of whatever wild beasts lay in their path, whether fawns, goats, bulls or lions.

Many people welcomed the Bacchae, accepted Dionysos into their hearts and joined his sacred dance. Those who did not were savagely punished. The king of Damascus in Syria was skinned alive; Lykourgos, king of the Edonians, was driven mad and killed his own son Dryas with an axe, chopping him down in mistake for Dionysos' sacred vine. (For this crime his people took him to a wild mountain-side, harnessed unbroken horses to his limbs and neck and had him torn apart.) The three daughters of Minyas, princesses of Boeotia (their names were Alkithoe, Leukippe and Arsinoe) refused to dance, even though the rest of their city had welcomed the god. They sat in the palace weaving. As they wove, Dionysos sent wild animals dancing through the room, turned the threads on their loom to vine tendrils and filled the air with Bacchic shouts and cries. Maddened, the three women sacrificed to Dionysos (but in their insanity they sacrificed Leukippe's son Hippasos, thinking him an animal), ran outside and were transformed into bats.

An even more terrible fate awaited Pentheus, grandson of Kadmos and king of Dionysos' own birthplace Thebes. Most Thebans accepted Dionysos as a god and went to join his dance on Mount Kithairon; but Pentheus sent soldiers to throw them into prison. Dionysos rescued them: the chains fell away and the dungeon doors opened of their own accord. Then the god hypnotised Pentheus into dressing as a woman and following him to the mountain-side to spy on the dance. There, Pentheus climbed a pine-tree to see better; but Dionysos showed him to the Bacchants as a wild animal and, led by Pentheus' mother Agaue, they uprooted the tree and tore him to pieces.

Gradually, as Dionysos' power spread across the world and more and more people accepted him as a god, his savagery grew less. When the women of Argos, led by Proitos' daughters, refused to welcome him, he at first drove them mad and made them rip their own children limb from limb; but when the priest Melampous pleaded with him, he restored their wits on condition that they joined the dance. On another occasion, a band of pirates kidnapped Dionysos and sailed away to sell him as a slave. He transformed the mast and yard-arms of the ship into curling vines, filled the hold with grapes and wine and showed himself to the pirates as a roaring lion. They jumped into the sea, were turned into dolphins and escorted the boat on its homeward journey, dipping and leaping beside it through the waves.*

Once he was universally accepted, Dionysos began to help mortals instead of harming them. His early childhood on Mount Nysa, home of the Muses, had given him a love of music and poetry; now he combined them and gave mortals the gift of drama: tragedy, comedy and declamation. He was a god of growing things and especially of vines: he showed mortals how to press grapes and ferment the juice into wine. He remained forever the god of ecstasy and intoxication; but now that people believed in him his dancing brought joy instead of grief.

6
THE · KINGDOM · OF
THE · SKY

The gods

In heaven the gods lived in houses and palaces, just as mortals do on earth. Though they could change their shapes as easily as we change clothes, they usually favoured mortal form: human visitors (if their eyes were not blinded by the gods' radiance) would have found them like ordinary men and women, though many times bigger. In their feelings and passions, too, they were like magnified human beings: their anger, dignity, wisdom, foolishness, generosity and greed were the same as ours.

The gods had two gifts denied to mortals: all-knowledge (and the power it brings) and immortality. Immortality came from *ichor*, a pale liquid which flowed in their veins instead of blood. They felt pain and could be wounded, but they never died and never aged. They looked after the affairs of the universe, and its beauties and pleasures were there for their delight. Sometimes there were squabbles; but on the whole the gods led carefree, untroubled lives.

Zeus was their king, and his palace on Mount Olympos was their court and gathering-place. Here they met for debates, for councils and above all for banquets. They ate ambrosia and drank nectar; they also enjoyed the rich smoke from sacrifices down on earth. From time to time, when they felt a craving for mortal food, they put on human shape and size and passed down to earth to enjoy human hospitality.

The first cupbearer of the gods, who poured their nectar at feasts and banquets, was Hebe, daughter of Zeus and Hera. But then, on earth, a son was born to King Tros of Troy. His name was Ganymede (Delight in Manliness), and he was handsome as no other mortal had ever been. Zeus knew that his beauty, being mortal, would one day wither and die; so he sent his eagle to snatch Ganymede up to heaven, gave him immortality and made him the gods' new cupbearer.* To charm away Hebe's jealousy, he allowed her to marry Herakles (another favoured mortal who became a god).

Darkness and light

The Titans Hyperion and Theia* had three children: Selene (Moon), Helios (Sun) and Eos (Dawn). Selene was secretive and shy. She loved Night's velvet dark, and galloped through it either on horseback or in a chariot pulled by pearl-white horses or silvery oxen. Soundless and aloof, she soared above the clouds. She hoarded her light: it was often pale and thin, and sometimes she veiled her face altogether and let Night's darkness rule.*

Her brother Helios and sister Eos were dazzling exhibitionists. Every morning, roused by their sacred bird the cock, they leaped out of bed and jumped into their chariots. Streaking the sky with rose-red fingers, Dawn galloped to the gates of Olympos to announce the coming of the Sun. Helios followed close at her heels, his horses prancing and shaking their fiery manes and his chariot filling all heaven with light. Dawn turned into Day and galloped beside him across the sky. When they reached the West they turned their horses loose to graze on the Islands of the Blessed, and set sail in a golden vessel on the river of Ocean, which carried them round the world from West to East; they disembarked and slept in the golden palace of Helios' son Aietes till the cock waked them to begin the next new day.

Helios the Sun was a busybody. His rays pierced everywhere and saw everything, and he gossiped and made trouble wherever he could. He was a cattle-farmer, with magnificient tawny herds in pastures far across the earth. He had two daughters, Prote (First) and Klymene (Famous), and one son, Phaethon (Blazing). One day Phaethon, showing off to his sisters, borrowed the Sun's fire-chariot and galloped off headlong across the sky. But he lost control: the horses ran where they would and the earth was alternately scorched (when they swooped too close) or chilled to ice (when they veered out into space). At last Zeus threw a thunderbolt and jolted Phaethon out and down like a shooting star. Phaethon drowned in the river Po in Italy (whose water runs orange to this day); the Sun's horses gal-

loped home; Phaethon's sisters were turned into weeping poplar-trees.

Eos was famous for her love-affairs. Once she slept with Ares the war-god, and jealous Aphrodite punished her by making her fall wildly in love with every handsome mortal who caught her eye. (The punishment lay in the fact that her lovers were mortal, and so, each time, she had to wach them gradually grow old and die.) Eos' human lovers were Kephalos, Kleitos, Ganymede, Tithonos and (most famous of all) Orion. Orion had raped the daughter of Oinopion of Chios, and in revenge Oinopion put out his eyes. An oracle told Orion to sail East, and promised that if he looked towards Helios at the exact moment when the sun-chariot rose up from Ocean, his sight would be restored. The oracle proved true; Orion regained his sight – and at the same moment Eos saw him and fell in love. They slept together on Apollo's sacred island of Delos. When Apollo found them, Eos hid in a cloud and Orion swam for safety to nearby Ortygia. But this island was sacred to Apollo's sister Artemis. Orion started swimming desperately back to Delos. Artemis set arrow to bow, took aim at his black seal's-head bobbing in the water and shot him dead.

The winds

The winds were the turbulent sons and grandsons of Dawn. They had vast, owl-brown wings, dragons' tails and billowing rain-cloud cloaks. Full of mischief, they roared and bucketed across the world and hurt whom they liked. Once their pirate-leader, the North Wind Boreas (Devourer), snatched mortal Orytheia from a procession in Athens, carried her away to his hideout and married her. (They had four children, Kalais and Zetes, dragon-winged sons, and Chione and Kleopatra, daughters in human form). On another occasion Boreas outraged Poseidon the storm-god by disguising himself as a stallion and running riot through Poseidon's herd of three thousand mares. Twelve foals were later born, white horses that raced among the waves without so much as dampening their hooves.

Poseidon slept with Arne, wife of the mortal Desmontes. When Arne's twin sons were born, Desmontes was so furious that he blinded her and shut her up in an underground pit. The children were left on a mountainside to die. But a shepherd rescued them and gave them to his employer, Queen Theaino, to bring up as her own sons; they were named Aiolos (Destroyer) and Boiotos (Herdsman) and grew up as princes in the palace. In the meantime, however, Theaino had two children of her own. She was afraid that the foundling princes would inherit the throne instead of these true-born sons, so she plotted with her own children that they should murder Aiolos and Boiotos and pretend that it was a hunting accident. The four princes set off for the hunt; they fought; Poseidon lent his own sons supernatural strength and they killed Theaino's children. When the news was brought to Theaino she stabbed herself dead. Aiolos and Boiotos went to their real home, killed Desmontes and rescued poor blind Arne from her pit. Boiotos settled in a farming area in Greece, later called Boeotia after him; Aiolos set sail to find his fortune, confident that his father Poseidon would look after him.

This was how matters stood. On the one hand there were the winds, proud and ungoverned; on the other there was Aiolos, seeking a kingdom. Zeus made his decision. With Poseidon's help he hollowed out a large floating island, Lipara, honeycombing its centre with caves and tunnels. Into these he forced the winds, and sealed the entrances. The winds raged and howled, but there was no way out. Above them Zeus built a bronze palace for Aiolos and his queen Enarete, and granted them long, contented life. Whenever the gods needed a wind to serve them, Aiolos took his trident (a gift from his father Poseidon) and prised open a vent-hole in the rock; the chosen wind shouldered its way to freedom and Aiolos blocked the hole behind it.

Ares and Aphrodite

One of the greatest scandals in the history of Olympos was the love-affair between Ares and Aphrodite. Aphrodite was married to Hephaistos,* who was a supremely skilful craftsman but also supremely ugly. Not only that, but his main interest was his work: he spent all day and half the night working in his smithy and had no time for a wife, not even the goddess of beauty herself. He made presents for Aphrodite – necklaces, ornaments, a set of golden tables that ran about of their own accord on tiny wheels – but he seldom spent time with her, talked to her or made love to her in their golden bedroom in the palace of Olympos.

Soon, therefore, Aphrodite found a lover: Ares. He had no skill in arts or crafts – in fact, few thoughts of any kind ever exercised his mind. But he was handsome, swaggering and strong, blessed with all the qualities Hephaistos lacked and exactly to lonely Aphrodite's taste. All day the two of them went about their business, pretending to care nothing for one another; as soon as it was night Ares ran to Aphrodite, threw down his bow and arrows and jumped into bed with her.

News of the affair was soon all over Olympos. The only god who knew nothing about it was Hephaistos, engrossed as always in his forge. At last the busybody Sun could contain the secret no longer and made it his business to tell Hephaistos everything.

'Go tonight,' he said. 'Catch them together. See for yourself.'

'What good will that do?' said Hephaistos. 'If it comes to a fight, Ares will win.'

'Don't fight him. Trick him,' said the sly Sun.

Working secretly, keeping what he was doing hidden even from the robots he'd invented to help in the smithy, Hephaistos wove a gossamer-fine, golden net, invisible and unbreakable. One afternoon, when Aphrodite was away from Olympos busying herself with mortal affairs, he went to their bedroom and hung the net all round the bed. Then he limped to his smithy and went back to work.

That night Ares came to Aphrodite as usual. He tossed down his bow and arrows and jumped into bed beside her. At once the net fell down and trapped them, naked and face to face. It clung like a spider's web; the more they struggled the tighter they were held.

Hephaistos called to the gods to come and see. (The goddesses, out of embarrassment, stayed away.) 'Zeus,' he shouted, 'Look at them! I insist that you punish them. I demand a divorce.'

'No,' said Zeus. 'It's not for me to interfere between god and wife. You must set them free.'

'Not till Ares is punished.'

'Set them free,' Poseidon said. 'I'll guarantee to end the affair and make Ares pay any fine you choose.'

'What if he won't?'

'I'll pay the fine myself, marry Aphrodite and take her off your hands.'

In the end, Hephaistos was convinced. He cut the net with a pair of golden shears, and set Ares and Aphrodite free. Naked and furious they ran from Olympos, Ares to his mortal friends the warlike Thracians, Aphrodite to Paphos, on her sacred island Cyprus. The laughter of all Olympos rang in their ears – and people on earth, hearing it, covered their ears at the violence of the storm.

Did Ares pay the fine? No. Did Poseidon marry Aphrodite? No. When it came to it, Hephaistos was so foolishly in love that he refused to let Aphrodite go.

7
THE · UNDERWORLD

The place

The Underworld lay below the earth. In form it was a mirror-image of the upper world, as darkness is a mirror-image of light, death a mirror-image of life. Just as the upper world was bounded by the swirling river Ocean, so the Underworld was bounded by the river Styx; it had mountains, spreading plains and deep cave-systems stretching down to the blackness of Tartaros, its lowest depth. It knew nothing of sunlight or the day's brightness; for most of the time its inhabitants groped in darkness lit only by phosphorescent corpse-light or the flicker of torches.

The main entrance to the Underworld lay in the far west of the world. There, on the banks of Ocean, the Kimmerians lived in a land unvisited by sunrise: day and night were forever the same to them. In this desolate place, through a grove of willows and black poplars beside the Gates of Evening and the Place of Dreams, flowed the fast-running river Styx, fed by its tributaries Acheron (Distress), Phlegethon (Blazing), Kokytos (Lament), Lethe (Oblivion) and Aornis (Birdless). To enter the Underworld, the souls of the dead had first to cross the river Styx in a leaking boat poled by the aged, ragged ferryman Charon. Before a corpse was buried in the upper world, a copper coin was placed under its tongue, to pay Charon's fare. Anyone unburied, or buried without the fare, was condemned to wander forever on the banks of Styx, begging Charon (in vain) to grant free passage. The area was thronged with souls, countless as autumn leaves.

Once across the Styx, the souls picked their way past Cerberus (Pit Devil). He was a gigantic, three-headed dog, the offspring of the

49

monsters Typhon and Echidne; day and night he prowled the entrance to the Underworld, ravenous, on guard for intruders from the upper world. Those dead souls who passed him and reached the White Rock in safety came next to the Fields of Asphodel. Here they waited in a numberless grey throng for their cases to be judged. Their judges were Rhadamanthys, Aiakos and Minos, and against their decisions there was no appeal. After the verdict, the souls passed on their way. Evil-doers were led to punishment in the depths of Tartaros; the good passed to happiness in Elysium; those who were neither good nor bad returned to live forever in the Fields of Asphodel.**

Styx and Hekate

Styx (Hate) was a river-goddess, daughter of Tethys and Okeanos. She was the wife of the Titan Pallas, and bore him four children: Zelos (Eagerness), Nike (Victory), Kratos (Might) and Bia (Force). During the war in heaven, when Zeus called all the immortals together to fight the Titans, Styx and her children hurried first to help. As a reward, Zeus made Styx's children his permanent servants (except for winged Victory, who served Athene). To Styx herself he granted power over all other gods: it was in her name that they swore their oaths.

Styx lived in a cave-palace at the edge of Ocean, where the sky-canopy was supported on silver pillars. For most of the time she was unvisited by mortals or by gods: for they hated her and feared her power. From a jagged rock above her palace, called Ocean's Horn, a spring of ice-cold water gushed out and formed a nine-branching river which clutched the whole Underworld in its chilly grasp. There was a tenth stream, called Oath of the Gods. If there was ever an argument in Olympos, and one god accused another of lying, Zeus sent his messenger Iris to fill a golden cup with this water. The accused god swore by the water that he or she was telling the truth, and drank. Anyone lying collapsed at once in a coma and lay unconscious for a year. On recovery, he or she was banished from the councils of Olympos, and from all the banquets and pleasures of the gods, for nine more years. Fearing this, few gods ever swore by the water of Styx and broke their word.

Hekate (She who works from afar) was a moon-goddess, daughter of Asterie (Starry) and cousin of Apollo and Artemis. When the Titans ruled, she had three-fold power (in land, sea and sky), and when Zeus defeated Kronos he let her keep her authority. Often mortals saw her galloping her moon-chariot across the sky, blazing torch in hand; her gifts to mortals she favoured were wealth, sporting skill, victory in battle and common sense. She was also connected with the earth's fertility, and together with Artemis helped women in childbirth. Often people placed her statues outside their houses, and touched them for luck as they went in or out.

Hekate was also the goddess of black magic and the queen of ghosts, more feared than any other spirit of the Underworld. Often she danced across the plains of Hades, whip in hand, a pack of ghosts and hell-hounds howling at her heels. Sometimes her dance spiralled into the upper world and was seen by terrified mortals in lonely places at dead of night. She was the goddess of crossroads, and her statues were placed on guard wherever three roads met. They had three faces, lion, dog, and mare: one for each direction. Travellers in daylight often found the remains of sacrifices at these statues' feet, where ghosts had walked and magic ceremonies had taken place in the secret dark. Hekate's offerings were blood, corn and milk, and her worshippers muttered spells in a language only they could understand.

Hades and Persephone

The ruler of the Underworld was Zeus's brother Hades; in addition, the Underworld itself was often known simply as 'Hades'. Hades' name meant 'invisible'. He seldom appeared to mortals or allowed them to build temples or make statues in his honour. He was master of everything under the earth, and was sometimes called Plouton (Wealthy) because of its mineral riches and its unquenchable power to make things grow.

For a long time Hades ruled alone: awesome, unapproachable, without a queen. Then he fell in love with Persephone, daughter of the harvest-goddess Demeter. She was a beautiful young girl (often known as *Kore*, or 'Maiden'); she lived on the island of Sicily, and spent her days singing, picking flowers and picnicking in green meadows with her servant-nymphs.

Hades asked permission for the marriage from his brother Zeus, and the two gods went to Demeter to ask for her daughter's hand. But Demeter was horrified to think of Persephone leaving the sunny earth for the shadows of the Underworld, and refused. There was nothing for Hades to do but steal Persephone. One day Persephone was picking flowers in the water-meadows of Henna in Sicily, when she saw a particularly beautiful narcissus. Its roots supported a hundred flowers; its scent filled the air and spread throughout heaven and earth. Eagerly Persephone plucked it – and at once the earth gaped open and Hades galloped up from the Underworld in a golden chariot pulled by coal-black horses, snatched her and carried her screaming down into the darkness. The earth's wound healed at once, and the water-meadows rippled in the sun as they had before. It was as if nothing had changed.

No one knew where Persephone had gone or who had stolen her. Hades had been wearing his helmet of invisibility; all Persephone's nymphs could tell her mother Demeter was of the ground splitting and of a hiss and roar like a whirling wind. Frantic, Demeter searched for nine days everywhere across the earth, a pine-torch blazing in each hand, stopping neither to eat nor drink. At last Helios the Sun, who goes everywhere and sees everything, told her that the thief was Hades, that Persephone now lived in his dark kingdom, and that Zeus knew and approved of what had happened.

Furious, Demeter swore to have nothing more to do with Zeus or with any other god. She threw off her immortal shape, disguised herself as an old woman and went out into the world of mortals, a beggar. She wandered from town to town, village to village; at length she came to Eleusis in Attica, where she was welcomed by King Keleos and Queen Metaneira.**

Without Demeter's protection, nothing grew. Across the whole world crops withered, trees died and the ground grew sour and sullen. It was as if the barrenness of the Underworld was reaching up to corrupt all healthiness above. People began to starve. At last their crying reached Zeus, and touched his heart. He sent Iris to make terms with Demeter. If she would bring back life to living things, she could beg Hades in return to let Persephone go.

Unexpectedly, Hades listened to Demeter's appeal. For all his grimness, he was also fair and just, and he pitied people's suffering. He agreed to let Persephone go; the black horses were harnessed,

52

and the earth gaped open ready for Persephone to leave. As she parted from Hades – sadly, for she had come to love both him and his sad people – he gave her a last gift, a pomegranate. In all her time in the Underworld, Persephone had neither eaten nor drunk; now, on the point of leaving, she ate a single pomegranate seed.

It was the gods' unbreakable law that if anyone ate food of the Underworld they were bound to live there forever. What could Persephone do? On the one hand, she was bound to Hades and his kingdom; on the other, she felt pity for her mother and the starving people in the world above.

At last Zeus settled it. For six months of each year Persephone was to live in the upper world and bring spring and summer to the waiting earth; for the other six months she was to live in the Underworld as Hades' queen, co-ruler of the shadow world. From that day on the pattern of growth and withering, the cycle of the seasons, was firm and fixed.

Orpheus and Eurydice

Orpheus was the son of a mortal (King Oeagros of Thrace) and an immortal (Kalliope, the muse of poetry). Most heroes had super-human gifts in war or prophecy; Orpheus' gift was for music. Apollo himself lent him his lyre and taught him to play. Orpheus' music attracted not only human listeners, but also the wild beasts of hills and forests. When he sang, rivers changed their courses and trees and boulders uprooted themselves and came to hear.

As a young man Orpheus visited Egypt, where the temple priests taught him their mysteries. He was one of the Argonauts who sailed with Jason to fetch the Golden Fleece; while he was on this journey he became a follower of the god Dionysos, expert in all his magic rituals. When he came home to Thrace he became king of Kikonia and took as his queen the Dryad (or oak-tree-nymph) Eurydice.

The Thracian countryside was barren and mountainous, and its people were savages. Eurydice's beauty was like a glimpse of the gods, a flower bringing colour to a desert. Many men would gladly have stolen her from Orpheus. One day she was bathing in the river Peneios, and a passing traveller, Aristaios,* tried to catch hold of her and carry her away. She ran from him – and in her panic trod on a snake and died of its venom. Aristaios fled; Orpheus' people buried Eurydice with honour, placing a coin under her tongue for Charon's fare.

For many days, grief for Eurydice tormented Orpheus. He neither ate nor slept; his lyre hung dusty on its peg; his songs were silent. At last he decided that since life without Eurydice was insupportable, he would lose nothing if he went down to the Underworld himself, alive, and begged Hades to give her back.

It was perilous: no mortal, and only a handful of the greatest heroes, men like Theseus, Odysseus and Herakles, had ever visited the dead and lived. But just as they had strength and daring to support them, so Orpheus had his lyre. There was a secret entrance to the Underworld at Aornos in Thesprotis: a narrow rock-passage round whose mouth a vapour swirled so foul that no birds ever flew overhead (hence the name Aornos, 'Birdless'). Here Orpheus sacrificed a black lamb to the gods of the Underworld, took his lyre, and crept into the silent, stinking tunnel.

After endless hours picking his way through the slimy dark, he came to the bank of Styx. The twittering ghosts drew back, overawed by the bulk of a living man. Charon was poling his oozing, rotting boat across the river, far away. The air was dank.

Orpheus lifted his lyre and began to play. His soft music seeped into every corner of the Underworld. The restless ghosts stood still; Charon leaned on his pole, listening; on the far bank, Cerberus closed his slavering jaws, lay down and thumped his tail; even the tormentors of the damned in Tartaros halted for a moment, to hear the song. When it was done, Charon brought his boat back to the bank, beat off the clamouring ghosts and cleared a place for Orpheus. Creaking at the unaccustomed weight and awash with water, the boat carried them across the Styx. Then Orpheus made his way through the Fields of Asphodel to Hades' palace.

He found Hades and Queen Persephone sitting in state, with the three grim judges of the dead and all their counsellors. 'Play again,' commanded Hades. 'Then ask for what you will.'

Orpheus played again, and once again the entire Underworld stopped still to listen. When his music was over, Orpheus knelt and begged Hades to release Eurydice.

'On one condition,' Hades answered. 'You must retrace your steps exactly, and lead her to the upper world without once looking back. If you see her, even once, you will lose her forever.'

Gladness leapt in Orpheus' heart. He started back the way he had come: through the Fields of Asphodel, past Cerberus, across the Styx in Charon's leaking boat. He kept his eyes fixed ahead, not daring to look back to see if Eurydice was really following. He left the banks of Styx and the bloodless ghosts, and began to climb the steep tunnel to the upper world.

There was no sound in the darkness but the drip of water from the walls and the scuff of his own footsteps. He could hear no one following; when he stopped and listened for Eurydice's breathing, there was silence. Shuddering, he set off again, playing his lyre softly to guide Eurydice's steps. He climbed up and up towards the daylight, all the while tormented by the fear that she was not there after all.

At last a pinhead of light appeared in the distance: the entrance. Orpheus quickened his steps. The higher he climbed, the more daylight filtered down into the tunnel. He could make out cracks and bumps in the rocky walls, and the gravel at his feet. There was still no sound of anyone following.

At last, at the very entrance to the upper world, his nerves could stand no more. He glanced quickly round, for just a fraction of a second, to glimpse Eurydice. At once a savage gust of wind, ice-cold, tore at his hair and flung him flat on the muddy ground. Coal-darkness; silence; emptiness of heart. He had broken Hades' condition, and lost Eurydice.

From that day onwards Orpheus rejected human company. He spent his time wandering in the fields and forests, playing desolate, grief-filled music for himself alone. He was as drained of human warmth as the ghosts of the Underworld were drained of blood; though he was still a living man, he belonged already to the dead.

At last Dionysos took pity, and ordered his Bacchants to end Orpheus' life. They came on him in one of their ecstatic dances, and tore him to pieces. They scattered his body across the fields, and placed his head in the river Hebros to float down to the sea.*

Now the other gods took a hand. Apollo sent the Muses to gather and bury the fragments of Orpheus' body. (His tomb was at Leibethra, at the foot of Mount Olympos; the nightingales there, filled with his spirit, sang more sweetly than anywhere else on earth.) His head, still crying 'Eurydice, Eurydice,' floated across the sea to the island of Lesbos, where it was buried in a prophetic shrine.

As for the inhabitants of the Underworld, they kept forever in their hearts the memory of Orpheus' singing, a dream of beauty to warm their eternal, empty lives.*

8
THE · KINGDOM · OF
THE · SEA

Poseidon and Amphitrite

When Zeus, Poseidon and Hades defeated Kronos and cast lots for kingdoms, Poseidon won the sea. He built an underwater palace near Aigai (a town on the sheltered coast of the island of Euboea), and set up court over the nymphs, water-sprites, fish and other creatures of the ocean. He rode proudly across his kingdom in a shell-shaped, golden chariot pulled by sea-horses, dolphins or white-winged stallions, trident brandished high, hair streaming in the wind. As well as the sea, he ruled all the fresh water in the world, and the gods and spirits of rivers, lakes, pools and fountains paid court to him. He often left his sea-palace and travelled across land to visit these servants. In four steps he could stride across the whole horizon; whales, seals and other sea-creatures gambolled in procession beside him. With one trident-blow he could strike rebellious river-subjects dry or open new springs from barren earth; he could sink continents beneath the sea or heave up islands and mountains where before there was nothing but smooth water. For this reason he was given the name Earthshaker, and people, mountains and forests trembled when he passed.

It was not Poseidon's nature to be content for long. He was jealous of his brother Zeus, and led the revolt of the gods against him. When this revolt failed and he had served his punishment (a year's enslavement to a mortal), he turned his attention to gaining power on land. He argued with Athene over Athens, and when he lost tried to claim another town from her: Troezen. As she had in Athens, Athene gave the townspeople of Troezen an olive-tree; Poseidon struck his trident on the ground and produced the first horse, which he claimed was a greater gift. Zeus divided Troezen between them –

a decision which still left them enemies. Poseidon next – and equally unsuccessfully – claimed Aigina from Zeus, Naxos from Dionysos and Corinth from the Sun. Finally he claimed Argolis from Hera, and refused to accept any Olympians as judges on the grounds that they were biased against him. So three river-gods, Inachos, Kephissos and Asterion, were chosen – and awarded Argolis to Hera. Poseidon punished them by drying up their waters with a trident-blow – to this day they are dusty and dry in summer – and stormed back to Aigai and his true kingdom under the sea. From this time on he kept aloof from the other gods, and his anger was savage and unpredictable, bursting out every so often in storms which sent huge waves crowding against the land.

Poseidon's violent nature made it hard for him to find a wife. His first choice was his sister Demeter: he hoped to make her his queen as Zeus had done with Hera. One day, when she was wandering the world distraught for the loss of Persephone, Demeter took the form of a mare and went to graze with a herd of horses in Arcadia. She hoped that her disguise would hide her from both mortals and gods. But Poseidon followed her, took the form of a stallion and raped her. Their children were a mare (Despoina, 'Lady') and a winged moon-stallion (Areion, 'Proud', later tamed by Herakles).* The rape enraged Demeter. She avoided Poseidon forever afterwards, and her anger even threatened innocent Arcadia, so that its people had to soothe her with prayers and sacrifice.

Poseidon next looked for a wife among the sea-nymphs, and particularly the Nereids. His first choice was Thetis; but then, like Zeus (who had also once been interested in her), he remembered the prophecy that she would bear a son greater than his father, and so abandoned her to the mortal Peleus and paid court to her sister Amphitrite instead.* At first Amphitrite was terrified, and fled to her grandfather Okeanos' underwater palace, near the Atlas Mountains at the world's edge. Instead of roaring after her and snatching her by force as he had done with Demeter, Poseidon used a new weapon: diplomacy. He sent dolphin-messengers* to speak gently of his love for her; their soft words won her heart and she agreed to be his queen. The wedding was held with great pomp – mortals who glimpsed it told of a moonlight procession of stags, panthers, lions, horses, bulls, rams and tigers, as well as every kind of sea-creature, each ridden by a Nereid, escorting bride, groom and their guests the gods across the wide, calm sea.

Marriage to Amphitrite finally made Poseidon satisfied with the kingdom of the sea. He still kept aloof from the other gods; he was still stern and unpredictable; his anger still burst out from time to time and shook the earth or shuddered across the sea in storms. But by and large he was content with his authority, and saved his fury for those who challenged it (for example, for Odysseus who blinded his Cyclops son Polyphemos); to most mortals he was generous, guiding their ships and filling their nets with fish. He and Amphitrite had many children, most of them mermen (called Tritons) or mermaids, with human bodies and fishes' tails.**

Sea-monsters

Like the kingdom of dry land, the sea-kingdom was peopled with creatures of every kind. Many of them were the children or grandchildren of age-old powers from before the time of the Olympian gods: of Ocean, the river that bounds the world, or of Pontos, the Sea, a relation of Darkness and Mother Earth themselves. Like many beings from the beginning of time, they were often uncouth monsters with hideous shapes, cruel minds and deadly powers.*

Pontos had three sons. One was Nereus, the gentle sea-god whose children were the Nereids. The second was Thaumas (Wonderful). His children included the rainbow-goddess Iris, messenger of the gods (who later married Zephyros the West Wind), and a group of three she-monsters called Harpies (Storm-winds or Snatchers). Their names were Aello (Hurricane), Okypete (Swiftwing) and Kelaino (Dark One), and in form they were gigantic seabirds with women's faces. They were filthy and ravenous, forever scouring the sea for prey; their wings darkened the sky, and anything they touched turned slimy and poisonous.

Pontos' third son Phorkys (Boar) was the father of some of the most hideous of all ocean-creatures. Three of his daughters were the Graiai (Grey Ones): Pemphredo (Wasp), Enyo (Warlike) and Deino (Dread). They had the bodies of swans or beautiful girls, but their hair was lank and grey and they had only one eye and one tooth between them, which they took turns to use. Their home was a lightless guard-post at the entrance to Kisthene, the land of rock-roses where their Gorgon-sisters lived. There were three Gorgons: Stheno (Strength), Euryale (Wide Sea) and Medusa (Cunning).* They had

61

women's bodies with stiff, golden wings, and their hands and feet were taloned with brass. Their faces were like frozen masks: staring eyes, tusks, grinning mouths and lolling tongues. For hair they had writhing snakes. A mere glimpse of their foulness was enough to choke the breath in people's throats and turn them to stone. Their heads had power to leave their bodies and float across the world, appearing eerily to mortals in nightmares or bringing terror on the battlefield.

Another of Phorkys' daughters was Scylla (Bitch); her mother was either the witch-goddess Hekate or the monster Lamia.* Scylla was originally a beautiful girl, a sea-spirit. But Poseidon slept with her, and his jealous wife Amphitrite filled Scylla's favourite pool with poisonous herbs. The next time Scylla bathed in the pool, she was turned into a revolting monster. From the waist up she kept human form; but from her waist sprouted twelve dogs' legs and six yapping heads with razor teeth and snaky necks. She became so ravenously hungry that she cared nothing for gods or mortals in her endless search for food. She stole and ate Herakles' cattle, and he killed her for it. But her father Phorkys burned her body at once and boiled the bones. This brought her back to life, and she made her home in a cave on a rocky cliff whose peak pierced the clouds and whose sides were washed glass-smooth by the ceaseless waves. From time to time Scylla reached down from her cave and snatched whatever prey she could find in the sea below: dolphins, seals, tunny – or sailors. (Passing creatures were forced to go within range because another sea-monster lurked just across the narrow strait: Charybdis, daughter of Poseidon, imprisoned by Zeus below the sea for stealing cattle. Three times a day, in a frenzy of hunger, she opened her whirlpool-gullet and swallowed the sea overhead and everything in it. Her den was marked by another glass-smooth cliff, not so tall as Scylla's, with a single fig-tree growing on top.)

There were other monsters, less hideous but no less dangerous. Among them were the Sirens, children of the river-god Acheloös. They could appear as bearded men or smooth-faced girls. They had seabirds' bodies, sometimes with talons, sometimes with lions' claws. They lived on a barren island, one of the entrances to the Underworld, and served Persephone, queen of Hades. When they swooped out to sea and sang, no living being could resist them: helplessly enraptured, their victims followed them to the island, were devoured and passed to the Underworld. Only the Argonauts and Odysseus ever outwitted them.

As well as of these repulsive monsters, the sea was also the home of many kindly and beautiful creatures. Among them were Atlas' daughters the Hesperides, who tended the fertile garden where Hera's golden apples grew. They were the sweetest singers in the sea, save only for the Oceanides, the sea-nymph daughters of Tethys and Ocean. No mortal ever caught sight of them; but on still nights under the stars their singing was sometimes heard by sailors, far in the distance across the endless sea.

The Old Man of the Sea

One of the most elusive of all ocean-beings was the Old Man of the Sea. Every traveller and sailor had heard of him, but few ever saw him face to face. Some said he was Nereus; others that he was Phorkys, and lived in an underwater palace near Odysseus' island of Ithaka. But most people identified him as Proteus (First One), the shepherd of the deep, whose favourite haunt was the sandy Egyptian island of Pharos.

As his name suggests, Proteus was immensely ancient, a god from before recorded time. No one knew his parentage; he seemed always to have existed, a power as limitless and unchanging as the sea itself. He was the protector of all sea-creatures, and herded them as a land-shepherd herds his sheep. His value to mortals was that he was a prophet who never lied: if you could catch him and persuade him to speak, what he told you of the future was certain to come true.

Catching Proteus was not easy. Like all the most ancient gods, he took a thousand different forms, changing shape as quickly as it took to think up a new appearance. Many mortals went to ask his advice, and gave up in despair. Others – a very few – were favoured with the help of his daughter Eidotheia (Shape-of-a-Goddess). She told them how to catch him. Every day at noon he swam to rest on the island of Pharos; there was a gust of wind, a ripple of dark water and he was there, lying on the beach at the cliff's foot. All round him was a herd of brown seals, pungent with the smell of the sea. If you lay hidden until he had counted the seals and settled down for his nap, you could pounce on him and hold him. Even then you could not be sure of him: he would wriggle and twist, taking on a dozen shapes – lion, snake, leopard, running water, tree – to try and break your hold. Only when he returned at last to the shape he had when you first took hold of him, would he give in and answer your questions.

Only two mortals were said for sure to have held Proteus and heard true prophecies. One was Menelaos, becalmed in Egypt on his way home from the Trojan War. Eidotheia disguised him and his men in seal-skins, rubbing them with ambrosia to drive away the sea-stink; after a long struggle, Proteus told Menelaos how to bring back the winds and sail for home. Aristaios consulted Proteus about the death of his bees, and Proteus told him what to do to start new hives.

Some people claimed that Proteus, for a time, took mortal form and was one of the Pharaohs of Egypt. This Pharaoh was renowned for his learning (particularly in astronomy), his justice and his hospitality. When Helen, Menelaos' wife, was stolen by prince Paris of Troy, they sailed to Egypt and were sheltered for a time in Proteus' court. King Proteus had two sons, Polygonos (Oftenborn) and Telegonos (Lastborn): they rashly challenged Herakles to a wrestling-match, and he killed them both.

Peleus and Thetis

One of the most glittering events in the history of the sea-kingdom was the wedding of Peleus and Thetis. Although many mortals made love with gods and had children with them, Peleus was the only mortal man ever to marry a god.* There were two reasons for the marriage. First of all, Thetis had long ago refused to sleep with Zeus when he came courting. Although she had helped Zeus at the time of the gods' revolt – it was she who fetched Briareus to untie the hundred leather knots – she took Hera's side afterwards in the arguments between the king and queen of heaven, and now she angrily refused to sleep with Zeus. He punished her by decreeing that she would never marry an immortal. This decision suited the Olympian gods because of the second reason for the marriage, the Fates' prophecy that Thetis' son would one day be greater than his father. Since no Olympian wanted a son who would outshine him, and since no mor-

64

tal can beget an immortal son, the gods decided that Thetis should marry a mortal prince, and chose Peleus for the honour.

What was honour for Peleus was disgrace for Thetis: no other immortal had ever been condemned to marry a being doomed to die. She refused to have anything to do with Peleus – and the gods (who disliked taking sides between marriage partners) gave him no help in courting her. At last Cheiron the centaur took pity on him and told him what to do. Every day, he said, Thetis rode on a dolphin's back to her favourite bay, Haimonia in Thessaly. Here, in a myrtle grove by a sandy beach, there was a cave where she slept during the heat of the day. All Peleus had to do was lie in wait, catch her and hold her until she agreed to marry him.

Peleus found his way to the cave, and hid. At midday Thetis rode her dolphin to the shore and settled down in the cave to sleep. At once Peleus seized her and held her tight. But Cheiron had not told him that Thetis would struggle to break free, changing shape to try to break his grip. He began by holding a naked girl; then, in an instant, she became a clawing lioness, a snake, a stream of water, a blazing fire, and finally a cuttlefish spitting ink. Torn, soaked, burnt and slimed, Peleus held firm, and at last Thetis gave in and agreed to marry him. The wedding was fixed for the night of the next full moon, and Hera sent invitations to all the Olympians, and to representatives of every other being in the universe.

The ceremony was held on Mount Pelion, lit as dazzling as daylight by the moon, stars and constellations who came as guests. The Muses sang a wedding-song, and the Fates sang a prophecy of the future. Thetis' Nereid sisters rose from the waves and danced on the shore with satyrs and centaurs from the hills. Twelve thrones were set up for the gods, and Hebe and Ganymede poured nectar and served a banquet of ambrosia. Hera held high the wedding-torch, and Zeus himself declared Peleus and Thetis man and wife. As wedding-presents the gods gave Peleus a suit of golden armour, a spear made by Hephaistos and a pair of winged stallions called Balios (Dapple) and Xanthos (Bay).

The feasting and dancing lasted until dawn: it was the twinkling of an eye for the gods, but they had to keep the party short for the sake of Peleus, who, being mortal, would not have lived to see the end of a full-scale, three-hundred-mortal-year Olympian weddingnight. There was only one sour moment, caused by the goddess Eris

(Argument) who had not been invited. Hera, Athene and Aphrodite were sitting talking; Eris rolled a golden apple across the sand towards them, and slipped away. Gallantly, Peleus ran to pick the apple up and give it to its rightful owner. At once he regretted it: for written on the apple were the words 'For the fairest' – and which of the three goddesses was he to choose? The goddesses themselves began to argue, and went to Zeus to settle it. He decreed that since Peleus refused, choice of the fairest must be made by another mortal man, prince Paris of Troy. (So the argument died down, for now – but later, that Apple of Discord and the Judgement of Paris led to the Trojan War.)

Peleus' troubles did not end with his wedding. Despite the gods' decree, Thetis was determined to make her children immortal. So, when each of her babies was born, she charred its bones clean of flesh, rubbed them with ambrosia and boiled them to remove any mortality inherited from Peleus. She did this six times altogether, and six of Peleus' sons were stolen from him to Olympos, where no mortal could ever tread. When the seventh baby was born, he rushed in on Thetis before she had time to finish the magic spell. The mortal part of the child was all charred away except for one ankle-bone. Peleus snatched it from the fire and so prevented his son from becoming fully immortal. Thetis was furious. She left Peleus and went to live in her underwater palace, where he could never follow her (because he was mortal and would drown).

The mortal child of Peleus and Thetis was named Achilles (Man of Grief). He grew up to be a great hero, helped by the fact that the whole of his body, except for one heel, had been three times purified (with fire, boiling water and ambrosia), and so could not be harmed by mortal weapons.*

9
GODS · AND MORTALS

Although it may seem that the gods were forever intervening in the affairs of mortals, nymphs, sprites and the other lesser beings in the universe, in fact these interventions were the exception and not the rule. The gods had immortal business to attend to; their scales of time and space were utterly their own (a mortal lifetime, for example, was to them no longer than a mayfly's lifetime is to a mortal; a god's single stride was a score of mortal kilometres); they treated the other beings in the world, for the most part, with indifference or amusement. They accepted sacrifice and listened – sometimes – to prayers, and their guiding hand could be seen in human activities such as farming, child-rearing and warfare; but most of the world's inhabitants lived their whole lives without ever once encountering a god.

The exceptions were those people whose appearance or behaviour was striking enough to catch an immortal's eye. It might be outstanding beauty, and result in a love-affair. It could be great goodness or wickedness, and result in reward or punishment. Often it was simple stupidity (for example, boasting that your hunting or singing was better than anything in Olympos); in such cases the god's reaction was swift and sharp. But whatever the cause, no lesser being could have dealings with the gods and not be changed.

Alcyone

Alcyone was the daughter of the wind-lord Aiolos, and she married prince Keyx of Trachis. It would have been the happiest marriage in the world, if Alcyone had not foolishly boasted that her love for Keyx was even greater than Hera's love for Zeus. At once Hera sent a

storm and drowned Keyx (who was sailing to consult an oracle). That
night, Keyx's ghost visited Alcyone and bitterly blamed her for his
death. Mad with guilt and grief, she threw herself into the sea and
drowned. Zeus took pity on the pair of them, and turned them into
water-birds. Alcyone became a kingfisher, Keyx a sea-gull. In memory of his daughter, Aiolos held back all the winds for a few days
each autumn, just before the outbreak of winter gales. This time of
calm and warmth was called 'halcyon weather' after Alcyone.

Tereus, Prokne and Philomela

Prokne and Philomela, the daughters of King Pandion of Athens,
were renowned for their singing, and were inseparable sisters. A visitor, King Tereus of Thrace, did their father a favour, and as a reward
was allowed to marry Prokne. He took her back to be queen of
Thrace, and their son Itys was born there.

After a year of marriage, Prokne began to pine for her beloved
sister Philomela. Tereus agreed to fetch Philomela from Athens to
live with them. But on the way home he committed an atrocious
crime: he raped Philomela, cut out her tongue to prevent her telling
anyone, and left her for dead. When he reached home he told Prokne
that her sister had died on the journey.

Some days later Tereus was told by an oracle that his son Itys was
doomed to be murdered by a blood relative. Tereus' only blood relative was his brother Dryas, and he galloped off at once to kill him
and so save Itys' life. While he was away, Philomela stumbled to the
palace, bedraggled, bleeding and tongueless. She had no voice to tell
her sister Prokne what had happened, so she embroidered the story
on a piece of cloth.

The sisters took savage revenge on Tereus. When he came home
from killing his brother, triumphant that his son Itys was now safe,
Prokne welcomed him with a dish of stew. When he'd eaten it Philomela appeared, bubbling and chuckling horribly with her tongueless mouth, and threw the bloodstained head of baby Itys on the
table. Itys had been killed by his mother – *his* blood-relative, not
Tereus' – and eaten by his father.

Tereus seized an axe and ran to kill the sisters. But before there
could be any more bloodshed, the gods changed all three of them
into birds. Tereus became a hoopoe, forever calling 'Pou? Pou?'

(Where? Where?) as he searched for his lost son; Philomela became a screeching, chuckling swallow; Prokne became a nightingale whose sweet, sad song forever included the syllables 'Itu, itu' in memory of the child she killed.*

Midas

Midas had dealings with the gods twice in his life, and each time his stupidity turned possible good luck into disaster. He was a Macedonian king, a famous gardener and rose-grower. One morning when his servants went to pull dead-heads from the roses, they found Silenos, king of the goat-footed Satyrs, snoring in a flowerbed. (He had been dancing in the revels of his master Dionysos; then he had drunk too much, felt sleepy and dozed off among Midas' flowers.) The gardeners entwined him with rose-chains and took him to Midas, who entertained him for five days as an honoured guest, until Dionysos came looking for him.* In return for this hospitality, Dionysos offered Midas any gift he chose to name.

Midas' greed drove every sensible request out of his mind. Without hesitation he asked that everything he touched should turn to gold. Dionysos sighed at his foolishness, but none the less agreed.

For the next few hours Midas was as happy as a child. He touched grass, trees, stones and flowers; he particularly enjoyed walking through his rose-gardens, turning his most perfect blooms to gold. But then came evening, and the evening meal. Midas found himself biting lumps of gold instead of bread or meat, drinking liquid gold for wine. Bitterly he realized his foolishness, and begged Dionysos to take back the golden touch. Dionysos told him to go and wash in the river Paktolos, in Asia. It was a long journey (especially for someone growing daily weaker for lack of food); but at last, thirsty and starving, Midas reached the Paktolos and plunged in. At once the golden touch was washed away – and to this day the Paktolos still runs with gold, carrying grains of gold-dust down to the sea.

The story of Midas' foolishness fascinated King Gordios of Phrygia (the Asian country through which the Paktolos flowed).* He offered Midas half his kingdom to stay in Phrygia – and Midas, delighted not to have to return to Macedonia and his jeering people, founded the city of Ankyra and settled there.

His life would have ended happily if he and his stupidity had not met the gods for a second time. He was walking one day on the riverbank when he overheard Pan and Apollo arguing about who was the better musician. Midas hid in the reeds to listen while they played in turn to Tmolos, the river-god. But when Tmolos declared Apollo the winner, Midas rushed out of hiding and shouted that *he* thought Pan's music best. Apollo punished him by giving him ass's ears.

Ashamed and embarrassed, Midas covered his head with a turban (a head-dress still worn in those parts to this day). He never took it off in public; only his barber knew the secret of his ears. But the barber was a gossip, and although Midas threatened to kill him if he told a living soul, he felt as the weeks passed that he had to share the secret or burst. Finally, at dead of night, he crept to the river-bank, dug a hole, whispered into it 'Midas has ass's ears' and quickly filled it in.

The seasons passed. A bank of reeds grew where the hole had been. And whenever the wind blew, they bent their heads to one another and whispered 'Midas has ass's ears!' The secret was out: all Phrygia soon knew that Midas had once again met an immortal god and made a fool of himself. Not even executing the barber soothed his embarrassment; in the end he drank bull's blood (an old Macedonian way of committing suicide) and choked to death.

Kainis

Poseidon made love to Kainis, and then offered her any gift she asked. She said 'Please turn me into a man – a warrior no weapons on earth can harm'. Poseidon agreed, and Kainis became Kaineus, king of the Lapiths.

The Lapiths were the first mortals to tame horses (thanks to their invention of the bit and bridle) and to ride them into war. They were an arrogant people – and Kaineus, their king, was the most arrogant of all. He set up a spear in the market-place, and declared that in future Zeus and the Olympians were deposed, and Might-in-War was god. Zeus ordered his servants the Centaurs to avenge this insult, and they fought a fierce battle against the Lapiths.* None of their weapons – arrows, spears and stones – had any effect on Kaineus, because of Poseidon's gift of invulnerability against weapons on earth. At last Zeus told the Centaurs to smother Kaineus

in a hole in the ground under a pile of logs. A grey-brown bird –
some say it was a cuckoo – flew out from the wood-pile, and the
priests declared it was Kaineus' soul and that he was dead,
smothered not by weapons on earth but by the earth itself. They
pulled the logs aside, and in the hole they found the body of a
woman – with the loss of his invulnerability Kaineus had turned into
Kainis once again.

Hyacinthos

Hyacinthos was a handsome Spartan prince, and Apollo fell in love
with him. But Hyacinthos already had a lover, the musician Thamyris. To get rid of *him*, Apollo told the Muses of Thamyris' boast that
he could outsing them, and the Muses punished Thamyris by stealing his voice, eyes and memory. This left the field clear for Apollo's
love-affair with Hyacinthos, and he showered the boy with presents
and taught him hunting, athletics, poetry and prophecy. He kept him
jealously hidden from the other gods; but one day the West Wind
caught a glimpse of Hyacinthos and fell passionately in love. He
gusted round Apollo and Hyacinthos as they practised athletics in
the meadows, trying to slip past Apollo and caress Hyacinthos'
cheek. One day he blew too hard: his breath spun away a discus
Apollo was teaching Hyacinthos to throw, and it cracked the boy's
skull and killed him. From his blood Apollo created the purple
hyacinth, which forever droops its head and is marked with the letters AI (Alas!) for grief.

Alope

Alope, daughter of King Kerkyon of Arcadia, was raped by Poseidon
and bore a son. She wrapped the child in a cloth and left him on a
mountainside to die. But a shepherd recognised the cloth as coming
from the palace, and took the baby to the king. The King was enraged that his daughter should have borne a bastard child; he
ordered his servants to brick Alope up in a cave to starve to death,
and to leave the baby on the mountain again to die. The child was
rescued for a second time – another shepherd found him and brought
him up as his own son, Hippothoös – but Alope starved in her pris-

on, and was buried by the roadside not far from Eleusis. Poseidon turned her into a fountain of fresh water, a welcome refreshment for travellers on that dusty road.

Europa*

Zeus was visiting Phoenicia in Asia Minor when he fell in love with Europa, daughter of King Agenor (and sister of Kadmos, who later founded Thebes). Europa and her maids were picking flowers in the water-meadows, while the king's royal cattle browsed nearby. Zeus disguised himself as a slow-moving, broad-browed bull, so tame that it allowed the girls to stroke it and even to garland its horns with flowers. Europa climbed boldly on its back to ride it – and at once bull-Zeus plunged into the sea and swam powerfully away, leaving the maid-servants wringing their hands and forlornly calling her name.

Still disguised as a bull, Zeus splashed ashore at last, at Gortyna in Crete.* Europa fell from his back and lay weeping on the sand – and bull-Zeus reared up and made love to her. They stayed together in Crete for several mortal years, and Europa bore Zeus three children, Minos, Rhadamanthys and Sarpedon. The king of Crete, Asterios, was childless, and he was easily persuaded to marry Europa and bring up Zeus' children as his own. So Zeus' and Europa's sons became princes of Crete, and founded one of the most powerful royal dynasties in mortal history.*

Phyllis

Phyllis was a Thracian princess, and her lover was Akamas. He went to fight at Troy, and every day throughout the war she went to the high sea-cliffs to watch for his return. Ten years passed; Troy fell; the victorious Greeks returned; but there was no sign of Akamas. In fact his ship had been holed in a storm and was delayed for repairs; but Phyllis knew nothing of this, and thought that he was dead. She mourned for nine days, refused food and finally died – only minutes before Akamas' ship reached land. Sadly he embraced her body – and Athene, touched by their piteous love, transformed her into

an almond-tree. Akamas set up a yearly almond-festival in her memory.**

Echo and Narcissus

Narcissus died as the result of an unusual love-affair: he loved himself. He was the most handsome youth in Greece; every girl and boy he met longed to be his lover. But he refused them all, saying that he was waiting for another being as perfect as himself. Everywhere he went, mortals and immortals alike pined for a kiss from him, for a kind word or a single glance: in vain.

One of Narcissus' would-be lovers was the wood-nymph Echo. She had once been pretty; but she angered a god and suffered for it. Zeus was visiting the wood-nymphs one day, and Hera heard of it. She came angrily down from Olympos, and Echo foolishly kept her talking while Zeus and the other nymphs slipped away.

Hera punished Echo by taking away her body and half her voice. She could never again be seen, and she could only speak by repeating the last words uttered by someone else. Lonely and miserable, Echo wandered the woods and hills, trying to make contact with anyone she saw. But her attempts at conversation seemed to travellers like an eerie, invisible mocking of their own words. They treated her as a joke or a trick and hurried on their way.

One day Narcissus was hunting in the woods, alone as always, when Echo saw him and fell in love. Invisibly she followed him, eager for him to speak so that she could echo him and answer. At last he shouted to his dogs 'This way! This way!'

'This way!' cried Echo joyfully.

Narcissus thought her voice the most beautiful sound he had ever heard – it was, after all, the echo of his own. He ran through the woods, trying to find the owner of the voice.

'Which way? This way?' he called.

'This way,' answered Echo.

Then, in a clearing, Narcissus found a pool of clear water. He knelt to drink – and in the water saw the perfect being he had wanted so long to meet. He smiled; the figure in the water smiled. He held out his arms; the figure in the water held out its arms to him.

For days Narcissus knelt by the pool in a haze of love, besotted by his own reflection. Echo watched tearfully as his love turned gradually to despair when his lover refused to come out of the pool to join him. At last, filled with the same hopeless passion as so many others had felt for him, he drew a dagger and stabbed himself. Wherever drops of his blood touched the ground, narcissus flowers grew: white, with a blood-red wound at the heart, their heads forever bent to gaze at their own reflection.

As for Echo, her longing for mortal company turned to bitter hatred. Instead of trying to make friends with travellers, she used her invisibility and mimickry to mock them, cheat them and if possible lead them from safety into danger.

Ixion

The mortal who sinned most greatly against the gods and suffered most severely for it was Ixion, king of the Lapiths in Thessaly. His father was Phlegyas, another criminal;* but Ixion outdid even him in wickedness. He was a raider and a thief: no rich men's goods, wives or daughters were safe from him. He stole Dia, daughter of Eioneus, and promised her father a huge bride-price if he came to the wedding. But when Eioneus arrived at Ixion's palace he walked into a trap: a pit dug in the ground, filled with red-hot coals and hidden with branches and a layer of earth. So Ixion not only never paid the bride-price, but also roasted Eioneus to death.

After this murder Ixion was an outcast. A man who killed his father-in-law was blood-guilty, and would bring pollution on anyone who sheltered him or fed him. No one in Thessaly, not even his own people, would speak to him or touch him until the gods purified his crime – and the gods refused. Only Zeus favoured Ixion. Perhaps he approved of a man bold enough to take what he wanted regardless of the consequences; perhaps he knew of some guilt in Eioneus for which his death was a just punishment. Whatever the reason, he finally listened to Ixion's prayers, and not only purified him from blood-guilt but even invited him to be guest of honour at an Olympian feast.

This was an unheard-of honour for any mortal, let alone a criminal and a murderer. The gods muttered, and many stayed away from the feast. Those who distrusted Ixion were right: for he drank too much and tried to rape Hera herself. Just in time, Zeus (who sees and knows all) replaced Hera with a phantom-goddess moulded from mist, called Nephele (Cloud). While Ixion was making love to Nephele, the gods seized him.*

For betraying Zeus, Ixion was given a punishment meant to remind other mortals of the lesson he had forgotten. He was chained to a blazing wheel which hurtled like a shooting-star from Olympos to the Underworld. On it was written in letters of fire the words 'Kindness deserves gratitude'; as the wheel revolved they burned into Ixion's flesh. There was no way to end his agony: Zeus set the wheel rolling in the Underworld till the end of time.

Leda

Leda was a woman of striking beauty, the wife of King Tyndareos of Sparta. One day Zeus and Aphrodite were walking beside the river Eurotas, when they found Leda bathing in a pool. Zeus was filled with lust; but he knew that Leda was true to her mortal husband (whose child she was already carrying), and would have to be tricked into making love. He persuaded Aphrodite to help him. She became an eagle (borrowing the form of Zeus' own sacred bird), and he became a swan. They spiralled through the air like hunter and hunted, and flew down to the bank of Leda's pool. Zeus lay feebly fluttering, as if exhausted by the chase; Aphrodite soared away like an eagle cheated of its prey. Leda, naked and wet from the river, took pity on what she thought was a helpless swan. She nestled it in her lap and stroked its neck to revive it. At once Zeus made love to her, soared into the air with beating wings and disappeared.

Some time afterwards, Leda gave birth to two identical swan-eggs. From each hatched a pair of human twins: two girls, Klytemnestra and Helen, and two boys, Kastor and Polydeukes (or Pollux).* The problem was, who was the father? It was thought at first that Klytemnestra and Kastor were mortal, the children of Tyndareus, and Helen and Polydeukes were the immortal children of Zeus. But later, when the children grew up, Kastor and Polydeukes were treated as immortals, the Dioskouroi (Sons of Zeus)*, and Klytemnestra and Helen remained on earth. Klytemnestra married King Agamemnon of Mycenae; Helen married his brother Menelaus, and was later stolen from him by prince Paris, an event which led to the most destructive event in mortal history up to that time, the Trojan War.

76

10
ORACLES · SHRINES
AND · PROPHETS

Delphi

The summit of Mount Parnassos in Phokis was more than 2500 metres above sea level, almost as high as Mount Olympos itself. (It was one of the few places not covered by flood-water when Zeus tried to wash the world clean of mortals: Deucalion beached his boat there, and it was on Parnassos that the new human race was born from stones.) The summit was divided into two peaks; one was a favourite haunt of Apollo and the Muses, the other of Dionysos and his dancing Bacchants. Any mortal who spent a night on either peak, spying on the dance, was found next morning gibbering and insane; by contrast, any mortal who drank from the Castalian Spring on the side of the mountain was inspired to write poetry.* About halfway up the mountainside, on a steep, winding road from the valley, stood the town of Delphi. It was named after Apollo's son Delphos, who founded it; it stood beside one of the most important oracles in Greece.

An oracle is a place where the gods speak directly to mortals, answering their questions and giving them advice. (Sometimes the answers are clear; sometimes the gods speak in riddles hard to understand.) The first god to give answers at Delphi was Gaia, Mother Earth. Shepherds, herding goats on the mountainside, noticed that some of their animals were missing. They found them lurching about in a cave like drunks. As soon as the shepherds went into the cave, they too were filled with ecstasy: Mother Earth breathed into them a spirit not their own. They came babbling down the mountainside – the first mortals to feel a god's prophetic power. Ever afterwards, anyone who visited the cave was entered by the god and prophesied.

When Leto gave birth to Zeus' children Apollo and Artemis, and jealous Hera sent the monster Python to kill her, it was in this same sacred cave that Apollo trapped the monster and killed it. From this time onwards, he took a special interest in the Delphic oracle. The shrine's first guardian was the goddess Themis (Order), and she was succeeded by mortal priestesses called Pythonesses (after Python). Temples were built at the cave-entrance, of all kinds of materials. (The first, of bees'-wax and feathers, blew away; the second, of woven ferns, rotted; the third, of laurel-branches, collapsed; the fourth, of bronze, was crushed in an earthquake; the fifth, of stone, survived and can still be seen today.)

To consult the Delphic oracle you visited the priestess in her holy cave, and put your questions. She sat on a tripod (a three-legged metal stool, which lifted her from the ground where ordinary mortals trod), and was filled with the spirit of the god. She gave Apollo's answers in shrieks and scattered words, and the priests wrote them down, turned them into verse and if necessary explained what they meant. The answers were sometimes hard to understand, and often deliberately two-edged. (For example, when King Croesus of Lydia asked what would happen if he invaded Persia, the oracle told him that he would destroy a great kingdom. Overjoyed, he invaded Persia, and a great kingdom was duly destroyed – his own.) But the Delphic oracle became famous for its wisdom and fairness, and grew to be one of the richest and most often visited shrines in Greece.*

Dodona

An oracle often consulted by gods as well as mortals was at Dodona in western Greece. Mother Earth sent out two sacred doves from her shrine at Thebes in Egypt. One of them settled at Ammon in Libya, and made that a sacred place. The other flew all the way to Dodona, where it perched on an oak-tree in the middle of a wooded hillside, and made the whole place an oracle. Later, Zeus was given control of both oracles by Mother Earth, and they became two of his favourite shrines.

At Dodona there was no sacred cave like the one at Delphi. Instead, the hills and woods themselves were the oracle. The oaks were home to thousands of doves, and the priests also hung tiny gongs and bells on the branches. To consult the oracle, you told the priests your question, and they made an offering and asked Zeus to grant an answer. The answer might come from the rustling of the oak-leaves, the doves' cooing, the tinkle of the gongs or the splashing of a stream beside a sacred oak. The priests listened to these noises, told you Zeus' answer and if necessary explained it to you.

Unlike Delphi, the oracle at Dodona concerned itself less with matters of state than with the ordinary problems of everyday life. For example, there was once a young man called Koresos who fell in love with a girl called Kallirhoe. Unfortunately she disliked him heartily, and wanted nothing to do with him. He asked Dionysos for advice; but instead of giving a clear answer, Dionysos sent a plague on the villagers, who went insane one by one and died. In desperation, they sent for help to Dodona. The oracle answered that the only ways to end Dionysos' anger were to sacrifice Kallirhoe or to find someone else prepared to die for her. Tearfully they prepared the girl for death; at the last moment Koresos sprang forward, announced that although she cared nothing for him he was happy to die for her, and killed himself. Kallirhoe, seeing him dead before her, was filled with the love he had waited for so long, and in her grief and despair killed herself as well. At once Dionysos lifted the plague. He turned Kallirhoe into a spring of clear water, and Koresos into a willow beside it, forever bending, lover-like, to caress the water with its branches.

On another occasion, Dionysos himself made his way to Dodona to consult the oracle. He was riding his favourite donkey, to which he had granted the power of speech. They were riding through countryside governed by Priapos, a scarecrow-spirit who looked after gardens, vegetable-plots and fields.* Suddenly Priapos sprang out and barred Dionysos' way. He claimed that the donkey's shadow had trespassed, crossing the boundary between public road and private field. The donkey began to argue; the argument ended in a fight, and the donkey was killed. Dionysos turned it into the stars called Asses (part of the constellation Cancer). What he did to Priapos, and whether or not he heard the answer he wanted from Dodona, the story fails to tell. The phrase 'to fight over a donkey's shadow,' meaning to argue about something trivial, became a proverb.*

79

Trophonios

The oracle of Trophonios was at Lebadeia in Boeotia. Its guardian spirit, Trophonios, son of the Argonaut Erginos, was one of the few mortals who turned into gods. He and his brother Agamedes were the stone-masons who built Apollo's temple at Delphi. When they asked for their wages, Apollo told them to spend the next week as his guests, wining, dining and enjoying themselves; on the last day of the week they would get their reward. They did as he said – and on the seventh day were found dead in bed.

Their death was not ingratitude or a cruel joke on Apollo's part: he had greater plans for them. Not long afterwards, the countryside of Boeotia was parched with drought. Every river and stream dried up; farm-animals, seeking water, sniffed dust and died; people withered like unwatered plants. They sent to Delphi for help, and Apollo told them to go to Lebadeia and look for a forest cave overhung with bees. Inside the cave, he said, Trophonios' spirit would give them an oracle.

They found the cave, climbed down inside, and the oracle told them how to channel an underground stream to carry water to the world above. After that, Trophonios and Agamedes were honoured as gods, Apollo's adopted sons. Temples were built to them in Lebadeia, and people came from all over Greece to consult the oracle.

Consulting Trophonios was not easy. At most oracles, all you had to do was ask your question, and the priests did the rest. But if you wanted Trophonios' advice you had to spend several days in Lebadeia fasting, praying and making sacrifice. Then, on the day of the consultation, you bathed in the chilly waters of the river Herkyna, rubbed yourself with oil and put on a plain cloth robe. You drank from two sacred springs, called the Fountain of Forgetfulness and the Fountain of Memory. After that, two boys led you to Trophonios' cave, a dark hole in the forest floor about eight metres deep. They showed you a ladder leading down into the darkness, placed a honey-cake in each of your hands and left you to continue on your own. Carefully balancing the honey-cakes, you climbed down the ladder to the cave-floor. In the centre of the floor was another hole, wide enough to admit only one person at a time. You had to wriggle into this, feet-first, until suddenly the walls of the tunnel disappeared and you slipped down into an echoing underground cavern. You lay there, dazed in the darkness, while the ghost of Trophonios, taking the form either of an invisible snake or of a spirit made from the bones and soil of Mother Earth herself, whispered secret words to you. When all was over (and the honey-cakes had disappeared), you had to find the narrow tunnel again, wriggle your way up through it and climb the ladder back to the open air, where waiting priests sat you on the Throne of Memory, listened to what you could remember of Trophonios' whispering, and explained what it meant.

Those who went through this ordeal usually came up white and shaking, as if they'd visited the underworld and spoken with ghosts. (For this reason, people used to say of dejected-looking friends 'He looks as if he's visited Trophonios'.) Despite its unpleasantness and difficulty, the oracle gave reliable answers, and became one of the leading Greek shrines. People often visited it in the same round trip that took them to Delphi, and an annual athletics festival was held at Lebadeia in honour of Trophonios and Agamedes*.

Asklepios

Oracles of a different kind were given at shrines of Asklepios (one of the most famous was at Epidauros in Argolis). Asklepios (or Aesculapius) was the son of Apollo and the mortal princess Koronis.* Foolishly, even when she was pregnant with Apollo's child, Koronis had another love-affair, with the mortal Ischys. For this Apollo and Artemis shot her dead. When she was lying on her funeral-pyre and the flames were already licking her corpse, Apollo suddenly remembered his son Asklepios. He cut open Koronis' womb and released the baby, just in time to save him from the Underworld.

Asklepios was brought up by the centaur Cheiron, who taught him medicine and the secrets of healing herbs. Athene also gave him two bottles of blood from the Gorgon Medusa. One was deadly poison; the other had power to raise mortals from the dead. But when Asklepios used the second bottle to raise Hippolytos, Zeus punished him by striking him dead with a thunderbolt. Later, however, Zeus relented, brought Asklepios back from the Underworld and gave him the rights and honours of a full immortal god.*

Because of his healing powers, people went to Asklepios' shrines not for advice about matters of state or family problems, but to be cured of illness. They hoped either to be healed on the spot or to hear an oracle which would tell them how to cure themselves. The

81

chief part of each shrine was a large courtyard or a Hall of Healing with an altar at one end. All the sick people lay down there to spend a night in the god's presence. They carried offerings of honey-cakes to feed his sacred snakes.

There was no light, and no sound but the uneasy tossing and coughing of the sick. At dead of night, without warning, Asklepios appeared, a shadowy figure surrounded by hissing snakes and accompanied by his daughters Iaso and Panakeia. They moved round the sufferers one by one, bending over them and either letting the snakes stroke them with their flickering tongues, or whispering to them how they might be cured. When everyone had been visited, the god and his assistants vanished. Next morning the sick people took Asklepios' words to the doctor-priests of the shrine, who either operated as the god advised or made up the necessary medicines and prescribed a course of treatment.

Melampous

Most of the priests who explained oracles were the servants of one particular god, and spent their whole lives working in a single shrine. But there were a few mortals, favoured more than usually by the gods, who roamed the world giving advice to anyone who asked. The gods spoke to them, sometimes directly, sometimes in omens and miracles, and they were skilled at prophesying and in all kinds of sacred rituals and magic arts.

One such mortal was Melampous of Pylos. He was the first human being ever to be given the powers of second hearing and second sight. His slaves were cutting down a tree one day, when they found a nest of snakes in the hollow trunk. Before Melampous could stop them they killed the parents, and he was only just in time to save the baby snakes. Remembering that snakes are servants of Mother Earth, he burnt the adults' bodies and buried their ashes, then took the babies home to rear. That night the baby snakes wriggled into his bed and began to lick his ears – and to his astonishment Melampous found that he could understand everything they said. Mother Earth had given him the gift of second hearing: from then on he understood the language of every living creature in the world. Later, Apollo also gave him second sight, the ability to interpret omens and foretell the future.

Melampous soon put his new skills to use. His brother Bias was in love with a girl called Pero. Her father had promised her to any man who stole the cattle of Phylakos, a nearby land-owner, and Bias asked Melampous to steal the cattle for him. Anyone else would have thought this a crime; but Melampous' special powers told him that if he stole the cattle he would be put in prison, but would be set free after one year and given the cattle as a gift. Accordingly, he stole the cattle, and was duly caught and thrown into prison.

For three hundred and sixty-four days Melampous sat in his prison cell. He listened eagerly to the conversations of the insects and spiders inside the cell, and of the birds and animals outside. In this way he learned all kinds of strange and useful facts – not least that birds and insects despise human beings, whom they think of as blundering, earthbound creatures with clumsy bodies and few brains.

On his three-hundred-and-sixty-fourth night in prison, Melampous overheard two woodworms congratulating each other on a job well done. The beam holding up Phylakos' palace roof was gnawed almost all the way through, and was sure to collapse next morning. Melampous shouted for Phylakos and told him this news. At first Phylakos thought that imprisonment had driven Melampous mad; but next day, when he cleared the palace of people and the roof fell in as prophesied, he was filled with respect for Melampous' magic powers and set him free. Phylakos' son Iphiklos was unable to have children; by listening to the conversation of a pair of vultures, Melampous found out a way to cure him – and as a reward Phylakos offered him any gift he chose. Melampous chose the cattle, drove them home and gave them to his brother Bias. Bias took them to Pero's father, and so was able to marry the girl he loved.

Melampous' next adventure concerned madwomen, the daughters of King Proitos of Argolis.* They had offended Hera by stealing gold from her statue to make jewellery, and in punishment Hera sent them insane. They thought they were cattle, and ran about the fields like cows plagued by flies, lowing, shrieking and trying to gore or trample passers-by. Melampous offered to cure them, for one third of Proitos' kingdom. Proitos refused: after all, although it was embarrassing to have daughters who thought themselves cows, it was hardly dangerous or worth such a high price to find a cure. But the madness spread – as Melampous knew it would – and soon every woman in Argos was raving in the hills, tearing sheep and cattle apart and threatening the life of everyone who passed. Proitos sent again for Melampous and offered him one third of the kingdom for a cure; Melampous replied that the price had doubled: he was to get one third, his brother Bias another third, and they were also to marry one of Proitos' daughters each. (By this time Bias' earlier wife Pero had died.)

Reluctantly Proitos agreed. Melampous and Bias rounded up all the cow-women and sent them stampeding to Sikyon, where they were washed clean of madness in a sacred stream. Proitos' daughters fled to a mountain cave; Melampous followed them, gave them water from the river Styx to drink, and cured their wits. He and Bias married one daughter each, and became joint kings of Argolis with Proitos. When Melampous died he was treated as a god, and shrines and temples were built in his honour, many of which became important oracles.

Kalchas*

Kalchas was another mortal favoured by Apollo. His reputation for wisdom, and for accuracy in interpreting the gods' sayings, was so great that when King Agamemnon was gathering allies to sail to Troy, he sent for him to join the expedition. Kalchas' value was shown at once: he told Agamemnon that the Greeks would fail unless they recruited Achilles, the hero-son of Peleus and the sea-goddess Thetis. Later, when the Greek fleet was becalmed at Aulis, he told them the cause and what to do. He also foretold the exact length of the Trojan War, by explaining the following omen: Agamemnon was sacrificing at Aulis when a huge snake, its back blotched with crimson, rose from the ground at his feet and slid across the beach to a plane-tree at the sand's edge. Here, on one of the top branches, was a sparrow's nest containing a mother and eight chicks. The snake ate them all – and then, before it could move, was turned to stone. Kalchas interpreted the omen to mean that Troy would resist for nine years, then fall like a stone in the tenth; to prove his words correct, Zeus sent a flash of lightning from a clear blue sky.

Kalchas sailed with the Greeks to Troy, and throughout the siege guided them with good advice. When the city fell he took his share of the spoils and sailed to Colophon in Asia Minor. This town was ruled by Mopsos, the prophet grandson of another famous prophet, Teiresias. It was here that Kalchas was doomed to die – as a result, for once, of ignoring information sent by the gods. They had told him that he would die on the day he met a greater prophet than himself. But he foolishly forgot this, and challenged Mopsos to a contest of prophecy.

The people gathered in a field by a fig-orchard, and the contest began. Kalchas pointed to the nearest fig-tree and challenged Mopsos to say exactly how many figs its branches held. 'Ten thousand and one,' said Mopsos. 'The ten thousand will fill a single container, and the one will be left over.'

'Prove it,' said Kalchas.

Mopsos' servants gathered the figs and counted them, and Mopsos' prophecy was proved exactly right. Now it was his turn. He pointed to a pregnant sow sniffing up windfall fruit in the orchard, and challenged Kalchas to predict exactly the number and colour of piglets in the litter. When Kalchas said he couldn't possibly know such a thing, Mopsos said that there would be ten piglets, one black male and nine black-and-white females. Next day the pigs were born and he was again proved right. Kalchas realised that he had met a greater prophet, and that this was the hour fated for his death. His body was buried at Megara in Achaia, where he was afterwards worshipped at an oracle. As for Mopsos, when *he* died the gods gave him immortality and an oracle at Malia, which became famous for the exactness and detail of its answers.

Teiresias

The greatest of all mortal prophets was Teiresias of Thebes. He was born an ordinary man, and was given magic powers as the result of a chain of bizarre events. One day when he was hunting he found two snakes coupling in a clearing. He hit them with a stick and killed the female snake. At once, by earth-magic (all snakes are protected by Mother Earth) he was changed into a woman. He remained female for seven years. Then, by chance, in the same clearing, he found another pair of snakes. This time he killed the male, and immediately changed back into a man.*

While Teiresias was a woman, he had several lovers; as a man, he made love to several girls. This made him the ideal person to settle an argument between Zeus and Hera about whether love-making gives more pleasure to the woman or the man. (Zeus said that the man gave more pleasure than he got, Hera said the opposite.) They sent for Teiresias and asked his opinion. From personal experience he agreed with Zeus, saying that the man gave nine times more pleasure than he got. Hera was so angry that she blinded Teiresias; but Zeus gave him the prophet's gift of second sight, and a lifespan of seven mortal generations.

Teiresias spent most of his long life in Thebes, where his prophecies helped and guided the townspeople. He had two special skills: he understood the language of birds, and could talk without fear to the ghosts of the underworld. His death, when it finally came, was as strange as the events of his life had been. He was walking in the afternoon heat, and felt thirsty. He gathered a handful of water from a spring and drank. Unfortunately the spring was Tilphoussa, noted for its icy coldness. The chill of the water froze Teiresias' blood, and he died and passed to the Underworld. Even there, the gods still favoured him: he kept his knowledge of the future, and any person bold enough to consult his ghost was rewarded with accurate prophecies. Teiresias also had two prophetic oracles on earth, on Mount Tilphoussa beside the icy spring, and at Orchomenos near Thebes.

11
THE · WORLD · OF MORTALS

Heroes

When the gods began to withdraw more and more from human affairs, leaving mortals to make their own decisions (and their own mistakes), one of the main reasons for their confidence in humanity was the existence of the race of heroes. Each hero was the child of one mortal and one immortal parent.* Because he was half mortal he shared all human feelings, hopes and fears (something no god could do, except from afar); because he was half immortal he had wisdom and strength more than other human beings. So long as heroes were in the world, the gods were able to forget mortals and concentrate, for better or worse, on their own affairs.

The Kalydonian boar

The first great gathering of heroes was the hunting-party assembled by King Oineus of Kalydon to kill a gigantic boar. Artemis, angry because Oineus had forgotten a sacrifice, sent the boar to plague the people of Kalydon. It trampled crops, gored cattle, and was too strong for any mortal to kill unaided. So Oineus sent word all over Greece that any hero who killed the boar would win its skin and tusks as prize: a valuable reward, since they had been created by a god and therefore had supernatural power.

The leader of the hunt was Oineus' son Meleager. The three Fates had attended his birth and given him presents. Klotho gave him courage; Lachesis gave him strength; Atropos gave him the chance of immortality, by pointing to a pine-branch burning in the fire and saying that he would never die so long as it stayed unburned. At once Meleager's mother Althaia snatched the branch from the fire and hid it. When Meleager grew up, he fell in love with Atalanta the Amazon, a follower of Artemis who claimed that she could run faster and hunt better than any man. She was one of the first guests – and the only female – invited to hunt the boar. The others included Kastor and Polydeukes, Theseus, Jason, Nestor, Admetos, Iphikles and over two dozen other heroes including two centaurs (Hylaios and Rhaikos) and Meleager's uncles Toxeus and Plexippos, two of the brothers of his mother Althaia.

The boar's lair was in a marsh filled with reeds and willow-trees. The hunters formed a line and began to pick their way through the marsh; they intended to flush out the boar and force it to run ahead of them until they cornered it beside the river.

Many of the hunters disapproved of Atalanta taking part. Meleager's uncles Toxeus and Plexippos were particularly angry. It was unheard-of (they said) for a woman to hunt with men; she would bring nothing but trouble. And they were right: as soon as the line of hunters moved into the high reeds, the centaurs Hylaios and Rhaikos rushed at Atalanta to rape her, and she shot them dead. Before anyone else could move, the boar broke cover and charged. It was as high as a man, with axe-sharp hooves and tusks a metre long. In its first charge it killed two of the hunters, disabled another and sent Nestor scurrying for safety up a tree. As it crashed away into the reeds, Iphikles threw his spear and grazed its shoulder, drawing a smear of blood.

Telamon and Peleus plunged after the boar. But Telamon tripped, and as the pair of them floundered in the reeds the boar charged again. Atalanta hit it with an arrow behind one ear and deflected it – luckily for Peleus and Telamon, but fatally for Ankaios who got in the way and was gored to death. The rest of the heroes surrounded the boar and began shooting arrows and stabbing with their spears. Peleus missed the boar and killed Eurytion; but several other heroes hit their target, and finally Meleager stabbed his spear into the boar's heart and it fell dead.

The boar's death was not the end of the matter. Who was to win the prize? Meleager's spear-thrust had finished the boar, but who was actually responsible for its death? Meleager himself awarded Atalanta the skin and tusks, saying that if her arrow had not deflected the boar's charge, the others would never have cornered it. Meleager's uncles angrily disagreed. Toxeus said that it was drawing

first blood that counted, and that the prize belonged to Iphikles. Plexippos said that it belonged to the person who actually killed the boar, that is to Meleager. Tempers rose until at last, in a furious rage, Meleager killed both his uncles.

When news of the deaths of Toxeus and Plexippos reached their two surviving brothers, they gathered soldiers and went to punish Meleager. But he held them all at bay, killed both princes and scattered their soldiers. Servants told Meleager's mother Althaia that all four of her brothers were dead, and that Meleager her son had killed them. Grim-faced, Althaia fetched the branch that protected Meleager's life and threw it on the fire. As the branch charred, Meleager began to crumple and fade, and by the time the branch had burned to ash, he lay dead and withered on the ground. The palace women gathered his remains and buried them, singing mourning-songs. Artemis turned them all into guinea-fowl (which still shriek and wail piteously to this day).

Many of the heroes went dejectedly home, disappointed at not winning the prize. But some thought they had found another, better prize: Atalanta. They flocked to her father's palace and demanded that she choose one of them and marry him. But Atalanta was a follower of virgin Artemis, and had sworn to have nothing to do with men; the Delphic oracle had also told her that marriage would end her human existence. In the end, to get rid of the suitors, she said that anyone who wanted to marry her should run a race with her. He would run unarmed; she would carry a dagger. If he reached the finishing-line first, she would marry him; but if she won she would stab him dead.

Many men accepted the challenge, ran the race and lost. Finally it was Hippomenes' turn. He was a favourite of the goddess Aphrodite, and she told him a trick to win the race. She gave him three of the Hesperides' golden apples, and told him to roll them one at a time in front of Atalanta as she ran. Atalanta stopped running each time to pick the apple up; Hippomenes was able to pass her, and so won the race.

Hippomenes' trick, to say nothing of the golden apples, melted Atalanta's heart and filled her with love for him. They ran into the woods to kiss and make love. Unfortunately they chose to do it in a place sacred to Rhea, and she changed them into lions and yoked them forever to her chariot. So the prophecy of the Delphic oracle came true: Atalanta's marriage ended her human life.*

Aiakos

Aiakos was the son of Zeus and the river-nymph Aigina.* He was born on the fertile island of Oinone; he grew up to be its king, and renamed it Aigina after his mother. This was a dangerous mistake. Up until then Hera had known nothing of Zeus' love-affair with Aigina, but the island's new name attracted her attention and she soon found out the whole story. Instead of punishing just the lovers themselves, she decided to take revenge by blotting out the island and all its inhabitants. She sowed the fields with stones, so that what had once been fertile land became sour and barren. The standing corn drooped and died; the islanders lived for a while on their stored provisions, but then began to starve. Hera added thirst to their misery: she filled every stream on the island with snakes, and sent a heat-wave instead of rain.

One by one the people of Aigina died. The sun-baked ground was too hard to dig graves, and the survivors were too weak to build funeral-pyres. Corpses lay everywhere, bloated in the sun; snakes swarmed over them; there was no sound but the buzz of flies and the cries of the dying.

Led by Aiakos, the few surviving inhabitants huddled in the temple. They were chiefly old people and a handful of children whose parents had kept them alive by giving them their own last scraps of food. There were no adults of child-bearing age; when the old people and children died Aigina would be as barren of inhabitants as it was of crops. Apart from the snakes and flies, the only other living beings left were ants: ceaselessly, tirelessly, they ran in busy columns up and down the trunk of a sacred oak-tree in the temple yard.

The old people and children lifted stick-arms and prayed to the gods for help. But their voices were thin, and no god heard. Then Aiakos gathered his last strength and cried in a despairing voice to his father Zeus.

Until he heard Aiakos' cry, Zeus knew nothing of what was happening in Aigina. But as soon as he saw the islanders' misery his answer was swift and sure. He shattered the heat-haze with a thunderbolt and ripped the sky apart for rain. Drops the size of acorns fell everywhere on the island; the once-parched water-courses brimmed with flood-water, and all Hera's snakes were washed out to sea and drowned. As the water ran over it, the hard-baked ground cracked open, so that the corpses of the dead were enfolded at last in graves.

91

Green shoots appeared; dried-up trees burst into bud.

As the rain continued, it penetrated the leaf-canopy of the sacred temple-oak and began streaming down the trunk. Soon it was running over the column of ants, washing them off the tree and plunging them to the ground. As each ant fell, it turned into a human being. Soon the temple was thronged with people, laughing in the rain: Zeus' children, Aigina's new inhabitants.

Aiakos called his new people Myrmidons (Ant-people).* He settled them in farms and houses all over Aigina, and soon the island was busy with marriages, childbirth and families. All was as before, except that Hera's stones still filled the fields. Crops were sparse, the earth was poor and grudging, and the people had to work with ant-like determination to grow enough food to live.

News of what had happened in Aigina soon spread. Visitors thronged to the island; the Myrmidons began to make a living from tourists as well as from their farms. King Aiakos, whose cry to Zeus had ended the drought and produced the ant-people, was honoured as a prophet and miracle-worker. When the whole of mainland Greece was struck with drought, the Delphic oracle announced that Aiakos was the only person who could bring about its end. Every town in Greece sent a messenger to Aigina. Followed by a huge throng, Aiakos went to the temple, sacrificed and prayed to Zeus. As before, Zeus answered by splitting the sky with a thunderbolt, and rain pelted down across all Greece.

Throughout his life Aiakos was one of Zeus' favourite mortal children, second only to Minos and Rhadamanthys of Crete. Zeus wanted to give the three of them immortality and to welcome them as gods into Olympos. But the Fates refused to lengthen their mortal lives, and in due course they died and passed to the underworld. Here Hades made them judges of the dead.†

Danaos and his daughters

Belos, son of Poseidon and Libya,* had two sons, Aigyptos and Danaos. Both married; Aigyptos fathered fifty sons and Danaos fifty daughters (known as the 'Danaids' or 'children of Danaos'). Because the brothers were twins, there was no way of settling which of them should inherit the throne when their father Belos died. They divided the kingdom between them: Aigyptos took Arabia and Danaos Libya. Then Aigyptos proposed that they should join the two kingdoms and rule together; they could mark their alliance by marrying his sons to Danaos' daughters. Danaos, however, had been told by an oracle that he would destroy all his sons-in-law but one, and that that one would destroy him. So he refused to allow the marriage. Aigyptos sent his sons with an army; Danaos and his daughters escaped by sailing frantically out to sea. Aigyptos, thinking they were sure to drown, sent no ships after them: instead he concentrated on taking over Danaos' half of the kingdom, which he named Egypt after himself.

Danaos and his daughters did not drown. Poseidon allowed their ship smooth sailing to the island of Rhodes. Here an oracle prophesied that Danaos would be made king of the next country he came to. He set sail again, landed at Argolis in Greece and claimed the throne.

Argolis already had a king, Gelanor. But he was unpopular with his people. The reason was that when Poseidon claimed power over Argolis from Hera and was refused (see page 60), he dried up all the rivers, and the countryside was parched with drought. The people looked to Gelanor for help, but he had none to give. It was one of Danaos' daughters, Amymone, who solved the problem and brought water back to the thirsty land. Poseidon made love to her, and then told her to fetch his trident from a nearby rock. When she pulled the trident from the rock, a spring of clear water gushed out, grew into a river (the river Lerna) and spread across the plain of Argolis to irrigate the countryside.

Apart from this ending of the drought, the gods sent an omen which made the people of Argolis eager for Danaos as king. The royal cattle were grazing peacefully in a field when a wolf attacked them and killed the bull which led the herd. Priests interpreted the wolf as Danaos and the bull as Gelanor. At once, Gelanor gave up his throne. Danaos built himself a palace at Argos, and a temple to Lycean Apollo nearby. (This was because he said that the wolf in the omen was actually Apollo in disguise. *Lycean* means 'wolf-like'.)

News of Danaos' new kingdom soon found its way back to Egypt. Aigyptos was furious that his brother had survived, and sent his fifty sons to Argos to kill Danaos and bring his daughters back as wives or slaves. The sons landed in Argolis and besieged the citadel of Argos. This was built on the only hill for kilometres around, and by chance was the only part of Argolis without its own water-supply. Danaos realised that when the water in his storage-tanks was finished he was bound to lose the siege, so instead of waiting he tricked Aigyptos' sons. He called a truce, welcomed them into the palace and smilingly agreed to let them marry his daughters. But secretly he gave each daughter a dagger and told her to kill her husband on the wedding-night.

The marriage took place and the fifty brides and fifty grooms went off to bed. Next morning, forty-nine daughters appeared before Danaos, each holding her bridegroom's sliced-off head. Only Hypermnestra was empty-handed. She had fallen in love with her bridegroom Lynkeus, spared his life and helped him escape to another town. Danaos could hardly punish his daughter for refusing to commit murder; but he ordered that she should still stand trial for disobedience. At the trial, Artemis lent Hypermnestra such powers of eloquence that she not only persuaded the jury to acquit her, but also talked Danaos into accepting Lynkeus as his son-in-law, welcoming him back in Argos and making him his heir.

The murdered bridegrooms were buried, and priests set about purifying Danaos' daughters of their guilt. In this, they failed. Although Danaos tried to find new bridegrooms among his own noblemen, there was hardly anyone willing to risk losing his head on the wedding-night. When the daughters eventually died they were condemned to eternal punishment in the underworld: they were set to drain a lake with sieves.

There was still the oracle which had made Danaos reluctant to allow any marriages in the first place, the prophecy that his son-in-law would one day destroy him. This came true: some years later Lynkeus killed him and seized the throne.*

Perseus

Most twins get on well with one another, but Akrisios and Proitos (Danaos' great-great-grandsons) began quarrelling in their mother's womb. All through their childhood they argued, and when they grew up and jointly inherited the throne of Argolis, their fights began to involve not just fists, but armies, swords and spears. Neither brother could win outright, and finally they agreed to divide Argolis between them. Akrisios took the citadel of Argos, and Proitos built himself a citadel at Tiryns. His workmen were seven Cyclopes, and they built the walls with mortarless blocks of stone the size of houses, too large to be lifted – or knocked down – by puny mortal hands.

Akrisios looked at Tiryns and was afraid. His brother had a son and heir, Megapenthes; but he had only one daughter, Danaë. Akrisios was afraid that if there was no king to succeed him after his death, his brother's son would seize the throne of Argos. He asked the Delphic oracle if he was fated to have a son, and was given the unwelcome answer that his daughter Danaë would bear a son who would kill him and take his throne. Now, many men had heard prophecies like this from Delphi, and had tried to prevent them coming true. Akrisios was no exception. He built an underground room, sealed from the outside and lined with bronze. In this he locked his daughter Danaë. She saw only one female slave, who brought her food and water; no one else was allowed near the dungeon on pain of death. This way, Akrisios hoped, Danaë would never meet a man and never conceive a child.

Zeus, who sees and knows everything, looked at Danaë in her dungeon and was filled with love. He visited her, pouring into the dungeon roof in a shower of golden rain. From this meeting Danaë conceived and bore a son, Perseus. Slaves told Akrisios that they could hear a baby crying in the bowels of the earth. Full of anger and fear, he unlocked the room, nailed Danaë and Perseus in a wooden chest and threw them into the sea.

But no mortal can drown a god's child unless the god so wills. Zeus' brother Poseidon carried the bobbing chest safely to the island of Seriphos. Here a fisherman, Diktys, caught it in his net. When he opened it, he found Danaë and Perseus peacefully asleep. He took them to his brother Polydektes, king of the island. Polydektes welcomed them with great kindness and gave them a home in his own palace. Here Perseus grew to adulthood.

As Perseus grew, Polydektes' kindness gradually turned sour. The children of gods are stronger and more handsome than ordinary mortals, and Polydektes began to fear that Perseus would outshine him and steal his throne. He also wanted to marry Danaë; but because her years in the underground dungeon had made her terrified of men, she refused – and there was no way of forcing her while Perseus was there to protect her.

At last Polydektes' chance came to rid himself of Perseus. He happened one day to be boasting about his own importance and the royal marriages he intended to make. 'Why,' he said, 'I intend to pay court to Hippodameia herself, princess of Elis – and I intend to take her the present of a horse from every man on this island.'

Perseus, not to be out-boasted, said 'I'll give you a present better than a horse. I'll kill a Gorgon and give you her severed head.'

'Agreed!' said Polydektes, snatching his chance.

Perseus had no choice but to carry out his boast. Of the three Gorgons, the only one with a trace of mortality was Medusa. But she could turn a man to stone with a single glance: even if he could find her lair, how would he get near enough to kill her and cut off her head?

At this point the gods took a hand. (They were not always so willing to help one another's children; but Perseus had done nothing to anger them, and they saw no reason not to support his quest.) They lent him prized possessions: Hades' helmet of darkness, Hermes' winged sandals, Athene's shield (polished to miraculous smoothness, as dazzling as a mirror) and Hephaistos' sickle made entirely of diamonds. They left all these things, together with a leather bag to carry the Gorgon's head, in a cave high in the hills of Seriphos. Perseus gathered up the shield, sickle and bag, and put on the helmet and sandals.

Wearing Hermes' sandals, Perseus was able to run in air as easily as people run on land. Each stride carried him many kilometres; Athene guided him to Kisthene, the land beyond Ocean where the Gorgons lived. Kisthene was a system of vast underground caves; its trees were stalagmites and its flowers were rock-roses formed by water-drops wearing away the stone. There was no light, and no sound except for the snuffle of the Gorgons, asleep in a distant cave.

The entrance to Kisthene was guarded by the Gorgons' sisters, the three Graiai. They had only one eye and one tooth between them: but the eye was enough to see intruders and the tooth enough to bite them dead. While two of the Graiai slept, the third took eye and tooth and stayed on guard; when her watch was done she woke one of her sisters and gave her the eye and tooth in turn.

While Athene kept out of sight, Perseus crept up beside the Graiai. Even in the pitch blackness their eye would have seen him, if Hades' helmet of even deeper darkness had not made him invisible. He crouched on the dank floor, waiting until the sister on guard woke her sister and passed her the tooth and eye. Then, in the in-

stant when both were blind, he snatched the eye and tooth and sprang back against the cave-wall. The Graiai fumbled towards him, venomous with rage. But he refused to return eye or tooth unless they showed him the tunnel to the Gorgons' lair.

Followed by Athene, Perseus picked his way down the tunnel: slowly, for he had no wish to turn a corner and stumble on the sleeping Gorgons. He could see nothing in the blackness, could guide his steps only by feeling the walls or by listening to the monsters' hideous breathing, which came nearer and grew more oppressive with every step he took. Soon there was a phosphorescent glow not far ahead, lighting up three bulky shapes in the darkness. Perseus opened his leather bag, gripped Hephaistos' sickle in one hand and Athene's mirror-shield in the other, and took another winged pace forward.

Now he was right on the Gorgons. He turned his back, so as not to look at them directly and be turned to stone. Guiding his movements by the dim reflection in the mirror-shield, he picked out Medusa. She was lying separately from her sisters, her deadly eyes closed, her slack tongue slobbering her face as she snored, her snake-hair coiled sleeping beside her head. Perseus, using the mirror-shield, had to work behind his back, reversing every normal movement. He raised the sickle and sliced down towards Medusa's neck. Even then, at the last moment, he would have missed; but Athene jumped forward and straigtened the blow. The sickle chopped through Medusa's neck, and as her head bumped to the ground its deadly eyes flicked open. Quickly Perseus snatched up the head by the nearest snakes, stuffed it into his bag and tied it tight.

There was confusion. From the spurt of blood from Medusa's neck two beings sprang up: an armed warrior (Chrysaor) and a winged horse (Pegasos). The clatter of Pegasos' hooves woke the other two Gorgons, and they towered up, eyes darting and snakes hissing. Keeping well out of their stony glance, Perseus leapt on to Pegasos' back and urged him up the tunnel towards the daylight far above. Athene followed. She was invisible, and Perseus was still wearing Hades' helmet of darkness: all the Gorgons could see was Chrysaor standing there, and the winged horse galloping away carrying nothing but a bulging leather sack. None the less, they sprang to attack; only the combination of Pegasos' speed and his own winged sandals saved Perseus' life. He soared on Pegasos past the Graiai, out of the cave-mouth, far beyond the Gorgons' reach. As soon as he was clear away, Perseus tossed down the eye and tooth which belonged to the Graiai. (They fell into Lake Tritonis in Libya, leaving the Graiai blind and defenceless forever.)*

Meanwhile, back on the island of Seriphos, King Polydektes had wasted no time. As soon as Perseus disappeared – no one saw him actually leave the island; he was last seen going into the mountain cave – Polydektes went to snatch Danaë and make her his queen. She fled to the temple of Athene: so long as she clutched the altar there, she was under the goddess' protection and no one could seize her or harm her. Polydektes countered this by setting a ring of armed men round the sanctuary, and simply sitting down to starve Danaë out.

So it remained for several days. Then there was a neighing and a whirr of wings overhead, and Perseus appeared in the sky on a wing-ed horse. He took the Gorgon's head from its bag and brandished it at the ring of men. At once Polydektes and his soldiers were changed into a stone circle around Athene's shrine; not only that, but all the people of the island who were staring up were also turned to stone, so that Seriphos became one of the rockiest islands in the whole Aegean Sea. Perseus rescued his mother Danaë (who had kept her eyes modestly on the ground and so avoided the Gorgon's glance), and left the island. He settled in Larissa, and gave the gods back their helmet of darkness, sickle, bag and winged sandals. In gratitude to Athene, he gave her Medusa's head, which she fixed on the front of her mirror-shield.

There was still the matter of the Delphic oracle given to Perseus' grandfather Akrisios long ago, years before Perseus was even born. Perseus knew nothing about it – he knew nothing of Akrisios' exist-ence – but he was fated to kill Akrisios and take his throne. This came about, seemingly by accident, at an athletics contest some years later in Larissa. The contest was a funeral games in honour of a dead king, and distinguished visitors included aged King Akrisios and his nephew King Megapenthes of Tiryns. Perseus competed in several events at the games, including the discus. As he threw his discus, a breeze blew it off course into the spectators, where it hit Akrisios's head and killed him.

Megapenthes (son of Akrisios' brother Proitos) now told Perseus the story of the twin brothers and their lifelong rivalry. He pointed out that Perseus, Danaë's son, was the rightful heir to Akrisios' throne of Argos, and that he could claim his kingdom now that Akrisios was dead. But Perseus refused to win a kingdom by murder, even if it had been foretold by an oracle and justified by Akrisios' cruel treatment of Danaë and her baby long ago. In the end he agreed to exchange kingdoms with Megapenthes. Perseus became king of Tiryns (ruling the eastern half of Argolis), and Megapenthes became king of Argos (ruling the western half). On the way to Argolis, flying on Pegasos, Perseus dropped his sword, and decided to build a new palace in the place where it fell. When it was built he called it Myce-nae, after the word *myces* or 'sword-hilt', and settled there.

After Perseus died – for even heroes, in the end, are mortal – he was taken into Olympos and honoured as Zeus' son.* His shrines were at Mycenae and on Seriphos, and he often appeared to mortals in the form of a gigantic warrior whose footprints were a metre long.†

12
SISYPHOS
AND · HIS · FAMILY

Sisyphos

Sisyphos, son of the wind-lord Aiolos, was a prince of Corinth – and a cunning rogue. He farmed cattle in the meadow-country on the Isthmus, and his neighbour was Autolykos, Hermes' son, another rogue. Autolykos went to his father (the god of trickery) and asked for the power to make black seem white and white seem black. He used it to steal Sisyphos' cattle: when Sisyphos' men came looking for black cows in Autolykos' herds they found only white ones, and vice versa. To prove who was stealing his cattle, Sisyphos had to think up a trick of his own. He branded all his cattle with his initial (C – the Greek capital S) – not on the hide, but on the underside of the hooves. The next time Autolykos' men raided Sisyphos' herd, a trail of Ss next morning led to Autolykos' byres, and the stolen cattle could be identified despite their colour-change.*

Sisyphos won a kingdom by treachery. His brother Salmoneus was king of Thessaly. Sisyphos raped Salmoneus' daughter Tyro, and she was so ashamed that she killed her baby sons as soon as they were born. Sisyphos gathered the townspeople together, showed them the children's bodies and said that they were Salmoneus' children, the result of incest with his own daughter. The people were so disgusted that they banished Salmoneus and made Sisyphos king.* (He later claimed that the Delphic oracle had made him lie about the children, to punish Salmoneus' crimes against *him*. What those crimes were, he never bothered to explain.)*

Sisyphos was a cruel tyrant. His method of executing enemies – not to mention rich travellers rash enough to risk his hospitality – was to peg them on the ground and crush them to death with stones.

101

He never bothered about right or wrong: if he thought he could get away with anything, he did it. In the end he went too far and cheated Zeus. When Zeus stole the river-nymph Aigina from her father and hid her, Sisyphos was the only person on earth who knew where she was, and he promised Zeus to keep it secret. But Aigina's father, the river-god Asopos, offered to pay for the information by creating a spring of pure water in Sisyphos' citadel; Sisyphos immediately broke his word to Zeus and told Asopos where to find the lovers. His reward from Asopos was the spring called Peirene; his reward from Zeus was death.

Even then, Sisyphos nearly managed to trick Death himself. Zeus sent his brother Hades to make sure that Sisyphos actually reached the Underworld. Hades told Sisyphos to hold out his wrists to be tied; Sisyphos pretended to be fascinated by the knot, and asked Hades to show him how to tie it; Hades held out his wrists, and Sisyphos tied him up and locked him in a dungeon. For days, now that Death was a prisoner, no mortal in the world could die. This was particularly awkward for Ares, god of war: all over the world men were being killed in battle, only to spring back to life and fight again. In the end Ares went to Corinth and untied Hades, and the two of them frog-marched Sisyphos to the Underworld. On the way, Sisyphos called out to his wife that she was on no account to bury his body; then, when he reached the Underworld, he went straight to Queen Persephone and complained that he had been dragged down to hell alive and unburied. He asked Persephone to allow him three more days in the upper world, to arrange his own funeral. Suspecting nothing, Persephone agreed – and Sisyphos went back to Corinth and took up his old life exactly as before. Zeus realised that the only person who could outwit such a rogue was an even greater rogue, and sent Hermes himself to deal with Sisyphos. Hermes devised the cleverest trick of all: no trick. Sisyphos was expecting glib argument or lies, and was on his guard against words. But instead of speaking, Hermes simply took Sisyphos by the scruff of the neck and bundled him down to hell.

The judges of the dead gave Sisyphos a punishment to suit both his trickery and his cruel method of killing people with boulders. They placed a huge rock just above him on a steep hillside; the only way he could prevent it rolling back and crushing him was to push it up the hill, and they promised that if he ever pushed it over the top and down the other side his punishment would end. With immense effort, time after time, Sisyphos heaved the boulder to the lip of the downward slope – and each time, just as one more push would have toppled it, the boulder tricked him, slipped out of his grasp and chased him all the way back down the hill. So he was doomed to make desperate efforts, and to be tricked, until the end of time.

Athamas

By contrast with Sisyphos, who had more than his share of the family brains, his brother Athamas was a simpleton. He was the king of Boeotia, a servant of Hera – until even she took advantage of his simplicity. When Ixion, the wickedest mortal in the world, repaid Zeus' invitation to a banquet in Olympos by trying to rape Hera, Zeus created the cloud-goddess Nephele, Hera's exact image, to cheat him. But after Ixion was caught and punished, there was no way of un-making Nephele: cloud or not, she was the immortal creation of an immortal god. She floated about Olympos, lonely and full of tears, confusing everyone by her likeness to Hera. At last Hera thought she had found a solution: she married Nephele off to Athamas and made her queen of Boeotia.

At first Athamas was delighted. He and Nephele had two children: a son, Phrixos, and a daughter, Helle. But as time passed the marriage soured. Nephele, who had lived in Olympos, found Boeotia drab and dull by comparison, and moped about the palace filling every room with drizzle. Athamas, for his part, grew tired of embracing a sulky cloud instead of a wife of flesh and blood. He found a mistress, Ino, and they had two children, Learchos and Melikertes. Athamas built the three of them a palace at the foot of Mount Laphystion – and kept it so secret that when Zeus had to find somewhere to hide his baby son Dionysos (son of Ino's sister Semele) from Hera's jealousy, he thought it the ideal place. Ino dressed baby Dionysos as a girl and brought him up among the palace women.

Unfortunately, even with Zeus' approval Athamas was too stupid to manage two families at once, or even to keep them apart for long. Soon he had to face a sullen cloud-goddess and an angry mortal woman, each determined to be rid of the other. Nephele complained to Hera that Athamas had cheated her and taken a lover; Hera's answer was to blight the crops so that Athamas' people would rise up and kill him. Then Ino bribed the Delphic oracle to say that

Nephele's and Athamas' son Phrixos had caused the blight (by raping his aunt Biddike), and that the only way to end it was for his father to take him to Mount Laphystion and sacrifice him.

Athamas could think of no arguments against the sacrifice. Sadly he tied Phrixos' hands and took him to the mountain. Phrixos' sister Helle went with them, weeping. They climbed to the mountain-peak, and Athamas built an altar of stones, laid Phrixos on it and drew his knife.

Just in time, Zeus noticed what was happening. He sent Herakles racing to the mountain-top, riding on a winged ram with a golden fleece. Herakles held Athamas' arm just as he was about to stab his son. He explained about the false oracle, and said that neither Phrixos nor Helle would be safe from Ino if they stayed in Boeotia. They should fly to safety on the back of the golden ram.

Phrixos and Helle sat on the ram's back and took hold of its crisp metal fleece. The ram soared into the sky and carried them away.* Athamas, by now utterly confused, went home to face Nephele. And he found even worse trouble waiting there. Hera had discovered baby Dionysos, hidden among Ino's palace women. She sent Ino mad and drove her out to wander in the hills; then, saying that Athamas was too stupid to deserve even a cloud for wife, she took Nephele back to Olympos.

So, at one stroke, Athamas lost his wife, his mistress and two of his children. He still had Ino's sons Learchos and Melikertes, but they were tiny children. He lived alone and unhappy for a year or two, hoping always that Ino would return; at last, convinced that she must be dead, he married another woman, Themisto, and made her his queen.

Athamas and Themisto lived happily for several years, and had two children. Then Hera restored Ino's wandering wits and sent her back to the palace. Once again Athamas was trapped between a pair of warring wives. For a while he tried to live with both, but their rivalry made it impossible, and in the end he gave way to Ino's insistence that she was his true wife, and sent Themisto away. Themisto, cheated and furious, plotted to kill Ino's two children so that her own sons would be brought up as princes in their place. She bribed one of the palace maids to dress her sons in black and Ino's in white; then, in the pitch-black night, she crept into the palace and stabbed the white-robed children dead. Unfortunately for her, the maid had told

Ino of the plot and Ino had changed round the children's clothes, with the result that the children Themisto murdered were her own.

They were also Athamas' sons, and their deaths sent him mad with grief. He was out hunting with Ino's son Learchos when the news was brought; in his insanity he took the boy for a lion and killed him; then he ran home, snatched up his last surviving child, Melikertes, and threw him into a cauldron of boiling water to try to make him immortal. Ino rescued Melikertes and fled. But in their haste they lost their way, fell over a cliff into the sea, and drowned.*

Broken with grief, Athamas left Boeotia forever. He went to the Delphic oracle and begged it to tell him a place where he could live the rest of his life in peace, unharassed by the gods. The oracle replied that the end of his wandering would come when wild animals shared their meal with him: there he would set up a kingdom and live in peace. Athamas set out on his wanderings (in the same northeasterly direction as Phrixos and Helle had flown on the golden ram). One day he came on wolves attacking a flock of sheep. The wolves scattered and Athamas, ravenously hungry, gathered torn scraps of sheep-meat and gorged himself. So the oracle came true. Athamas named the area Athamania, sent for Themisto to be his queen, and settled in peace at last.

Bellerophon*

Sisyphos' grandson Bellerophon was originally called Hipponous. He inherited his grandfather's fierce temper, and one day had a violent argument with his brother Belleros and killed him. Horrified, he made a vow never to show emotion again, took the name Bellerophon (Belleros-killer) as a reminder of his crime, and fled from Corinth.

Bellerophon visited Tiryns, the rock-fortress built by Cyclopes for King Proitos. Queen Anteia fell in love with him and invited him to sleep with her. Bellerophon took this as a test of his vow not to give way to emotion, and refused. No one had ever before refused Anteia anything (she was so stubborn that she was nicknamed Stheneboia, 'Strong as a cow'), and she ran to her husband Proitos and accused Bellerophon of rape. Proitos was reluctant to punish Bellerophon himself (for fear of offending Zeus, who protects visitors). So he

asked Bellerophon to carry a sealed message for him to King Iobates of Lycia. Bellerophon, glad of any excuse to leave Tiryns, willingly agreed.

He might have been less willing if he had known that Iobates was queen Anteia's father, and that the king's message told him about the rape and asked *him* to deal with Bellerophon. Iobates sent Bellerophon on a series of deadly quests. (If he survived, his innocence would be proved; if he failed, his death would end the matter once and for all.) For his first task, Iobates told Bellerophon to kill Chimaira, a fire-breathing monster which lived on a nearby mountain, terrorising local farmers and scorching their land bare of crops and herds.*

Bellerophon accepted without a flicker of emotion. But inside he was paralysed with dismay. How could any man kill Chimaira without immortal help? He went to the prophet Polyeidos to ask advice. Polyeidos gave him a bow, a quiver of arrows and a spear tipped with a large block of lead instead of a point. He told him to go to the fountain of Peirene in Corinth. He would find Pegasos (the winged horse born when Perseus killed Medusa) drinking there; he should tame him, bridle him and fly on his back to fight Chimaira. Bellerophon slung the bow and quiver over his shoulders, picked up the spear with its boulder-sized block of lead and made his way secretly to Corinth, which he entered at night to avoid being seen. He climbed to the Fountain of Peirene in the citadel – and there in the moonlight was Pegasos, drinking placidly from the pool, stretching his wings and whinnying for pleasure.

Bellerophon laid down the weapons and walked gently towards Pegasos, trying not to startle him. But as soon as Pegasos scented him his eyes rolled white and he snorted and reared in alarm. Bellerophon tried to climb on his back; but the more he tried, the more Pegasos flapped his wings and reared away. Soon Bellerophon was exhausted. He was just about to give up, when suddenly the fountain was bathed in immortal radiance, and Athene appeared. At her coming Pegasos grew calm, drooped his head and stood quiet and still beside the pool. Athene disappeared as suddenly as she had come, the light paled again to moonlight, and at his feet Bellerophon found a golden bit and bridle, Athene's gift. Pegasos accepted the bit and stood quietly while Bellerophon bridled him, collected the weapons and climbed on to his back. Then, silent as an owl, he soared into the sky towards Chimaira's lair.

107

Soon, in the darkness below, Bellerophon could see the red flicker of Chimaira's fires. He reined Pegasos in and they hovered directly above the volcano's jaws. Chimaira sensed Pegasos' wing-beats above her, woke from sleep and leapt to defend herself. Her serpent's tail writhed; her razor-hooves struck sparks from the rocks; her lion's jaws spat fire. Pegasos flew above, just out of reach, while Bellerophon fired arrow after arrow. The arrows weakened Chimaira; but she rallied her strength and leapt at Pegasos again, opening her fiery jaws to char him dead. Bellerophon lunged with the only weapon he had left, the lead-blocked spear. The lead stuck like a stone in Chimaira's throat; she belched flames to dislodge it – and a stream of molten metal ran down into her lungs and choked her. Bellerophon heaved her carcase into the glowing volcano, remounted Pegasos and flew to tell Iobates that the first task was done.

Chimaira was dead; the next task was to deal with Chimairos. He was no more than a mortal, a simple pirate; but he terrified his victims by taking Chimaira's name and sailing against them in a ship with a lion's head at the prow, a snake's tail at the stern and armed with a machine for catapulting fire. Bellerophon dealt with him – and with the adversaries Iobates sent next against him, Solymoi and Amazons – by pelting them from the sky with stones.

Iobates began to panic. Bellerophon conquered every enemy he faced. What if he next demanded Iobates' kingdom? Hastily Iobates chose a handful of trusted soldiers and laid ambush. Bellerophon dismounted from Pegasos and let him loose to browse. Then he walked unarmed towards the palace – and Iobates' soldiers attacked. The gods gave Bellerophon superhuman strength; he killed all the soldiers with his bare hands. At this Iobates, seeing that Bellerophon was under heaven's protection, gave in at last, let him marry his daughter Laodamia and gave him half his kingdom.

Up till now, Bellerophon had kept his vow and avoided emotion. But Iobates showed him the secret message he had brought from King Proitos, and he learned for the first time that Anteia had falsely accused him of rape. The violent temper inherited from his grandfather Sisyphos boiled up in him as it had long ago when he killed his brother. He bridled Pegasos, flew to Tiryns, snatched Anteia thousands of metres into the air and dropped her to her death. Then, full of his own hot-headedness and the excitement of flying, he decided to soar still higher and visit the gods themselves.

But no mortals can ever enter Olympos unless a god invites them. Zeus sent a fly to sting Pegasos; Pegasos reared; Bellerophon plunged to earth like a shooting star. He landed in a thorn-bush at Aleion (The Plain of Wandering) in Asia Minor, and broke both legs. The thorns also put out his eyes, and he spent the rest of his life as a lame, blind beggar wandering the desert. As for Pegasos, he was put to work in Zeus' chariot-team, pulling his new master about the sky to hurl his thunderbolts.†

13
THE · VOYAGE · OF
ARGO

The Argonauts

When Phrixos flew to Colchis on the golden ram, King Aietes welcomed him, shared his kingdom with him and let him marry his daughter Chalkiope.* Aietes did this out of greed, not generosity: he wanted the ram's golden fleece. But Phrixos gave the fleece to some priests of Ares, who hung it in the gardens of a temple guarded by a dragon. For this, Aietes murdered Phrixos and refused to bury his body. Months and years passed; the flesh rotted from Phrixos' bones; his ghost wandered on the banks of the river Styx, begging Charon to ferry it to the underworld. In the end it took to appearing before Phrixos' relatives miles away in Iolkos, wringing its hands and demanding that they travel to Colchis and give his body proper burial. Their reward, it said, would be the golden fleece; if they did nothing, Iolkos would be poor forever.

The king of Iolkos was Phrixos' cousin Pelias. He was an old man, and had ruled for many years. He won his throne by force and kept it by murder: first he stole the throne from his half-brother Aison; then, when the Delphic oracle said that a descendant of Aison would one day kill him, he ordered his soldiers to murder every baby in the palace. Now, twenty years later, the oracle spoke again, telling Pelias to beware of a young man wearing only one sandal – and soon afterwards just such a young man arrived in Iolkos, said he was Aison's son Jason and demanded Pelias' throne.*

It would have been easy for Pelias to deal with Jason by having him arrested and killed. But the people of Iolkos were greatly impressed by Jason's appearance (he wore a leopard-skin, carried two hunting-spears and had long golden hair): some even wondered if he was a god in disguise. Pelias therefore decided to dispose of him by cunning instead of force.

'If a man came to you,' he said, 'and you knew from an oracle that he was to cause your death, what would you do?'

Jason answered unhesitatingly 'I'd send him to Colchis to fetch the golden fleece.'

'*You* fetch it, then!' said Pelias.

Jason sent messengers to all the heroes in Greece, inviting them to join the expedition. Fifty accepted, and gathered at Iolkos to make preparations. They needed a strong, swift ship because Colchis lay in the far north, in stormy seas near the river Ocean at the edge of the world; to get there they would have to sail through dangerous waters filled with sea-monsters, whirlpools and a gateway of clashing rocks which swallowed unwary travellers like snapping jaws. They asked Argos, a follower of the craftsman-god Hephaistos, to build the ship, and he named it *Argo* (Swift) after himself. He built it of pines from Mount Pelion, and also made fifty broad-bladed oars, one for each of the Argonauts (or 'sailors on *Argo*') as the heroes called themselves.*

When *Argo* was ready, the Argonauts dug a channel down the sand, laid wooden rollers under her keel and hauled her into the water. They fitted the oars and loaded food, wine and fresh water. Then they sacrificed to Apollo, spent the night feasting and singing (led by Orpheus), and set sail at dawn.

The voyage to Colchis

Argo's first port of call was the island of Lemnos. Here the Argonauts found a threatening army on the shore, made up entirely of women. Some months before, the women of Lemnos had offended Aphrodite, and she punished them by making them stink so much that their husbands disowned them and sailed to the mainland to find new wives. On the night they came back, the women of Lemnos slaughtered them as they slept.* Now, mistaking the Argonauts for a war-party from the mainland, they snatched up knives, sickles and pruning-hooks and ran to defend themselves. The Argonauts moored out of range, and Echion made a speech explaining who they were and asking for hospitality. He was so persuasive that the Lemnian women not only allowed the Argonauts ashore, but fell in love with them and entertained them as guests and husbands for a whole year. (As a result of this the island was filled once more with children, among them the twin princes Euneos and Thoas, sons of Jason and Queen Hypsipyle.) Many of the Argonauts would have stayed in Lemnos forever if Herakles, after a year and a day, had not driven them back on board ship and forced them, mutinous and grumbling, to continue their voyage.

Their next landfall was Arkton, Bear Island. Its king, Kyzikos, had just married a girl called Kleite and was holding his wedding-feast. He was delighted to welcome such noble guests – and the Argonauts repaid his hospitality with a fine wedding-present. In the mountains of the island lurked a tribe of giants, each with six arms and the body and head of an enormous bear. That night they roared down on the banqueters, and broke up the feast by hurling rocks. The Argonauts held them at bay while Herakles, kneeling for better aim, fired arrows and shot them dead. The grateful islanders loaded the Argonauts with so many presents that, next day, when *Argo* was ready to sail, she lay low in the water and could hardly move. Jason and Herakles, the strongest men in the crew, bent to their oars and at last sent her skimming on her way. All day they travelled north, following the coastline. But when night fell a black storm blew up, drove *Argo* helpless before it, and finally grounded her on an unknown beach. Wearily the Argonants landed – and the local people mistook them for pirates and attacked them in the darkness with clubs and spears. There was a pitched battle, and the Argonauts killed many of the inhabitants, including their leader. Next morning they were horrified to discover that they'd been blown all the way back to Bear Island, and killed King Kyzikos himself. In despair, Kyzikos' young bride Kleite hanged herself.

Grief-stricken, the Argonauts helped the islanders bury the bodies and hold funeral games. Then they tried to set sail again – and were prevented by another, even fiercer storm. For twelve days they watched impatiently as winds howled, rain streamed down and waves snarled against the land. Then the gods told Jason that Rhea, patron goddess of the island, was angry because the Argonauts had killed her servants the bear-giants, and unless they won back her goodwill they would never sail. Jason told Argos to carve a wooden statue of the goddess; then, in the teeth of the storm, he and his men set it up in a grove of oaks, sacrificed to Rhea and danced round the altar clattering spears on shields. This ceremony satisfied Rhea; she held back the storm and allowed the Argonauts to sail.

As *Argo* butted her way through calm seas, the Argonauts' relief changed first to excitement and then to boisterous high spirits. Just for fun, Jason challenged Herakles to a rowing match, and the rest of the crew laid bets and cheered them on. The veins knotted on their foreheads; their oars arched like bows; neither would give in. Then, without warning, Herakles' oar snapped and he fell flat on his back in the bilge. The Argonauts' laughter filled the sky. They decided to beach *Argo* and make camp while Herakles cut another oar. While the others busied themselves with wineskins and cooking-fires, Herakles and his page-boy Hylas set off into the woods to find a suitable tree. After a while Hylas grew bored, left Herakles and went exploring on his own. He found a pool of water and bent to drink – and the water-nymphs pulled him down to live with them in their underwater cave. When Herakles came back to *Argo* (carrying a pine-tree ripped up roots and all), Hylas was nowhere to be found. Herakles searched all night, plunging further and further into the woods, away from *Argo*. Next day, when the Argonauts were ready to leave, there was no sign of him. There was a long argument: should they wait or sail without him? In the end Kalais and Zetes persuaded the others that it was best to sail.*

The next port of call was Bebrykos. Its king, Amykos, was a savage who insisted on boxing to the death with the strongest man on every ship that called – and among the Argonauts was Zeus' son Polydeukes, the finest boxer in the world. Polydeukes and Amykos were well-matched, but in the end Amykos fell to a punch just above the ear. At once his people attacked the Argonauts with clubs and stones, and forced them to run for *Argo*, cut the mooring-rope and row for their lives. They made for Salmydessos on the mainland. This time they were met on the shore by palace servants begging them, for their own good, not to land. King Phineus,* they said, had angered the gods and been punished by blindness and starvation. He was corpse-thin; every time he sat down to eat, two Harpies flew down and snatched the food from his lips. Phineus' servants said that this was no hospitality to offer visitors; but Kalais and Zetes (who were the winged sons of the North Wind, afraid of no other creature in the sky) promised to chase away the Harpies and save Phineus' life. The servants prepared a banquet, and it was no sooner

114

on the table than the Harpies appeared, screeching and flapping their monstrous wings. Kalais and Zetes soared to the attack, chased the Harpies halfway across the world to the Strophades or Whirling Islands, and would have killed them there if the gods had not sent Iris with a promise to pardon Phineus if Kalais and Zetes spared the Harpies' lives. In gratitude for this, Phineus told the Argonauts how to deal with the dangers they still had to face, and especially how to avoid being crushed by the clashing rocks. Then he loaded them with gifts and saw them on their way.

The clashing rocks (Symplegades) were guardians of the mouth of the Black Sea and the secret kingdoms beyond. They stood on each side of the water-gully which separated Greece from Asia; they were living beings in the form of rocks, threatened by the gods with death if any unauthorised ship slipped past. For this reason, whenever anything living tried to pass between them they clashed together with enormous force, crushing and splintering whatever lay in their path. This was the obstacle *Argo* faced, and Phineus had told the Argonauts the one slim chance that might get them through. As soon as they came in sight of the narrow straits, and felt the current tugging like a giant's grip on *Argo's* keel, Euphemos released a dove, which flew straight for the opening between the rocks. Orpheus played an urgent rhythm on his lyre, and the crew took up its beat with their oars and churned the sea to foam. The rocks sensed the dove's slight presence, gathered themselves and hurled themselves together. There was a thunderous crash, a funnel of foam, and the sea-bed growled and shook. But for all their fury, the rocks nipped only the very tip of the dove's tail feathers. Like lions rounding on a herd, they parted and gathered for another attack. Orpheus quickened his beat, and *Argo* plunged between the rocks like an arrow fired dead-centre down the gap. It was like sailing into the mouth of an enormous fish: the Argonauts saw stone jaws closing on either side, and shuddered. Then Athene swept down from Olympos, perched *Argo* on a tidal wave and hurled her through. The rocks clashed closed – too late: their jaws tasted nothing but the tip of the superstructure at *Argo's* stern. At once the gods' threat of punishment came true: the rocks split apart, died and froze forever to the sea-bed; the Argonauts were the last mortals ever to see them move. As soon as they could they landed, beached *Argo* and made a thanksgiving sacrifice.

From now on it was plain sailing to Colchis. The only threat came as *Argo* passed the desolate island of Ares, where the Stymphalian birds roosted on the barren rocks. The birds were bronze-feathered and bronze-taloned, and fed on human flesh: they rose clattering from the rocks and swooped on *Argo*. Their method of attack was to drop bronze feathers from above, like arrows; but the Argonauts, who had been warned by Phineus what to do, locked shields above their heads like a metal roof. When the rattle of bronze on bronze ceased, they unlocked the shields and began clashing them against their spears. The birds scattered like frightened starlings flocking from a hawk. *Argo* passed safely on; the only injury was to Oileus' shoulder, which one of the falling feathers grazed.

The golden fleece

Argo sailed on to Colchis. Soon the Argonauts could see Aietes' golden palace gleaming in the distance, like a huge fire-basket glowing among shaggy pines. Their hearts sank. How could they outwit Aietes, steal the golden fleece and escape from such a place as this?

From Olympos, Hera saw their doubts. The expedition was under her especial protection. When Poseidon, long ago, was looking for a kingdom, he tried to steal Argolis from her. She vowed vengeance – and her vengeance took the form, now, of helping Jason win back his throne from Poseidon's son Pelias. Hera's ally, Aphrodite, also had a score to settle with Helios the sun-god, who told her husband Hephaistos of her love-affair with Ares. Nothing would please her more than to see Helios' son Aietes lose the golden fleece.

Neither Hera nor Aphrodite wanted to risk the gods' anger by helping the Argonauts openly; so they decided to make use of Medea, Aietes' daughter. She was a priestess of Hekate, with magic powers: if the goddesses made her fall in love with Jason, she would do their work for them and take the blame. They went to find Aphrodite's son Eros, god of desire. He was playing knucklebones with Ganymede, and winning; he didn't want to leave his game to run errands, but Aphrodite bribed him with a shooting-star, a golden ball which had once belonged to baby Zeus. Eros picked up his bow and arrows, flew down to Colchis and stood by a pillar in Aietes' palace, invisible, waiting for the Argonauts.

Aietes was amazed to hear that strangers had escaped the clashing rocks and were now mooring their ship and making their way to his palace. He was still more amazed when they came before him, fifty stalwart heroes, and politely asked him to hand over the golden fleece, since it rightfully belonged to them. Instead of killing them on the spot (and so risking not only the anger of the gods, but also a war-expedition from each of their families), he set their leader Jason three tasks. First he was to yoke two fire-breathing bronze bulls (one touch of whose breath would char him to ash) and plough the Field of Ares; then he was to sow the ploughed field with serpent's teeth and single-handedly destroy the army which grew from them; then he was to kill the fleece's dragon-guardian. Jason, as sure as Aietes that these tasks were impossible, nevertheless agreed, and the whole company sat down to a banquet, while Orpheus played and sang for them.

In the shadows, Eros set arrow to bow, took careful aim at Medea, and fired. The arrow pierced her heart with love for Jason. When the feast was done and the Argonauts had settled in the visitors' rooms to sleep, she went secretly to Jason and promised to help him if he, in return, would marry her and take her back to Greece. She gave him a jar of oil: it was distilled from magic herbs and would protect him from the bulls' fiery breath.

Next morning Jason rubbed himself with the oil from head to foot. Then he dressed, took his shield and spear and walked with the other Argonauts to the Field of Ares. The people of Colchis thronged to watch; Aietes, his noblemen and the Argonauts took their places on polished thrones at the field's edge; Aietes signed for the contest to begin. Servants brought Jason a bronze helmet full of serpent's teeth, and led him towards the underground cave where the bulls were kept. Their fiery breath would have melted any normal pen; even the boulders of their cave glowed red-hot and the ground was black and lifeless for metres round.

Jason found a cool spot and put down the helmet of teeth and his shield and spear. Then he stripped off his clothes and plunged into the bulls' cave. There was a roar and a trampling of bronze on rock; the earth shook; flames eddied in the cave-mouth. Aietes' people gasped with pity for Jason, and Aietes looked round at the Argonauts, well satisfied.

Then the people gasped again, this time in amazement. The bulls came quietly out of the cave, necks bent, yoked and submissive. Behind them, guiding the plough, was Jason – and not so much as a hair was singed. He drove the bulls to the edge of the field, calmly set them in place for the first furrow, and began to plough.

All morning and half the afternoon, while Aietes' people cheered and Aietes ground his teeth in rage, Jason ploughed furrow after furrow until the field was done. Then he unyoked the bulls, slapped their bronze flanks and sent them clanking back to their cave. He picked up the helmet and walked up and down the new furrows, sowing serpent's teeth like seed. Nothing happened until the sowing was done and the first shadows of evening slanted across the field. Then there was a whirr and rush, and armed men grew in the furrows as thick as standing corn. They turned on Jason. He threw a stone and hit one of them; the wounded man turned on his neighbour and accused him of attacking him; the neighbour accused *his* neighbour; soon all the warriors were at each other's throats. Jason picked up his shield and spear, waited until most of the warriors had killed one another, then finished off the survivors and bowed in triumph to Aietes.

In front of his people, Aietes had to pretend to be pleased. Smiling through his teeth, he invited the Argonauts to another feast; tomorrow, he said, if Jason successfully completed the third task, he would win the fleece. But once again, when the feasting was done, Medea went to Jason in the darkness of night. She had with her her brother Apsyrtos, a wide-eyed child. She told Jason that Aietes was planning to rise with the Sun at dawn, send soldiers to burn *Argo* and murder the Argonauts in their beds. Quickly Jason woke the others, and Medea led them out of the palace and down to the harbour by secret paths. The Argonauts hurried to prepare *Argo* for sailing. Jason, Medea and Apsyrtos went to the Garden of Ares, where the golden fleece hung glinting on a leafy oak. It was guarded by a dragon, an earth-monster whose thousand coils snaked through the garden and choked the entrances. Jason drew his sword, and at the sound the monster hissed alert and opened its fiery jaws. Its gullet gaped in front of him, wide enough to swallow *Argo* and all her crew; but before it could pounce Medea whispered a sleep-spell and shook magic drops in the monster's eyes. Instantly it crashed to the ground asleep; its coils slumped; the way from the garden was clear. Jason threw the golden fleece round his shoulders like a lion-skin. Then he, Medea and Apsyrtos ran to the harbour. They jumped on board *Argo* and shouted to the Argonauts to row.

They had very little start. The priests of Ares found the dragon asleep in the Garden and raised the alarm, and Aietes came swooping after *Argo* in a fast warship. He would have sunk her and killed

118

her crew, if Medea (whose love for Jason drove every other thought from her head) had not found a hideous way to slow him down. She took Jason's sword and sliced her own brother Apsyrtos to pieces. Then, one by one, she dropped the pieces overboard – and Aietes had to stop, each time, to fish them out for burial. So *Argo* slipped away and was soon beyond pursuit.*

The journey home

Apsyrtos' murder freed *Argo* for a time from mortal pursuit; but it brought down on her the fury of the gods. They snatched her up in whirlwinds and tossed her from sea to sea; the Argonauts were lashed by sleet or parched by endless sun. They were terrified; their strength and skill were useless; they were helpless, the gods' toys.

At last *Argo* herself rebelled. When she was built, Athene had pegged into her a beam of sacred oak which gave her the power to speak and to prophesy; now she used it for the first and only time. Medea was blood-guilty, she said, and Jason was her accomplice. They should leave the ship at once and go to the floating island of Aiaia, where Aietes' sister Kirke had power to purify them. In the meantime the other Argonauts should sail south to Drepanon and wait for them.

Jason and Medea took the golden fleece, and the rainbow-goddess Iris carried them to Aiaia on storm-wind's wings, her cloak scattering gleaming dew-drops across the sky. When they were gone, Hera made Aiolos the wind-lord hold back his subjects, and Thetis and her sea-nymphs guided *Argo* south. Gambolling like dolphins, they led her past the Wandering Reefs, past the needle-cliffs where Scylla and Charybdis lurked, past the water-meadows where the Sun's white cattle grazed. The Argonauts saw the Sirens singing in the distance, and would have been drawn to their deaths if Orpheus had not play-ed his lyre and drowned the Siren-song. (Even so, sharp-eared Boutes heard the merest breath of Siren-music, and was so enrap-tured that he plunged into the sea and would have drowned if Aphrodite had not picked him up and dumped him back in *Argo*, sulky and spluttering.) At last they reached Drepanon and beached the ship. King Alkinoös came to the shore to welcome them.

There was no such welcome for Jason and Medea in Aiaia. Kirke had been terrified by a nightmare: her palace was burning, and the only way she could put out the flames was by swamping them with the blood of a murdered child. She knew at once who Medea was (for the Sun's children and grandchildren all have dazzling, flashing eyes). But the crime of child-murder revolted her, and although she was bound by the gods to purify Jason and Medea – that was the message of her dream – she wanted them away from her island as soon as possible. She killed a new-born pig, sprinkled them with its blood and said prayers to the gods of death. Then she turned away from Jason and Medea and waited for them to leave. Once again they were gathered up on the wind's wings, and carried to the other Argonauts in Drepanon.

As well as the Argonauts, they found trouble there. The warfleet from Colchis had finally caught up with *Argo*, and its admiral demanded that Jason give back the fleece and hand Medea over for punishment. Jason answered that the fleece was his by right, and that Medea had been purified of guilt. Neither the Colchians nor the Argonauts wanted to settle the argument by force, so they asked King Alkinoös to judge between them. That night Alkinoös' queen told Jason what the decision was to be next morning: if he and Medea were married they could take the fleece and leave in peace; if not, Medea was to be handed back to her father for punishment. At once Jason and Medea held a hurried marriage ceremony in a mountain cave. The Argonauts prepared a wedding-feast, and Jason and Medea spent their wedding-night on a couch spread with the golden fleece. Next morning King Alkinoös gave judgement in their favour; the Colchians sailed angrily home, and *Argo* was free to leave.

The Argonauts rowed briskly, eager for the homes they had not seen for months; a soft breeze filled their sail and once more Thetis calmed the waves and gave them fair sailing. They only stopped once: in Crete, for fresh water. As they drew near the shore, they were pelted with boulders by Talos, guardian of Crete. He was a bull-headed giant, forged in bronze by Hephaistos as a present for King Minos. Three times each day he paced round the island, hurling rocks to repel visitors; any still foolish enough to land he scorched to death in his fiery grip. He could not be harmed by mortal weapons. Hephaistos had filled him with ichor, the god's immortal blood, and it pumped round his body in a single, throbbing vein. He had only one vulnerable spot: the hole in his heel where Hephaistos had poured in the ichor, sealing it with a bronze stopper. No sailors had ever landed on Crete against Talos' will and lived; but now, while

Argo bobbed out of range, Medea sang a sleep-spell to make Talos drowsy, and Poias shot the pin from his ankle with an arrow. The ichor gushed out and Talos crashed dead to the ground. The Argonauts landed, filled their water-jars and sailed for Iolkos.*

Jason and Medea

When *Argo* first sailed for the golden fleece, King Pelias of Iolkos was overjoyed. He thought he had sent Jason to certain death and cheated the oracle which foretold that he, Pelias, would die because of one of Aison's sons. But then Jason's elderly parents, Aison and Alkimede, unexpectedly produced another child, Promachos. Pelias dashed out the baby's brains on the palace floor; Alkimede hanged herself and Aison drank hot bull's-blood and died.* Once again Pelias rejoiced; he was secure on the throne at last, and he had a son and heir of his own, Akastos, to follow him.

When the returning Argonauts landed in Iolkos (secretly at night, for they distrusted the welcome Pelias might have in store for them), a servant told Jason of his parents' and brother's deaths. Jason wanted the Argonauts to storm the palace at once, find Pelias and kill him. But Medea had a safer, much more cunning plan. She left the Argonauts in hiding, and went to Pelias' palace disguised as a priestess of Hekate. She said she had the power to turn age back to youth, and demonstrated it by cutting an aged ram into thirteen pieces, boiling them and making a lively lamb leap from the pot. Pelias was completely taken in. He asked Medea if she could work the same magic on human beings. She said yes, laid him down on a butcher's block, gave knives to his daughters Alkestis, Euadne and Amphinome and told them to cut him up for boiling. Alkestis refused, but Euadne and Amphinome eagerly set to work – and caused their father an agonising death.

The Argonauts now entered Iolkos in triumph. Royal funeral games were held for Pelias, and contestants and visitors came from every part of Greece.* The golden fleece was publicly displayed, and the priests made offerings so that long-dead Phrixos' ghost could rest in peace. When the games and ceremonies were over, the Argonauts went home to their own cities. Jason and Medea left Iolkos to Akastos (a nobler and more honest king than his father Pelias), and sailed in *Argo* to Corinth. They beached *Argo* in an inlet on the shore, and

121

Jason built a temple to Hera on the summit of Akrocorinth, the mountain-ridge behind the city, and held a thanksgiving festival there in her honour every year.

Jason and Medea ruled in Corinth for ten contented years. As time passed, however, Jason's love for Medea began to wither. She was still consumed with love for him; but as she grew older (and preoccupied with their children, seven sons and seven daughters)*, his eye began to wander and he found a mistress: Glauke, daughter of King Kreon of Thebes. Soon afterwards, he announced that he intended to divorce Medea and make Glauke his queen. At this, Eros' arrow-wound in Medea's heart began to fester, and her love for Jason turned into its mirror-image, hate. She sent Glauke wedding-presents: a crown and a golden wedding-dress. But they were smeared with poison, and when Glauke put them on they burst into flames which engulfed the palace and killed Glauke, her father Kreon and all the wedding-guests. Jason escaped by jumping out of a window; Medea fled to Akrocorinth, to the temple of Hera.

In despair, Jason went to the beach and sat down in the shade of *Argo*, under the prow, where the superstructure had been built round the beam of prophetic oak. The oak was still solid and whole; but the lesser wood, the pine-planks from Mount Pelion, had begun to rot and crumble. All at once *Argo* settled in the sand, the superstructure caved in and the oak beam fell on Jason's head and killed him.

Medea stayed in Akrocorinth as high priestess of Hera. Zeus fell in love with her and offered to sleep with her – and when she refused, his queen Hera rewarded her by giving her immortality. She left Akrocorinth in the sun's golden chariot, and travelled first to Thebes and then to Athens, where she married King Aigeus. (She bore him a son, Medos, who later went to Colchis, made peace with his grandfather Aietes and founded a vast new kingdom in the south, called Media after himself.) When Theseus became king of Athens, he finally drove Medea out, and she went to live in the Underworld, in the Elysian Fields. Hades made her the goddess of rebirth: souls who had earned a second or third mortal life stepped into her cauldron, had their former mortality boiled away and were born again in the upper world.†

14
HERAKLES

Herakles' childhood

After they became lords of the universe, the gods successfully defended themselves against giants, monsters and supernatural creatures of every kind. But Zeus knew that however powerful the Olympians were, Mother Earth's dark relatives Sea, Night and Chaos still lurked in the recesses of creation, and that one day gods and mortals could be swept aside just as Zeus and his brothers had swept aside the Titans. He decided therefore to create a son, a hero who would combine the finest qualities of men and gods, who would act as the gods' champion, defy the shadow-world and keep its creatures cowed.

To be the mother of such a champion Zeus chose the noblest of all mortal women: princess Alkmene of Mycenae. Since she would never betray her husband Amphitryon to make love with anyone else, even the king of the gods, Zeus waited until Amphitryon was away from home, fighting the Teleboans;* then he disguised himself as Amphitryon and made love to Alkmene in her husband's place. The love-making lasted for three mortal nights: Zeus made Helios stable his sun-horses and stay at home, while the Moon lingered and Sleep sealed mortal eyes. Human beings leapt up refreshed after their three-day sleep; Amphitryon (the real Amphitryon) defeated the Teleboans and hurried home, only to find his wife pregnant with Zeus' child.

For nine months Zeus kept Alkmene's pregnancy secret from his jealous queen, Hera. But Hera still found out in the end, thanks to the goddess Ate. Ate had the power of intoxication, like wine: she could make even a god lose his wits and say or do what he might afterwards regret. Now, under her influence, Zeus boasted that the man-child about to be born in Mycenae would be the prince of every-one around him. At once Hera sent Eileithuia, goddess of childbirth, to hold back Herakles' birth. Eileithuia sat outside Alkmene's door and clasped her hands tightly round her knees. This spell prevented Alkmene from giving birth – and in the meantime Hera helped another Mycenean princess, Nikippe, to give birth to a seven-months' child. His name was Eurystheus, and as soon as he was born Zeus' boast came true: he became the prince of everyone around him. (When Zeus heard of his birth he grabbed Ate angrily by the hair and threw her from Olympos to earth, where she has plagued mortals ever since. She fills their minds with arrogance, until they challenge the gods and suffer for it.)

There was still the matter of Alkmene's unending pregnancy. Hera meant to leave Eileithuia sitting on guard until Alkmene and her unborn child died of starvation. But Alkmene's maidservant Galanthis ran suddenly in and cried 'A boy! A boy!', and Eileithuia jumped up in surprise and broke the binding-spell. Angrily she changed Galanthis into a weasel; but she was too late to stop Alkmene giving birth, at last, to twins: Iphikles, the mortal son of Amphitryon, and Herakles, the son of Zeus.*

The first Hera knew of Herakles' birth was when she woke up one night and found him lying in her arms, suckling from her breast. (Hermes had secretly put him there, on Zeus' orders: for any baby who sucks a goddess' milk is guaranteed immortality.) Angrily Hera flung Herakles away; drops of her milk splashed far and wide across the sky, and became the Milky Way. Zeus laid Herakles in a cradle beside his twin Iphikles. Later that same night Hera sent a pair of snakes sliding into the cradle to eat the children. Iphikles' screams woke the palace; but when the servants came running, they found baby Herakles gurgling cheerfully, with a strangled snake in each chubby fist.

After this it was clear that Herakles needed no protection, either from mortals or from gods. He grew up as the prince of Mycenae, and was educated like any mortal prince – except that many of his teachers had been taught by the gods themselves. Eurytos, grandson of the archer-god Apollo, taught him to shoot; Kastor and Polydeukes taught him sword-fighting and boxing; Autolykos taught him wrestling-tricks; Eumolpos the priest and Linos, brother of Orpheus, taught him lyre-playing and the skills of prophecy.

Although Herakles was half mortal, he had the strength of an immortal god. He grew to be two metres tall; he could eat a haunch of meat and a basket of bread at a single meal; he had the temper of a lion. One day he argued with Linos during a lyre-lesson, hit him furiously with the lyre and killed him. At this Amphitryon, his mortal foster-father, banished him to a cattle farm where he could do no harm, and Herakles spent the rest of his childhood there, learning the skills of farming, until he was eighteen.

Herakles at Thespiai and Thebes

Herakles pastured his cattle in the foothills of Mount Kithairon. He made friends with his neighbours, the herdsmen of King Thespios of Thespiai, and they told him about a fierce lion on nearby Mount Helikon: it savaged the king's cattle and had eluded every mortal hunting-party sent to track it down. As soon as he heard this, Herakles cut himself a club (from a wild olive-tree ripped up roots and all), went straight to King Thespios and offered to kill the lion.

Thespios had fifty daughters, and he wanted each of them to bear a child fathered by a god's son. So he arranged for every one of them to sleep with Herakles. Each day, for fifty days, Herakles tracked the lion, and each night he took a different girl to bed. (Only one of Thespios' daughters refused to sleep with him. Later, she became a virgin priestess of his temple in Thespiai.) By the time Herakles caught and killed the lion,* forty-nine of Thespios' daughters were pregnant. All of them bore sons – twins, in the case of the eldest and youngest – and when this army of children grew up they were enough to colonise the whole island of Sardinia.

Leaving the Thespians at last, Herakles shouldered his club and walked to Thebes. On the road he met a party of soldiers, and asked where they were going. Their leader said they were King Erginos' men, on their way to collect tribute from Thebes. If the Thebans refused to pay, Erginos' orders were to chop off the ears and nose of every man in the city. Herakles said 'If that's the tribute Erginos wants, let him have it!' He cut off the soldiers' ears and noses, strung them round their necks and sent them home. Erginos, enraged, set out to sack Thebes and kill Herakles. He had many more men than the Thebans, and his cavalry covered the Theban plain; but Herakles found two underground water-tunnels, built to allow the river Kephissos to drain into the sea, and blocked them with boulders; the river flooded the plain and drowned Erginos' cavalry. Erginos and his foot-soldiers advanced along higher ground – but Herakles ambushed them in a gully and killed them. Then he led the Thebans against Erginos' city, captured it and forced the inhabitants to accept Theban rule.*

King Kreon of Thebes rewarded Herakles by allowing him to marry his daughter, Princess Megara. (Her sister married Herakles' twin brother Iphikles, and their son Iolaos later became Herakles' companion-in-arms.) Herakles and Megara had several children and lived a calm and happy life in Thebes.

Calm and happiness, however, were very far from what Hera had in mind for Herakles. She could not kill him, since he had sucked the milk of immortality from her own breast, but she could hinder and harass his mortal life. She began by clouding his mind with madness: he raged through the palace and the servants fled before him. His sons were practising sword-fighting in the palace yard; Herakles snatched a sword and began lunging at them in insane frenzy. When they jumped clear he took a bow and arrows, shot them dead and burned the palace round them. Megara, their mother, died in the flames.

After such a crime, no human could purify Herakles or fix his punishment. He went to the Delphic oracle for judgement. The priests gave him medicines to clear his mind, and the oracle pronounced his fate: he was to serve King Eurystheus of Mycenae, and carry out whatever ten tasks Eurystheus chose for him.* Herakles was furious: Eurystheus (the seven-months' child Hera had caused to be born ahead of him) was a cowardly blusterer, protected from other men only by Zeus' promise that he would be prince over everyone around. He was jealous of Herakles, and with Hera's help would think up tasks as difficult, insulting and dangerous as possible. Nevertheless, this was Herakles' punishment and he had to accept it. The gods gave him presents to help him: Hermes gave him a sword, Apollo a bow and a quiver of unerring arrows, Hephaistos a bronze-headed club and a breastplate, Poseidon a team of horses, Zeus a shield and Athene a royal robe. Herakles kept the bow and arrows; but he gave everything else to his companion Iolaos, preferring to do battle with his olive-club and the strength of his own two hands.

The tasks

Eurystheus first sent Herakles to skin the Nemean lion. Selene the moon-goddess had created this monster: she moulded sea-foam into a lion's shape, and breathed life into it. Its claws were razors; its skin was weapon-proof. It ate human flesh, and had killed or frightened away the local people for miles around. It took Herakles thirty days to track the lion to its mountain lair.* The monster had recently kill-ed, and was sleepy after its meal, or it would never have let Herakles near. He clubbed it hard – not on its weapon-proof skin but on the end of its nose. The lion sneezed in surprise and backed into its cave. Herakles ran in after it and strangled it. He skinned it with its own razor-claws – the only things sharp enough to cut the hide – flung the skin round his shoulders and made a cap from its gaping jaws.* Then he shouldered his club and went back to Mycenae. Eurystheus' ser-vants told their master that Herakles was walking up the slope to the Lion Gate, and wearing the lion – and Eurystheus (who had never expected to see him alive again) completely lost his nerve. He buried a huge bronze jar in a hole in the ground; then he climbed inside and hid, trembling, until the royal steward gave Herakles his next task and Herakles went away.

Herakles' second task was to kill Hydra. This she-monster lived in the bottomless Lernean swamp near Argos. She had a dragon's tail, a dog's body and nine snapping heads on serpents' necks. One of the heads was immortal and safeguarded Hydra's life. The others were mortal – but whenever one was cut off, two more grew in its place. Hydra's breath was poisonous: the merest whiff of it would freeze your lungs and cause instant death. Herakles and Iolaos crept through the swamp to Hydra's lair. Herakles shot fire-arrows to wake Hydra up, and she slithered at them, hissing, across the swamp. Herakles filled his lungs with a huge breath of air – it would have to last, because of Hydra's poison-breath – and fell furiously on the monster, battering her with his club. But for each head he crushed, two more grew. Steadily Hydra advanced, until Herakles was slip-ping and stumbling on the swamp's very brink. As he teetered there, Hera sent a giant crab to nip his ankles and tumble him in. Choking for breath, Herakles tripped over the crab and fell to his knees. Hydra reared for the kill – and just in time Iolaos beat her back with a blaz-ing branch. Herakles jumped up, took another deep breath of air and stamped the crab dead. Then he leapt at Hydra again. This time, each

127

time he crushed one of the heads, Iolaos ran in with the blazing branch and seared the stump before any more heads could grow. At last only Hydra's immortal head was left. Herakles snatched Iolaos' sword and sliced through the slimy neck. The head hissed on the ground in front of him, still alive; but without limbs it was harmless, and he buried it under a boulder, chopped up Hydra's body and threw the pieces into the swamp. He dipped his arrows in Hydra's blood: from this moment on, even their smallest graze was fatal. This was the evidence he took to Eurystheus to prove that the task was done.*

Eurystheus next sent Herakles to catch the Keryneian hind. She was a dappled deer with bronze hooves and golden antlers (which made many hunters mistake her for a stag). She was sacred to Artemis, and could run faster than any other living thing. Herakles could easily have shot her to slow her down; but his orders were to bring her back unharmed. He chased her for a year, across the whole world from the Garden of the Hesperides in the south to the land of the Hyperboreans in the north. At last, thinking Herakles far behind, the deer lay down to rest – and Herakles caught her, tied her legs and carried her to Mycenae slung across his shoulders as shepherds carry lambs. He showed her triumphantly to Eurystheus, then set her free to run back to her mistress Artemis.

Annoyed that Herakles had found this task so easy, Eurystheus told him to track down another fast beast and bring it back alive. This time, instead of a harmless deer, it was a man-eating boar which terrorised the people by the river Erymanthos.* To Eurystheus' surprise, Herakles (who had learned hunting from Apollo himself) found capturing the boar no trouble at all: he tracked it to its lair, startled it with a sudden shout and drove it up the mountain to the snowline where it stuck fast in a drift. He fastened it with chains, laid it across his shoulders as he had the deer and carried it to Mycenae. Eurystheus watched in terror from his jar: was Herakles going to unchain the boar there and then, and let it rampage through Mycenae? Just in time, as Herakles was walking up to the Lion Gate, a messenger from Iolkos caught him up and gave him Jason's invitation to join the expedition for the golden fleece. Herakles dropped the boar, called to his page-boy Hylas and marched off to Iolkos. (No one knows what Eurystheus did with the boar. Its tusks were later found hanging in Apollo's temple at Cumae in Italy, but how they got there is a mystery.)

Herakles travelled with the Argonauts until Hylas was lost and the rest of the crew sailed without him. Then he angrily abandoned the expedition and went back to Mycenae. To punish him for breaking off from his tasks, Eurystheus gave him next what he hoped would be a particularly unpleasant job. King Augeias of Elis was the son of Helios the sun-god, and like his father kept huge herds of cattle. They were immortal, and enormously fertile: none ever died, and every day thousands more calves were born. Because Augeias never cleaned out his cattle-pens, the dung was beginning to overflow and choke the fields for kilometres around. This was the filth that Eurystheus set Herakles to clean. He imagined him forking the dung into carts and laboriously dragging it away: a disgusting job that would take him years. But Herakles bet Augeias one tenth of all the cattle that he could do the whole job in a single day, without dirtying so much as a fingernail. He knocked down the wall of the cattle-pen, and diverted the river Alpheios through the yard. The water gushed across the countryside, and in a single flood carried all the dung from pens, farms and fields far out to sea. When the cleaning was done, Herakles returned the river to its course and rebuilt the broken wall.

After the second task (the killing of Hydra) Eurystheus complained that Herakles had only succeeded because of Iolaos' help; now he objected that the fifth task had been completed not by Herakles at all, but by the river-god Alpheios. He ordered Herakles to undertake the sixth task single-handed – and then gave him a job he thought impossible. The Stymphalian Marshes in Arcadia were infested by a flock of man-eating birds, numberless as the souls of the dead in the Underworld; they had bronze beaks, talons and feathers, and killed their prey by dropping razor-sharp feathers from above and then swooping and tearing it to pieces with their talons. Eurystheus told Herakles to kill these birds, or at least drive them out of the marshes forever. So long as Herakles wore the skin of the Nemean lion, he was safe from the birds' attack; but he could find no way to dislodge them from their marshy nests. He tried to frighten them with arrows; but although each time he fired one of the birds fell dead and the rest flapped uneasily, they knew he could hardly kill them all, thousands upon thousands, and soon settled back on their nests. Soon all Herakles' arrows were fired, and he shook his empty quiver angrily at the birds. Its bronze casing rattled against the bow – and at once the birds rose in a dense, squawking cloud, flapping and

clattering their metal wings. Herakles ran up and down, rattling his weapons and shouting at the top of his voice. The superhuman din – a god's voice and weapons made by gods – drove the birds away at last. They flew off in a bronze cloud that glinted in the sun (and settled on the barren island of Ares where the Argonauts later found them); Herakles went to tell Eurystheus that the Stymphalian Marshes were free of them for good.

Eurystheus' answer was to send Herakles to Crete to capture Poseidon's fire-breathing bull, the father of the Minotaur. Herakles confused the bull by standing with his back to it, wearing his lion-skin cloak. The bull took him for a lion and charged, snorting fire; as soon as he felt its scorching breath, Herakles turned, caught hold of its horns and somersaulted on to its back. Then, however much the bull arched its back and bucked, he kept fast hold of its horns and rode it until it was as tame as a broken horse. Then he drove it into the sea, forced it to swim to Mycenae and presented it to Eurystheus: a sorry sight, its spirit broken and all the fire gone out of it. Eurystheus tried to sacrifice it to Hera, but she refused such a pathetic offering and sent the bull whimpering north, where it took refuge among wild cattle on the plain of Marathon.

After a fire-breathing bull, flesh-eating horses: the four savage mares of King Diomedes of Thrace. Diomedes kept them locked in bronze stables and tethered with iron chains; he invited unwary visitors to dinner, killed them and fed the mares their flesh. But Herakles routed Diomedes' army with a roar, clubbed Diomedes senseless and fed him to his own mares. Then, while they were docile after their meal, he unchained them, harnessed them to Diomedes' chariot and galloped back to Mycenae. Eurystheus hastily told him to take the mares to Mount Olympos and offer them there to Hera;* their descendants were still pointed out to tourists in the time of Alexander the Great.

By now Eurystheus was finding it hard to think up monsters for Herakles to attack, and he gratefully accepted a suggestion from his daughter Admete that Herakles' next task should be to bring back the belt of Hippolyte, queen of the Amazons.* The Amazons were warrior-women of Pontos, on the Black Sea shore; Hippolyte's golden belt was a gift from her father Ares, a sign that she was more powerful than any other woman in the world. To reach the Black Sea, Herakles built a ship and gathered a crew of heroes, just as Jason had done when he went for the golden fleece. They sailed north, and after many adventures came to Pontos – where to their surprise the Amazons, instead of fighting, welcomed them and took them as lovers. But Herakles knew that the Amazons always ended by killing or enslaving the men they loved; so he took hostages and demanded Hippolyte's golden belt as ransom. The Amazons attacked; there was a battle and many were killed, including Hippolyte herself. Herakles stripped the belt from her body, leapt on board ship and shouted to his men to row. They made their way south – once more with many adventures – and returned triumphantly to Mycenae after a whole year away. Herakles handed Admete the golden belt; his ninth task was done.

Eurystheus now sent Herakles on an even longer and more dangerous journey, to the island of Erytheia on the brink of the world, where the river of Ocean whirls in the far west. The island's ruler was the Titan Geryon. From the waist upwards he had three bodies, each with its own arms and head. His companions were the cowherd Eurytion and Orthros, an enormous two-headed dog. They looked after Geryon's herd of cattle, whose hide glowed red like the setting sun – and it was these cattle that Eurystheus sent Herakles to steal. Herakles travelled to the western edge of the Mediterranean Sea, to the narrow neck of land which joined Europe and Africa. There was no way through from the Mediterranean to the river of Ocean, so he set to work to make one, battering the rocks apart and levering up the continents. Helios the sun-god stopped to watch; his rays beat down until Herakles, sweating, threatened to shoot him unless he went away. Helios laughed and offered to lend Herakles the golden ship which carried him round the stream of Ocean from west to east each night. Herakles set two massive stone slabs (the Pillars of Herakles) at the sides of the channel he had gouged between the continents, embarked on the sun-ship and sailed on the river of Ocean to Geryon's island. He found Geryon's cattle drinking at a river-estuary. The watch-dog Orthros ran snarling towards him, and he clubbed it dead. Then Eurytion the herdsman shouted for Geryon, and ran to attack. Herakles had just time to club Eurytion to the ground when Geryon himself lumbered into view: monstrous, vast, a living hill. His three bodies kept him safe from most attacks: unless you killed all three at once the uninjured body fought while the others recovered from their wounds. Herakles solved this problem by running round and shooting Geryon from the side. His shot was so powerful that the arrow not only passed through all three of

Geryon's bodies and left him dead, but also grazed Hera (who had come to help Geryon) and sent her weeping back to Olympos. Herakles loaded Geryon's cattle into the sun-ship, sailed back to the Pillars of Herakles, returned the ship to Helios and drove the cattle overland all the way to Mycenae.*

Herakles had now completed ten tasks, as the Delphic oracle had ordered. But Eurystheus refused to set him free. He said that because Herakles had accepted help for two of the tasks – from Iolaos when he fought Hydra and from the river-god Alpheios when he cleaned Augeias' cattle-yards – he still had to perform two more tasks single-handed. Eurystheus said this chiefly out of greed: while he had Herakles in his power, he wanted him to steal the golden apples of the Hesperides (Mother Earth's wedding present to Hera when she married Zeus). Only four of the apples had ever been seen in the world – the apple of discord thrown by Eris at the wedding of Peleus and Thetis and the three golden apples Hippomenes used to win the foot-race against Atalanta. Herakles had so far succeeded in doing everything Eurystheus asked, however difficult – why should he not also succeed in stealing the greatest treasure in the world? Herakles had no idea where the golden apples grew; so he went to ask Proteus, the Old Man of the Sea, and pinned him down while he wriggled into a thousand shapes and tried to break free. At last Proteus gave in and told him where the apples were (in the garden of the Hesperides in the Atlas Mountains, guarded by the serpent Ladon), and how to pick them and escape unharmed.* Herakles travelled to the Atlas Mountains and found the garden and the apple-tree, protected by Ladon's thousand coils. Instead of picking the apples himself, Herakles (as Proteus had advised) climbed to the mountain-peak where Atlas supported the sky on his shoulders. He offered to hold the sky for a moment, if Atlas would go down and pick three apples. Atlas gestured at Ladon, who was watching from below with venomous snake's eyes. Herakles answered by shooting Ladon dead – and Atlas gladly passed him the sky and bounded off down the mountain, stretching his aching arms and hallooing with joy. He picked three apples, and called up to Herakles, offering to take them to Eurystheus if Herakles would hold up the sky for a day or two more. But Herakles – who had been warned by Proteus to expect this trick – answered that he'd be delighted to hold the sky, if Atlas took it back just for a moment while he made a cushion for his neck. Foolishly Atlas took back the sky, and Herakles picked up the golden apples and left him where he stood.* He carried the apples back to Mycenae and offered them to Eurystheus. But Eurystheus (who suddenly began to wonder what Hera might do to *him*, if he received her stolen property) was terrified. He begged Herakles to dispose of the apples – anywhere he liked, so long as it was far away. Herakles gave them to Athene, and she handed them back to their proper guardians, the Hesperides.

Embarrassed by his own cowardice, and more jealous of Herakles than ever, Eurystheus now set him the last and most dangerous task of all: to go down to the Underworld, capture Cerberus and bring him back alive. (He hoped that Hades would be more than a match for Herakles, and would keep him in the Underworld forever.) Guided by Athene, Herakles picked his way down the dark tunnels to the world of the dead, shouldered past the souls on the banks of the river Styx, and threatened Charon with a clubbing unless he ferried him across. Reluctantly, Charon made room in his boat and poled Herakles across the Styx. (Hades later punished him for this by locking him in a dungeon for a whole year, during which time no souls at all were able to cross to the Underworld.) Herakles splashed ashore and found himself in a jostling, inquisitive crowd of ghosts, including a hero in full war-armour, Meleager, and the Gorgon's head (which floated above them like a deadly moon). In alarm, Herakles set arrow to bow; but Meleager told him he was in no danger from empty ghosts: no shadows could harm a living man. Herakles strode on through the twittering ghosts, and found Cerberus whining and cringing by his master Hades' throne. Hades gave Herakles permission to take Cerberus to the upper world, provided he first caught him and held him, unarmed, wearing only his lion-skin cloak. Herakles put down his bow – and at once Cerberus leapt for his throat, snarling, his three pairs of jaws snapping and his serpent-tails arching to strike. Herakles caught him by the neck and squeezed till the branching heads began to droop and loll; the serpent-tails' venom dribbled harmlessly against his lion-cloak. At last Cerberus gave in, and Herakles fastened him with an iron chain and led him, docile as a puppy, through the cowering shades back to Charon's boat, across the Styx and up the rock-passages to the upper world. As soon as Cerberus sensed sunlight he flattened his ears and whined; his jaws slavered, his eyes glittered like sparks from a blacksmith's anvil and his snake-tails hissed and writhed. But Herakles dragged him on, snarling and tugging against the lead, across the green fields to

Mycenae, where Eurystheus was in the middle of a sacrifice. Eurystheus saw Cerberus, dropped the knife and ran, squeaking with fear, for the safety of his underground pot. Herakles unchained Cerberus and let him run back to Hades; then he demanded a share in Eurystheus' sacrifice as a sign that his tasks were at last complete. Eurystheus had no choice but to agree – but even so, instead of the slice of honour, he gave Herakles the handful of offal reserved for slaves. Herakles scowled and roared, and Eurystheus told his sons Perimedes, Eurybios and Eurypylos to attack him off guard and kill him. But Eurystheus' sons were no more a match for Herakles than any of the monsters and giants had been, and he easily killed all three. Then – since he could do nothing to Eurystheus himself, thanks to Zeus' promise that Eurystheus, at least while he stayed in Mycenae, would be more powerful than anyone around – Herakles left Mycenae and went back to Thebes.*

Later adventures

By successfully carrying out Eurystheus' tasks, Herakles proved his immortal powers and purified himself from the crime of murdering his children. But he still had to win Hera's favour, and he still had scores to settle with several mortal enemies.

The first of these was King Laomedon of Troy. When Herakles and his crew sailed to capture the belt of Hippolyte, queen of the Amazons, they passed a rocky headland not far from Troy, and were surprised to see a naked girl there, chained to the rocks. King Laomedon had offended Apollo and Poseidon – their punishment for leading the gods' revolt against Zeus was to build Laomedon a city, Troy, but when it was finished he refused to pay the promised wages, a herd of cattle – and for this Apollo sent a plague on the city and Poseidon a ravenous sea-monster. The gods' price for setting the city free was that Laomedon should feed his own daughter Hesione to the monster. Herakles made a bargain with Laomedon that he would kill the monster if Laomedon let him marry Hesione and gave him his two immortal chariot-horses as a wedding-present. (These horses were Zeus' gift to the Trojans in exchange for prince Ganymede. They ran so fast that they could gallop across standing corn without bending it and could skim the sea dry-shod.) The sea-monster surged to attack Hesione, and Herakles leapt down its gullet and stamped

135

about inside for three days, clubbing and stabbing until at last the
beast lay down and died. Then he leapt out again – the fight had
shrivelled his hair and left him bald – and demanded his prize. But
Laomedon (who never kept promises) refused him Hesione, and fob-
bed him off with two ordinary chariot-horses from the royal stables.
Then he hastily retreated behind Troy's god-built walls, leaving
Herakles to sail disappointed on his way.

It was this insult that Herakles now set out to punish. Instead of
attacking with a warfleet, in daylight, he took five companions only
(Iolaos, Peleus, Oikles, Deimachos and Telamon*), and they landed
secretly, at night, from a single boat. Leaving Oikles on guard, they
crept to the city wall. Herakles sent the sentries scurrying with a sudden roar, and battered a gigantic hole in the wall with his club. Hastily Laomedon tried to gather his soldiers. But they were panic-stricken
in the darkness, fighting an enemy of whose size and numbers they
had no idea; from the start the battle went the heroes' way. Laomedon ran to his stables and began to harness his immortal mares; but
Herakles ran after him and shot him dead. He killed every one of
Laomedon's sons except for the youngest, Podarkes, a baby. (He sold
him next day in the slave-market; Podarkes' sister Hesione bought
him and changed his name to Priam, 'Bought Leader'.) Herakles gave
Hesione to Telamon as a prize of war and sacked Troy, leaving it (for
a time) as harmless as a country village. He set baby Priam on the
throne (a helpless king for a helpless state), loaded Laomedon's
horses and sailed home.

Next, Herakles went to Elis to settle his score with King Augeias.
Before he cleaned the cattle-yards, he bet Augeias one tenth of all the
cattle that the job would take no more than a single day. But when
the yards were cleared Augeias made the same objection as Eurystheus (that the river Alpheios, not Herakles, had done all the work)
and refused to pay. Now Herakles took an army to Elis and demanded the cattle. Augeias laughed in his face: he was protected by his
monstrous nephews Eurytos and Kteatos, and thought he had nothing to fear. Eurytos and Kteatos were twins, born from a single
silver egg and joined together at the waist. They were not immortals
(like Herakles' twin half-brothers Kastor and Polydeukes), but they
had more than mortal strength and easily outmatched Herakles' army.
In fact, in a single day, taking advantage of a sudden illness which
forced Herakles to leave the fight, the two of them killed three hundred and sixty of his men, including his mortal half-brother Iphikles.

They would have slaughtered his whole army, except that the festival of the Isthmian Games began and both sides stopped fighting and went to take part. Herakles, however, took no notice of the truce: he ambushed Eurytos and Kteatos as they rode to the games, and shot them dead. Then he gathered a second army, captured Elis, executed Augeias and set Prince Pyleus on the throne. He used his share of Augeias' cattle to pay for another huge festival, the Olympic Games, which he set up in honour of his father Zeus. The Games were held every four years at Olympia. At the first festival no one dared compete with Herakles, and he won every event; but later the Games became the largest athletics festival in Greece, and every town and city sent competitors.

Herakles' illness at Elis was a shadow of the madness which had long ago made him kill his children – and now it grew in his mind again and made him commit another crime. King Eurytos of Oichalia (Apollo's grandson, who taught Herakles archery) announced a shooting contest: the winner would marry his daughter Iole. With his divine bow and unerring arrows, Herakles easily won – but Eurytos refused him Iole, saying that he would never allow his daughter to marry a madman and child-murderer. Only one of Eurytos' sons, Iphitos, stood up for Herakles; the others stole his weapons and threw him out of the palace. Herakles went home to Tiryns, vowing vengeance – and from that moment the fingers of madness began to grip his mind. A few weeks later Iphitos came to Tiryns to apologise for his brothers' behaviour, and Herakles took him to the highest tower and threw him down.*

Like murdering a kinsman, killing a guest was a crime no mortal power could purify. Once again Herakles went for advice to the Delphic oracle. But Apollo was angry at the death of Iphitos (his great-grandson), and refused to answer – and Herakles, carried away by madness, seized the holy tripod and tried to wrench it out of the shrine. He and Apollo began a superhuman tug-of-war, dragging the tripod backwards and forwards across the shrine as the worshippers scattered. At last Zeus threw a thunderbolt between them and put an end to it. He himself decreed Herakles' punishment: he was to be sold in the slave-market and serve his new owner for a year, doing whatever he was ordered. The slave-price was to be paid to Eurytos, as blood-money for Iphitos. Hermes took Herakles to the slave-market and put him up for sale. But no one dared to buy – who wants to risk a god for slave? At last Queen Omphale of Lydia paid

Hermes eighteen thousand drachmas and took Herakles off to her kingdom. She took away his club, stripped him of his lion-skin and dressed him as a woman. Glowering, Herakles had to sit spinning with the female slaves, or carry Omphale's sunshade when she walked outdoors.* From time to time, when bandits attacked the kingdom, Omphale dressed him in his lion-skin and sent him to deal with them;* but always afterwards, until a full year was past, he had to return to his work among the female slaves.

After his year's service to Omphale, Herakles had only a short time left on earth. He was finding it harder and harder to contain immortal strength in a mortal body. The effort – though it never again led to criminal madness – often made him impatient and irritable. Once, when he was accidentally splashed with water at a banquet by his host's young son, he lost his temper, slapped the boy and killed him. On another occasion, to hurry up a slow servant, he tapped him with one finger and broke his neck. He travelled restlessly from place to place, righting wrongs, deposing tyrants and helping good and innocent people. But he felt more and more a visitor in the world of mortals, favouring them with his presence rather than making them his friends. Not only that, but the main obstacle to his entry into Olympos, Hera's enmity, had been unexpectedly removed: one day Herakles rescued her from some drunken satyrs, and in return she agreed, at last, to accept him as Zeus' son.

The oracles at Delphi and Dodona made predictions about the end of Herakles' mortal life. The Delphic oracle said that he would be killed by his own dead enemy; the oracle at Dodona said that fifteen months after he married a fifteen-year-old girl he would either die and ascend to Olympos or live the rest of his life in peace on earth.

Herakles' young bride was Deianeira, the daughter of King Oineus of Pleuron. It was when he met the ghost of her brother Meleager in Hades that he promised to marry her; but when he went courting he found a rival suitor, the river-god Acheloös (a giant with a serpent's tail, a man's body and a bull's head, from whose beard and mane streams of river-water unceasingly flowed). The two gods fought for Deianeira. Acheloös wriggled like a serpent, wrestled like a man, and finally lowered his head like a bull and charged. This was the end of the fight: for Herakles remembered how he had tamed the Cretan bull, and took hold of one of Acheloös' horns to vault on to his back. The horn snapped off in his hand, and Acheloös, disfigured and ashamed, withdrew from the fight and left Deianeira to

Herakles. (Later, he bought back the horn by presenting Herakles with the Horn of Plenty; Herakles in turn gave this to Ploutos, the blind god of wealth.)

Herakles and Deianeira set out for home. On the way they came to the river Euenos, and a passing centaur, Nessos, offered to take Deianeira on his back and carry her across. But when they reached the far bank, thinking he was out of Herakles' reach, Nessos tossed Deianeira to the ground and tried to rape her. Herakles fired an arrow and injured him fatally. Dying, Nessos whispered to Deianeira to take some handfuls of his blood-stained woolly coat and weave them into a shirt for Herakles: if he wore it he would never fall in love with another woman. Nessos died, and Deianeira plucked the wool and took it home. She and Herakles settled at the court of King Keyx of Trachis, and lived there comfortably for fifteen months. Then Herakles, forgetting the prophecy of the oracle at Dodona, decided to go to Oichalia and punish Eurytos and his sons for their insults after the archery contest. Deianeira was afraid that he might fall in love with Eurytos' daughter Iole; so she wove Nessos' wool into a shirt and gave it to Herakles' servant Lichas. She told him to keep the shirt safe until Oichalia was destroyed, but to be sure to give it to Herakles if he ever saw him paying too much attention to Iole.

Herakles killed Eurytos and his sons and sacked Oichalia. Iole, hoping to die rather than be taken prisoner, leapt from the battlements; but her skirt billowed out and saved her life, and Herakles chained her up with the other slaves. Then he prepared a thanksgiving sacrifice – and Lichas gave him the Nessos-wool shirt to wear. As soon as Herakles put it on, the prophecy that his dead enemy would kill him began to be fulfilled: for Nessos' shirt, stained with Nessos' blood, was poisonous; it blistered his flesh and made it bubble as if on fire. In a last explosion of fury, he picked Lichas up by the heel and hurled him into the Euboian Sea (where the gods changed him into a rocky island and so saved him from a miserable, unburied eternity of wandering on the shores of Styx). Grinding his teeth in agony, Herakles begged his son Hyllos to take him to Mount Oita in Trachis, build a funeral pyre and let him die.

Hyllos, helped by Herakles' nephew Iolaos, built the pyre, spread Herakles' lion-cloak over it and dressed Herakles in his armour. Herakles was bent with agony, and his poisoned flesh smoked and seethed. He lay down on the pyre, leaned his head on his club, and begged his friends to light the fire and leave. But none of them could bring themselves to do it, and in the end Herakles had to call to a passing shepherd, Philoktetes, and bribe him to light the pyre. (He paid Philoktetes by giving him his bow and unerring arrows; later Philoktetes and the bow were vital to the Greeks at Troy.)

As soon as the first smoke from Herakles' funeral pyre reached Olympos, Zeus threw a thunderbolt to end Herakles' agony and burn his mortality away. Hyllos, Iolaos and their men watched dry-mouthed as pyre, lion-cloak, club and armour were instantly consumed. Herakles slipped from his mortal flesh as a snake casts off its skin, and for a moment they saw him in the radiant wholeness of an immortal god. Then, as thunder rolled and lightning split the sky, he stepped into the chariot of his father Zeus and soared up to Olympos to take his hard-won place at the banquets of the gods.†

15
THESEUS

The Cretan labyrinth

The Athenian inventor Daidalos was to mortals what Hephaistos was to the gods. No problem ever baffled him; everything he designed, to help people or just to give pleasure, was simple, effective and ingenious. Until his time, ships had only oar-power; he invented sails and so gave them wings. He showed people how to split logs not with axes but with hammers and wedges. He made beautiful dolls, like miniature statues with flexible, jointed limbs. His only rival was his twelve-year-old nephew Talos. Talos looked at the way potters laboriously built up their pots from strips of clay; he invented the potter's wheel and gave them speed and symmetry unknown before. One day, playing with a fish's jagged backbone, he used it to cut a twig in half; he copied the bone's shape in bronze and invented the saw. At this Daidalos, raw with jealousy, took him for a walk on the steep rocks of the Acropolis, led him to the edge and pushed him over. Then he fled with his young son Ikaros to Crete, where King Minos (who was no friend of the Athenians) gave him refuge.*

Daidalos settled in Crete, and the islanders were as delighted by his inventions as the Athenians had been. But once again his craftsmanship led to trouble. Queen Pasiphaë was angry with the goddess Aphrodite for encouraging King Minos' many love-affairs,* and refused to sacrifice; Aphrodite punished her by making her fall in love with an enormous, fire-breathing white bull.* Pasiphaë asked Daidalos to devise some way of helping the bull make love to her. Daidalos was reluctant; but he was a refugee and she was the queen – how could he refuse? He built a cow-shaped wooden framework and covered it with hide. Then he and Pasiphaë trundled it into the bull's field, and Pasiphaë climbed inside the hollow body and waited.

141

The bull waddled over, sniffed the cow and inspected it. Then, clumsily, he mounted it and mated with it – and so mated with Pasiphaë lying inside.*

When Minos discovered what had happened, and that Pasiphaë was pregnant, he hurled Daidalos into prison and ordered his advisers to find a solution, fast. They told him to build Pasiphaë a hiding-place, so that no one would ever see her again or know what mis-shapen child she bore. Minos bargained with Daidalos: the hiding-place in exchange for freedom and a ship from Crete. Once again Daidalos had no choice but to agree. He designed a vast under-ground palace, hundreds of rock-carved rooms linked by a spider's web of passages: a labyrinth, a maze whose secret only he and Minos knew. When it was finished Minos locked Pasiphaë in the innermost room, far underground, and there she gave birth to her child: the Minotaur, a monster with a man's body and a bull's neck and head. Its bellowing boomed through the tunnels and terrified the islanders – and because no one who went into the maze was ever seen again, a rumour grew that the monster fed on flesh.

Daidalos asked Minos to keep his part of the bargain. But Minos, afraid that Daidalos would tell the labyrinth's secret, refused him freedom and set guards on the harbour to stop him sailing. That night, in desperation, Daidalos devised the cleverest of all his inventions. He stitched feathers to ribs of willow and made four man-sized wings, jointed with wax. He fitted one pair to his son Ikaros' shoulders and strapped the others on himself. Next morning, as the first upcurrents of air climbed with the rising sun, he and Ikaros soared into the sky, and the islanders mistook them for gods and worshipped them.

Unfortunately, Ikaros began to imagine himself a god as well. The joy of flying bubbled up in him and drove out every other thought: he banked and spiralled on the updraughts, climbing higher and higher into the heat-haze. The higher he went, the hotter the sun beat on his face – and on the wax fastenings that held his wings. The wax softened, loosened and slid apart, and Ikaros' wings spun in a flutter of feathers down to the marble sea. His mouth split in a scream; his arms flailed; he fell like a stone and drowned. (The stretch of water was later called the Sea of Ikaros in his memory.)

White with grief, Daidalos flew on to Cumae in Italy. From there he made his way to a tiny village in Sicily, and settled there. He knew that Minos would never rest until he found him and killed him to safeguard the secret of the labyrinth. But his son was dead, thanks to his inventions – what else had he left to lose? He built temples in Ikaros' honour, delighted the village children with toys and tricks, and waited grim-faced for the day that was sure to come.

After years of searching, Minos' spies at last brought him word of buildings of miraculous craftsmanship in a remote part of Sicily, and he knew that that was where Daidalos must be. He proved it by a trick: he took a twisted, conical triton-shell (as full of passages as the Cretan labyrinth itself) and offered a reward to anyone who could thread a string all the way through. It was a problem far beyond ordinary mortals, and the Sicilians naturally took the shell to Daidalos. He drilled a hole in the closed end, and smeared the outside with honey. Then he fastened a thread of spider's silk to an ant, and laid it in the shell's wide mouth. Attracted by the honey, the ant picked its way through every cranny and tunnel inside the shell – and so the trick was done and Minos knew that he had his man. But that night, while Minos bathed, Daidalos poured boiling water down secret pipes and scalded him to death. So Daidalos was never taken back to Crete: he stayed in Sicily, where he made many wonders, including a golden honeycomb, exact in every detail, for Aphrodite's temple on Mount Eryx. Minos' body was carried back to Crete and buried with royal honour – and the secret of the labyrinth was buried with him. The monstrous Minotaur lived on, still howling and roaring underground, as if the earth itself was bellowing. The islanders devised a ceremony to appease it, in which acrobats danced and leapt, somersaulting across the horns of bulls. At the end of the ceremony human victims were sent into the labyrinth, and disappeared.

Theseus and the sword

King Aigeus of Athens had no children, and was afraid that after his death his kingdom would be snatched by one of his quarrelsome brothers Nisos, Lykos and Pallas, or by one of Pallas' fifty warrior-sons. He asked advice from the Delphic oracle, and the priests told him not to unfasten the wineskin's foot until he reached the Acropolis, or he would cause his own death. Aigeus found this advice incomprehensible, and went to ask his friend Pittheus, the prophet-king of Troizen, if he could explain it. On the way he visited Medea in Corinth. She was tormented with rage because her husband Jason had taken a new wife; she told Aigeus that if he promised her shelter in Athens she would end his childlessness. Aigeus (who knew nothing about her murderous plans) eagerly agreed.

In Troizen, King Pittheus was delighted to see his old friend, and gave a banquet in his honour. Aigeus enjoyed himself so much that he forgot the Delphic oracle's advice: wineskin after wineskin was unfastened and drained, and he staggered drunk to bed without ever telling Pittheus why he had come. Not only that, but the bed he staggered to belonged to Pittheus' daughter Aithra. He slept with her – and then in the sober dawn, rather than face her father, slipped out of Troizen and hurried back to Athens. Before he went, he buried a sword and a pair of sandals under a rock, and told Aithra, if she proved to be pregnant and bore a son, to wait till the boy grew up and then tell him about the sword. If the gods gave him strength to lift the rock and find the sword he should go to Athens, where he would be welcomed as Aigeus' son and heir.

Aithra *was* pregnant, and in due course Theseus her son was born. She hid his real father's name: she said that Poseidon had slept with her and the child was his. So Theseus grew up doubly honoured, as a prince of Troizen and as the son of a god. When he was sixteen his mother told him the story of Aigeus and the buried sword. The rock was too big for four grown men to lift; but Theseus laid a pine-trunk across a smaller boulder and levered it up without effort. He found the sandals and sword, brushed off the dust and buckled them on. Then he set off for Athens to claim his inheritance.*

While Theseus was growing up in Troizen, Medea had murdered Jason's wife and children and fled from Corinth to Athens, where she demanded that Aigeus keep his promise of protection. Aigeus was delighted to see her, and even made her queen, certain that her magic would end his childlessness. (He had completely forgotten the advice of the Delphic oracle.) He and Medea ruled Athens for sixteen years, and had one son, Prince Medos. When Theseus arrived Aigeus paid him no more attention than any other visiting prince (for he had no idea that his drunken night in Troizen long ago had produced a child). But Medea knew, and decided to kill Theseus before he could challenge her own son's right to the Athenian throne. She told Aigeus that Theseus was a spy; then she laced a wine-cup with poison and served it to Theseus at supper. But before he drank the slaves brought in a dish of roast beef, and he drew his sword with a flourish to carve the meat. Aigeus recognised the sword as the one he had hidden years ago in Troizen. He leapt up and smashed Medea's poisoned wine-cup on the floor. Theseus ran to kill Medea, but she surrounded Medos and herself with a mist of invisibility and so escaped. (Medos went to Asia, where he founded the kingdom of Media; Medea went to the Underworld, where Hades welcomed her with honour.)

As soon as the fifty sons of Aigeus' brother Pallas heard that Medea and her magic were gone, leaving Athens protected only by an aged king and a beardless boy, they raised an army and swarmed to the attack. Theseus fought them off single-handed: he killed twenty-five of them, and the others called off their soldiers, made peace and slunk away. After this all the Athenians honoured Theseus as their saviour-prince – and Poseidon (whose son he had once been claimed to be) gave him the chance to prove his superhuman powers by performing what seemed like a miracle. The fire-breathing white bull of Crete, father of the Minotaur, had long ago been captured by Herakles and forced to swim to the mainland, where it took refuge among wild herds on the plain of Marathon, not far from Athens. It was a weak shadow of the monster Herakles had tamed; but it still breathed fire, still pawed the ground with bronze-tipped hooves, and was more than a match for any mortal strength. A hundred men had tried to capture it, and had been gored or scorched to death. But Poseidon told Theseus how to outwit the bull. He stood unarmed and waited for it to charge, then agonisingly twisted his fingers in its nostrils, caught hold of its horns and wrestled it to the ground. Then he sprang round and vaulted on to its back. He let it gallop itself exhausted, and when its spirit was broken tied a rope through its nose, led it to the Acropolis and sacrificed it there.

The Minotaur

When he came down from the Acropolis, Theseus found a weeping procession making its way out of Athens towards the port of Phaleron. At its heart were seven young men and seven girls, dressed in mourning and surrounded by tearful relatives and friends: they were the victims chosen for the Minotaur, the Athenians' payment for murdering Minos' son Androgeos (see page 250).

Theseus had just killed Poseidon's bull. Why, he wondered, should the Minotaur not make equally easy prey? He told one of the

seven men-victims to stand aside, and announced that he would sail to Crete in the young man's place. Aigeus was filled with despair: one minute a son arrived from nowhere, and the next he sailed off to fight the Minotaur, a journey from which no one ever came back alive. But there was no way to change Theseus' mind. Aigeus gave him a sail of purple-red, and told him to hoist it on the way home if he killed the Minotaur; then he stood with the other parents at Phaleron, watching forlornly until the ship was out of sight.

The gods gave Theseus fair winds, first to Delphi (where he sacrificed to Apollo) and then south to Crete. Minos sailed out in a war-galley to meet the Athenians. He walked up and down inspecting them, arrogant as a slave-dealer in the market. He chose Periboia, one of the prettiest of the seven girls, and told his soldiers to take her to his bedroom in the palace. But Theseus lifted his club and forced them back. 'No son of Poseidon, as I am,' he said, 'stands by while a tyrant rapes young girls.'

Contemptuously, Minos pulled a gold ring from his finger and tossed it into the sea. 'If you're Poseidon's son,' he said, 'dive overboard and fetch that ring.'

Theseus dived over the side. The sea closed over him, and the watchers on the ship groaned (the Athenians) or chuckled (the Cretans) to think him dead. But as soon as he plunged below the surface, a pair of dolphins, Poseidon's messengers, guided him gently with their snouts to Poseidon's palace on the ocean floor. Nereids and Tritons frolicked round him, and Amphitrite herself, queen of the sea, welcomed him and gave him a tunic of sea-purple, a golden crown rose-patterned with rubies (her own wedding-gift from Hephaistos), and lastly Minos' ring.

Theseus took the presents, swam up with his dolphin escort and surfaced beside the ship. He climbed on board, wearing the crown and tunic; not a hair on his head was damp. He handed Minos his ring, and there was no more argument. Minos went ashore in a rage, without Periboia, and the Athenians were herded off their ship and tossed into prison. Next day the bull-leaping ceremony would begin.

Princess Ariadne, Minos' daughter, had gone with her father to meet the Athenians, and the sight of Theseus climbing from the sea in his purple tunic and golden crown had set her on fire with love. That night she unlocked Theseus' cell and said she would help him kill the Minotaur, if he promised to take her back to Athens and make her queen. She gave him a spindle of thin, strong thread.

Daidalos had made it, and it held the secret of the labyrinth. Everyone imagined the labyrinth as a horizontal maze, a one-storey honeycomb of corridors. Daidalos' secret was simple: instead of being horizontal, the labyrinth was vertical, its tunnels spiralling downwards like the chambers in a triton-shell.* To find the heart, therefore, you fastened one end of Ariadne's thread to the opening, put the spindle down and let it roll. It would find its own level, unwinding downwards until it came to the bottom chamber where the Minotaur lurked. To reach the surface again all you had to do was climb up the rock-passages, guiding your way by the dangling thread.

While everyone in the palace slept, Theseus fastened the thread at the labyrinth's mouth and let the spindle roll away into the darkness. Then he slung his club round his shoulders and began to clamber down, gallery by gallery. Ariadne followed, wearing Amphitrite's golden crown; the gold glowed to light their way. The air was rank with corpse-smell; their fingers dislodged bones and greasy scraps from the crevices; there was no sound but the Minotaur's snoring from far below.

At last the thread ended and their feet crunched on the bone-strewn floor, deep in the earth's belly. The Minotaur's stink filled their nostrils; in the dim golden glow they could see its limbs humped in sleep, and its bull's mane matted and foul with blood. Theseus edged forward, lifted his club and smashed it down again and again until there was no more breathing, no movement, nothing but his thudding heart and the whisper of Ariadne's dress in the darkness behind him. Suddenly, in the stillness, he was filled with choking panic, and scrabbled on the filthy floor until his hands closed on the dangling thread. Then he and Ariadne clambered back up the long tunnels to the sweet outside air.

They opened the cells and freed the other Athenians. The young people gaped at them: they were grim-faced, filthy with blood and dung. Theseus beckoned to them to follow, and ran through the darkness to the harbour. There were no guards – no one but Daidalos had ever escaped from Crete, and even he had needed wings. As soundlessly as possible, the Athenians scuttled every Cretan ship, scrambled on board their own boat and started pulling on the oars. By dawn, when the Cretans were gaping at empty dungeons and a trail of blood from the lip of the labyrinth to the drowned ships in the harbour, the Athenians were beyond pursuit.

They landed on the island of Naxos to draw fresh water. Ariadne fell asleep on the sand, and Theseus, overcome with love, placed on her head Amphitrite's golden crown. Its glow attracted Dionysos from Olympos, and he too was seized with love for Ariadne, more than for any mortal he had ever seen. He blurred Theseus' and his companions' minds with forgetfulness: they looked about them in surprise, with no idea where they were or why they were there; then they boarded ship and sailed. Ariadne woke up and found herself alone on the empty beach. She began weeping and cursing Theseus, calling on the gods to punish him for betraying her. Then Dionysos appeared, dancing over the sand-dunes with his maenads and satyrs tumbling after him. He spoke gently to Ariadne, charmed all memory of Theseus from her mind, and filled her with love for him alone. She became his queen and consort, the companion in his revels over all the world.

Theseus sailed on for Athens. But forgetfulness still fogged his mind, and blotted out his promise to Aigeus that he would hoist a purple-red sail if he was coming back alive. So Aigeus, gazing out to sea, saw a black sail on the horizon, and in despair jumped from the Acropolis and killed himself.* (In this way the long-forgotten prophecy of the Delphic oracle came true: by unfastening the wineskin's foot long ago in Troizen, he started a chain of events which led, years later, to his death.)

Phaidra and Hippolytos

After Aigeus' death the Athenians made Theseus king. His first act was to strengthen his people and build up their community. Until his time the Athenians had lived in a scatter of villages, each with its own laws and boundaries. Theseus drew them into a single city-state centred on the Acropolis. Unity gave strength, and Athens soon became the leading city in that part of Greece.

Once the city was secure, Theseus began to join other heroes on their expeditions and adventures. In particular, he was invited to the wedding of Peirithoös king of the Lapiths, and helped him in the battle which followed against the Centaurs. Theseus and Peirithoös became friends, and took part together in many adventures. They were two of the heroes who hunted the Kalydonian boar; they sailed with Herakles to steal the belt of Hippolyte, queen of the Amazons. On the way, Herakles besieged the Amazon town of Themiskyra. But it was well fortified, and had stores of food and wells of water inside the walls: there was little hope of taking it by force. In the end it fell by treachery. Princess Antiope was standing on the battlements looking out at the besiegers, and as soon as she saw Theseus the gods filled her with love for him, just as they had Ariadne in Crete. That night she unlocked the gates and let the invaders in. Themiskyra was captured, and Antiope travelled with Theseus as his mistress.

Later, after Herakles had killed Hippolyte and taken her belt back to Mycenae, the Amazons set out to punish Antiope's treachery. By now she had gone back with Theseus to Athens, married him and become his queen. The Amazons rode all the way south from the Black Sea to Athens, and attacked the city. The Athenians withdrew to the Acropolis, and the Amazons set up camps on two hills facing it, the Pnyx and the Areiopagos (or Hill of Ares). The siege lasted for four months. The Amazons made constant attacks on the Acropolis, but its walls were too steep to climb and the Athenians easily beat them off. The Athenians, too, made raids, and there was fierce fighting on the flat ground between the three hills. At last Theseus' friends Herakles and Peirithoös came with reinforcements, and in a final battle killed all the Amazon invaders or drove them out.

Theseus and Antiope ruled Athens peacefully for several years, and had a son (called Hippolytos after the Amazons' long-dead queen Hippolyte).* But after King Minos of Crete was killed by Daidalos, Theseus decided to make an alliance with Minos' son Katreus, the new king, and to divorce Antiope and marry Katreus' sister, Phaidra, princess of Crete. The wedding was held in Athens – and in the middle of the wedding-feast Antiope burst in with a band of armed Amazons to kill Theseus, Phaidra and all their guests. There was a confused fight, tumbling among the wine-jars; it ended when Theseus killed Antiope and her supporters fled.

The gods did not punish Theseus immediately for murdering Antiope; but Ares (Antiope's father) and Artemis (her patron goddess) were none the less watching, and though their vengeance was delayed for years it stayed sure and sharp. The reason for delay was that they were waiting until Theseus' son Hippolytos grew up. As soon as he reached manhood, they made his step-mother Phaidra fall wildly in love with him. She spied on him as he exercised; she pined;

she wept; she behaved less like a queen than like a giddy girl. In the end she sent Hippolytos a letter begging him to come and make love to her. He refused, haughtily* – and at once the gods turned Phaidra's love to its mirror-image, hate, and their revenge on Theseus for Antiope's murder began. Phaidra sent Theseus a letter saying that Hippolytos had raped her; then she disarranged her clothes, overturned the furniture as if there had been a struggle, and hanged herself. Theseus found her body and sent guards to arrest Hippolytos. The boy fled in a chariot, galloping down the coast road beside the Saronic Gulf. In his fury Theseus prayed to the gods to kill his son – and Poseidon curled a huge wave into the shape of a roaring bull and terrified Hippolytos' chariot-horses. They reared, and the chariot was overturned; Hippolytos was tangled in the harness and dragged to death.

Theseus' madness and death

After the deaths of Phaidra and Hippolytos, Theseus began to suffer from the same kind of madness as afflicted another hero, Herakles. With his friend Peirithoös, he made an audacious plan: they would each kidnap a new queen, a daughter of Zeus, and marry her. Their first choice was twelve-year-old Helen of Sparta, twin sister of Klytemnestra and half-sister of Kastor and Polydeukes. They rode to Sparta, tethered their chariot-horses and slipped into Artemis' temple. No one noticed them because the temple was crowded with visitors for a festival. Helen was in a group of girls dancing the goddess' sacred dance; Theseus snatched her up while Peirithoös stood with drawn sword and kept back the priests. So they stole Helen and defiled Artemis' holy festival. They hid her in the village of Aphidnai near Athens, and drew lots to see who was to marry her. Theseus won.

Next they had to steal another daughter of Zeus for Peirithoös – and Peirithoös proposed that they go down to the Underworld and kidnap Hades' queen Persephone. In his madness, Theseus agreed. They slithered down oozing tunnels to the banks of Styx, and instead of tricking or forcing Charon to ferry them, blandly told him that they were on their way to steal Persephone. Charon recognised the gods' madness in their minds, gave them free passage and left them to

151

Hades' mercy. They hammered on Hades' door and demanded Persephone. Hades pretended to welcome them, and invited them to sit down and eat, before they took Persephone and started the arduous journey back to the upper world. But the seats he offered them were the Thrones of Lethe. Anyone who sat in them instantly forgot who he was or why he had come to the Underworld – and his flesh fused with the rock until he could never get up again. As soon as Theseus and Peirithoös sat down, they stuck; a banquet was laid before them, out of reach; snakes hissed; Cerberus snarled; the Furies scourged them with iron-tipped whips.

Theseus and Peirithoös would have sat on in torment until they were totally engulfed in stone, if Herakles had not come down to the Underworld on his journey to steal Cerberus. He recognised the whimpering wraiths of his old companions, clubbed the Furies aside and took Theseus by the armpits to haul him free. Theseus had already grown into the rock; as Herakles tugged, his flesh was ripped from his bones and stuck to the throne in lumps. He slumped, gasping and bleeding, while Herakles went to rescue Peirithoös. But the ground roared and split apart, and a voice boomed from the depths. 'Leave him! The plan was his, not Theseus', and he has all eternity to pay for it. Leave him and go!'

Terrified, in agony, alone, Theseus hobbled back to the upper world on his rags and bones of legs. He had been four years in the Underworld, and in that time Kastor and Polydeukes had rescued their sister Helen, invaded Attica and set up a new king in Athens (Theseus' nephew Menestheus, once banished and now triumphantly returned). There was no place for Theseus in Athens: his former citizens discarded him. He left the city and limped away.

Theseus' death, like so many events of his life, happened without reason or explanation. A ship's captain bound for Crete felt pity for him and took the poor sick cripple on board. But on the way to Crete, the ship put in at the island of Skyros, and King Lykomedes recognised Theseus despite his tatters and deformities, took him to a rocky precipice and threw him over. There was no reason for it – except that Lykomedes was a follower of Artemis, the goddess whose servants Theseus had wronged throughout his life.

Centuries later, at the battle of Marathon, Greek soldiers reported that Theseus' ghost had come fully armed to help them, and had scattered a whole wing of the Persian army. The Delphic oracle advised the Athenians to collect Theseus' bones from Skyros and bury them in their own city, with honour. In an ancient burial-mound on Skyros they found a gigantic human skeleton and an ornate bronze sword. Sure that the bones were Theseus' (and that the sword was the one he rescued from under the rock at Troizen), they carried the remains back to Athens and buried them in the temple called the Theseion. Theseus has lain there, guarding and protecting the city, ever since.†

16
THEBES

Kadmos and Kadmeia

When Zeus disguised himself as a bull and stole princess Europa of Phoenicia, her father Agenor sent her brothers across the world to look for her. Each brother took a different direction; one travelled overland, two by sea; only the youngest, Kadmos, had the sense not to wander aimlessly but to ask the Delphic oracle where Europa was. The oracle told him to forget Europa; instead he was to buy a cow and drive it until it collapsed with exhaustion. Where it lay down, he was to build a city.

Kadmos and his servants left Delphi, and came down from the hills into meadowland filled with the grazing cattle of King Pelagon (one of the oldest inhabitants of the world, the last survivor of the clay-people moulded by Prometheus). The king's cowherds gave them food and a night's shelter, and in the morning sold them the prize animal from Pelagon's herd, a cow marked with a silver moon-circle on each brown flank. Driving the cow before them, Kadmos and his servants set out across the plain. They walked for a day and a night without rest, and still the cow showed no sign of weariness. It was not until the end of the second day, as they were plodding across rising ground at the plain's edge, that the cow's legs buckled and it collapsed exhausted on its right side, exactly as the oracle had foretold.

Kadmos piled stones for an altar, ready to sacrifice the cow, and sent his servants up the hill for water. But the water-spring was guarded by an enormous, fanged snake, an earth-monster from the bowels of the Underworld. It snatched Kadmos' servants and tore them to pieces. While it ripped and gnawed their flesh, Kadmos crept up behind it, lifted a boulder full-stretch and smashed its skull.

As the snake twisted and died, the rocks and trees began to glow with radiant light, and the goddess Athene appeared in full armour. She told Kadmos to sow the snake's teeth like seed-corn, and lent him her golden helmet to gather them. Kadmos sowed the teeth, and as soon as they touched the ground an army of men grew from them, unfolding and stretching like sprouting weeds. Kadmos tossed a pebble among them, and they leapt for each others' throats and fought till all but five lay dead. The five survivors knelt and promised Kadmos loyalty. Their names were Chthonios (Earthman), Echion (Snakeman), Hyperenor (More than Man), Oudaios (Born from the Soil) and Peloros (Giant Snake); together they were called the Spartoi (Sown Men), and they founded the Theban race.

As punishment for killing the gods' sacred snake, Kadmos had to spend eight years as a slave in Olympos; but when his time was done Zeus gave him a sign of particular favour: although he was mortal, he was allowed to marry the goddess Harmonia, daughter of Ares and Aphrodite. The wedding, attended by all the gods, was a dazzling event.* The marriage-feast was held in the rich meadows through which the moon-marked cow had wandered; Kadmos called the place Boeotia (Cowland) after her. When the wedding-celebrations were over and the gods had gone back to Olympos, Kadmos and the Sown Men set to work to build a citadel; they called it Kadmeia, and it quickly became the heart of a thriving town.

Kadmos and Harmonia had five children. Their daughter Agaue married Echion, one of the Sown Men, and the son of that marriage, Pentheus, eventually became king in Kadmos' place. Another of Kadmos' daughters, Semele, gave birth to the god Dionysos, Zeus' son; but the townspeople refused to accept him as a god, and Dionysos took a bloody revenge on Pentheus and Agaue (see page 39). After this, Kadmos and Harmonia left their city in a chariot pulled by two moon-marked calves; in extreme old age they settled as king and queen of Illyria, and when the time came for their mortal lives to end the gods changed them into snakes and carried them away to live in the Islands of the Blessed.

Amphion and Zethos

When Kadmos left Kadmeia, the throne passed to his son Polydoros and from Polydoros to Labdakos. Labdakos died when his son Laios

was only one year old – and the descendants of the Sown Men re-
fused to be ruled by a one-year-old baby. They gave the throne to
Nykteus (son of the Sown Man Chthonios), and banished Laios to
Pisa in southern Greece, where he was brought up by King Pelops.

Nykteus had a beautiful daughter, Antiope. He guarded her like a
jailer – he remembered how the daughter of his namesake, King
Nykteus of Crete, was driven insane by the gods, slept with her own
father and was then turned into an owl, and he was determined that
there would be no such scandal in his family: Antiope would make
the respectable marriage her ancestry required. Unfortunately, before
this could happen, Zeus saw Antiope, slipped past Nykteus' guards
and made love to her. Antiope soon found that she was pregnant,
and ran away to Sikyon, where she married King Epopeus – and
Nykteus was so overwhelmed with shame that he gave his throne to
his brother Lykos and killed himself. Lykos took an army to capture
Sikyon and punish Antiope for causing her father's death. He found
that her children by Zeus, the twins Amphion and Zethos, had
already been born and spirited away (they were hidden in a herdsman's cottage in the hills, and grew up as his sons). Lykos threw
Antiope into prison, and for twenty years he and his wife Dirke treated her as cruelly as if she were a captured slave. But at last Antiope
escaped, found her grown-up sons and begged them to take revenge.
The twins, like all Zeus' children, had more than mortal strength:
they killed Lykos and all his guards, and punished Dirke by tying her
to the horns of a wild bull, which dragged and tossed her to death.

Amphion and Zethos made themselves joint kings in Lykos'
place. They enlarged Kadmos' old citadel Kadmeia and built a new
city round it. Zethos laid out the streets, using ordinary building
skills; but Amphion, who was a musician trained by Hermes himself,
played so cleverly on his lyre that stones leapt into place of their own
accord to form the walls. Amphion married Niobe, daughter of Tantalos; Zethos married the nymph Thebe, and called the new city
Thebes in her honour.

Amphion and Zethos both died as their grandfather Nykteus had
done, as a result of sorrow caused by their own children. The children of Niobe and Amphion were so beautiful that Zethos' wife
(some say it was Thebe, others a second wife called Aëdon) was filled
with jealousy and crept into the nursery one night to murder them.
But in the darkness she mistook one cradle for another, and the baby
she killed was her own son Itylos. (The gods turned her into a night-

ingale, just as they did Prokne after she murdered Itys: she has sung mourning-songs for Itylos ever since.)

When Zethos found his son's body he killed himself for grief. But his sister-in-law Niobe felt no grief at all. She had no thoughts in her head but of her own children's beauty; she was forever comparing them favourably with every other child on earth. In the end she boasted that they were more beautiful even than the son and daughter of the goddess Leto, and Leto's children (Apollo and Artemis) punished her by shooting her children dead. At this, Amphion, the children's father, was driven insane by grief. He gathered an army and marched on Delphi, intending to revenge himself on Apollo by slaughtering his priests. But Apollo scattered the army, and killed Amphion with a single shot – and although Amphion was Zeus' own son, Zeus punished him for challenging the gods by taking away his immortality and banishing him to the Underworld. (He turned Niobe into a mountainside, and she forever wept streams of tears in memory of her children and of her boasting which caused their deaths.)

Laios and Oedipus

While this was happening in Thebes, banished Prince Laios (the rightful heir to the Theban throne) was growing up at the court of King Pelops in Pisa. He was educated in all princely sports, including archery, wrestling and especially chariot-racing. As he grew older he began to prefer the company of drivers and charioteers to that of anyone else; he fell in love with a handsome charioteer called Chrysippos, King Pelops' bastard son, and scandalised everyone by giving him presents and sending him love-poems as if he was a girl. Even worse, when news came from Thebes that Amphion and Zethos were dead and that the throne was Laios' for the taking, he asked Chrysippos to marry him and go with him – and when the boy refused he threw him into a chariot and galloped off with him. Chrysippos struggled free, jumped from the chariot and broke his neck.* Laios fled to Thebes – and when news of his son's death reached Pelops he cursed Laios, calling on the gods to prevent him ever having a son, or if he did, to make sure that that son was also his murderer.

Knowing nothing of the curse, Laios reached Thebes and was acclaimed as king. To ensure the loyalty of the Sown Men, he married Jokasta, the great-grand-daughter of Pentheus son of Echion. But the marriage was childless, and as time went on the descendants of the Sown Men, led by Jokasta's brother Kreon, began demanding that Laios should either provide an heir or give up the throne. Laios went to Delphi for advice, and the oracle told him that Jokasta was pregnant, but that if the child ever grew to manhood he would murder his father and marry his mother. To cheat this prophecy, Laios snatched Jokasta's baby the moment he was born, fastened his ankles with a golden pin, put him in an earthenware pot and left him on Mount Kithairon to freeze to death.*

But what man can cheat the gods? A shepherd heard the baby crying, took pity on him and carried him home. He pulled out the pin and bandaged the child's wounds, then gave him to his wife to nurse. They called him Oedipus (that is, *Oidipous* or Swollen-foot), and looked after him until he was old enough to crawl. Then, because they guessed from the golden pin and expensive swaddling clothes that he was a rich man's son, perhaps even a child of the palace, they dared keep him no longer, and the shepherd gave him to a visiting cowherd from Corinth. The cowherd took the child home to his master King Polybos. Polybos and his queen Periboia had ruled Corinth for many years; they were aged and childless, and treated Oedipus as a gift from the gods. They gave him a royal education, and brought him up as their own son and heir.

Oedipus grew up convinced that Polybos and Periboia were his parents. He was therefore horrified when a drunken banquet-guest one day jeered at him for being a foundling, a stranger with no claim at all to the Corinthian throne. He went to Delphi to consult the oracle. But Apollo's terrible answer to his question 'Who am I?' was 'You are the man fated to kill his father and marry his mother' – and Oedipus vowed never to go back to Corinth, so that he could never harm Polybos or Periboia. He hurried from Delphi, avoiding the Corinth road and travelling east instead of south. He came to a narrow track, where the road passed between cliffs before forking at a crossroads to Daulis and Phokis. An old man in a chariot was coming the other way, and there was no room to pass. The old man shouted to Oedipus to make way; Oedipus stood firm; the old man galloped straight at him and beat him on the shoulders with his driver's whip. Oedipus snatched the reins and overturned the chariot. He tangled the reins round the old man's legs; the horses galloped away and dragged the old man to death.

Oedipus the king

Some days later, Oedipus came to Thebes. He found the city in the grip of the monstrous Sphinx, a supernatural being with a lion's body, eagle's wings, a serpent's tail and a woman's face. (It was Hera's revenge on Thebes for the murder, years before, of the charioteer Chrysippos.) It posed the people a riddle: 'What has four legs in the morning, two at noon and three in the evening, and is weakest when it has most legs?' Each day they failed to answer, the Sphinx snatched up a Theban child and devoured it. Laios had gone to ask the Delphic oracle for help; but he had not returned, and in their desperation the people offered the throne, and marriage to Queen Jokasta, to anyone at all who could solve the riddle.

Oedipus had just come from Delphi, and fresh in his mind was the riddle carved on Apollo's temple there, 'Know yourself', and its answer 'Know that you are man'. He realised that the same answer, 'Man', fitted the Sphinx's riddle: a man has four legs in the morning of life (when he crawls on all fours as a baby), two at noon (when he walks upright) and three at evening (when he leans on a stick). He went to the market-place (where the Sphinx perched every day to cackle its riddle and pick its victim) and shouted the answer in the monster's face. Screeching with rage, the Sphinx flew up, darkening the sky; but it was fated that if ever its riddle was answered it must die, and it threw itself down on a rocky hillside (later called Sphikion, or Phikion, after it) and broke its neck.

Oedipus was proclaimed king and saviour of Thebes. He married Jokasta, and ruled happily and securely for many years. Although Jokasta was much older than he was, she was still of child-bearing age, and they had four children: two sons, Eteokles and Polyneikes, and two daughters, Antigone and Ismene. No one remembered Laios, the old king. There was a rumour that he had died in a chariot accident, or been murdered by robbers on the Daulis road; but while the city was prosperous and its king was strong, who had thoughts to spare for that?

But if the Thebans forgot Laios, the gods remembered him. Even though he was a guilty man, and his sufferings had been ordained by the Fates, his murder was still a crime and was not to go unpunished. Oedipus knew nothing of it, but he was caught in a trap and there was no escape. When the time came to spring the trap, the gods sent plague on Thebes. The crops withered; cattle and people died; the air was greasy with the smoke of funeral-pyres. In their agony the townspeople gathered in front of Oedipus' palace and begged him to help them. He had freed them from the Sphinx; he was the only man who could end the plague. Oedipus sent messengers to Delphi, and they brought back word that the cause of the plague was Laios' murderer, still prosperous in Thebes. The way to end it was to hunt him down and punish him. Oedipus swore to find the murderer; he sent for Teiresias the prophet and ordered him to consult the gods and name the guilty person.

At that moment a messenger from Corinth, an old cowherd, came to Thebes with what he thought was happy news. King Polybos and Queen Periboia of Corinth were dead: there was no more risk from the oracle that Oedipus would kill his father and marry his mother. When Jokasta heard about the oracle, she laughed. Was that all Oedipus was frightened of? All oracles lied; none should be taken seriously. The Delphic oracle had told her old husband Laios that he would be killed by his own son – and his son had been exposed and died in infancy; Laios had been killed at a crossroads, by total strangers.

But now the old cowherd identified Oedipus, by the scars on his ankles, as the baby long ago rescued from Mount Kithairon and taken to Corinth. The riddle was becoming clearer – and finally Teiresias spoke and made all plain. Oedipus was the son of Laios and Jokasta, and Laios' murderer. His wife was his mother, and his children were his brothers and sisters. All the oracles were true; there were no more riddles; the gods' trap was sprung. In a frenzy of guilt, Jokasta hanged herself; Oedipus cut her down, took a golden pin from her dress – it was a match for the pin which had pierced his ankles long ago – and jabbed it into his eyes, again and again, until he was blind.

For a time, afterwards, Oedipus lived on in Thebes, a human husk, sitting in a corner of the palace and staring ahead with blood-caked, empty eyes. His sons (and brothers) Eteokles and Polyneikes despised him – and one day, instead of serving him the king's portion of meat from a sacrifice, they gave him a slave's helping in its place. Oedipus threw the meat down and cursed his sons: he prayed to the gods that Eteokles and Polyneikes might decide their inheritance with iron, and go to the Underworld on a single day, each killed by the other. Then, leaning on a beggar's stick (like the old man in the Sphinx's riddle), unable to see how his own people shrank from him, he picked his way out of Thebes for good.*

The seven against Thebes

As soon as Oedipus was gone his sons began a bitter quarrel for the throne. They could have ruled Thebes jointly, as Amphion and Zethos had done; but neither would agree to share. Eteokles (the elder) proposed that they should take turns, rule for one year each and spend one year in exile; Polyneikes refused, saying that he could never trust Eteokles to hand over the throne when his year was up. He offered to give up his claim to the throne altogether, if the Thebans gave him the gods' wedding-presents from the marriage of Harmonia and Kadmos long ago, the silver-embroidered dress of Athene and the necklace of Hephaistos. These were Thebes' greatest treasure, stored and cherished for three generations. But they were not worth keeping, if the price was civil war: reluctantly, the priests took the dress and necklace from their place of honour and gave them to Polyneikes, who stuffed them under his arm, mounted his horse and galloped out of town.

Whatever his promises, Polyneikes had no intention at all of giving up the throne. He went to Argos, told King Adrastos that he had been unjustly banished, and asked him to help win back the throne. Adrastos willingly agreed,* and gathered an army led by seven champions: Adrastos and Polyneikes themselves, Tydeus, Kapaneus, Hippomedon, Amphiaraos and Parthenopaios.* They marched north, led by Adrastos on his winged horse Areion. Their soldiers swept across the plain like floodwater, and the sun glinted on their spearpoints as if on waves surging to swamp the land.

They camped in Nemea, and asked King Lykourgos for food and water. Lykourgos sent his slave Hypsipyle to lead them to a water-spring. Hypsipyle had once been queen of Lemnos; now she was a slave, the nursemaid of Lykourgos' baby son Opheltes. An oracle had prophesied that if Opheltes touched the ground before he was old enough to walk, he would die; Hypsipyle therefore had to carry him everywhere, and never to let him out of her arms. But in her eagerness to point out water to the visitors, she forgot these orders and put baby Opheltes down. It was just for an instant – but in that

162

instant a snake reared out of the earth and savaged him. By the time the Argives beat it off, Opheltes was dead and his body torn and mutilated.* To ward off bad luck, the Argives buried him with royal honours and held week-long funeral games. Then they continued northwards. Tydeus galloped ahead, reined in before the walls of Thebes, and arrogantly ordered the Thebans to surrender and give Polyneikes back his throne. The Thebans indignantly sent fifty men to capture Tydeus. Single-handed, Tydeus killed them all but one, and sent him whimpering home with news of the others' deaths.

Adrastos and Polyneikes marched their army up and ringed Thebes with spears. There were seven city gates, and the attack on each was led by one of the seven Argive champions. Inside the city, seven Theban champions led the defence: Melanippos, Polyphontes, Megareus, Hyperbios, Aktor, Lasthenes and Prince Eteokles. Eteokles prayed to the gods to fight for the just cause, and when Teiresias prophesied that the Thebans would win if a royal prince sacrificed his own life for the city, Menoikeus, son of Kreon, jumped from the battlements and killed himself.

The battle began, and at once Zeus sent an omen to gladden the Thebans' hearts. Kapaneus, the most fiery of the seven Argive champions, was filled with madness: he shouted that he would fall on the Thebans like a thunderbolt, so hot that in comparison Zeus' thunderbolts would seem like feeble rays of winter sun. He climbed a scaling-ladder to jump down into the city; but Zeus hurled a real thunderbolt, and feeble as winter sun or not, it toppled Kapaneus blazing to the dust. The Thebans threw open the gates and attacked. Three more of the seven Argive champions were killed at once, and another of them, Tydeus, was stabbed in the belly by a spear. He lay gasping and spitting blood; his protectress Athene ran from Olympos with a cup of nectar which would give him immortality. But Amphiaraos (who was jealous of Tydeus) cut off the head of the Theban spearsman who had wounded Tydeus, and gave it to him saying 'Eat his brains!' Tydeus sucked out the brains, and Athene was so sickened that she went back to Olympos and left him to die. Amphiaraos laughed with satisfaction – and while his attention was distracted the Theban warrior Periklymenos ran at him with lifted spear. Amphiaraos leapt into his chariot and fled. But his gloating over Tydeus had left his enemy time to get close, and there was no escape. In the nick of time Amphiaraos prayed to Zeus to spare him the dishonour of being stabbed in the back, and Zeus split open the earth so that he and his chariot rode headlong into the Underworld and disappeared. When King Adrastos saw this, and realised that with five of his champions dead the expedition was doomed, he leapt on to his winged horse, shook the reins and soared from the battlefield. The Argive army fled.

Now, on the plain, only the brothers Polyneikes and Eteokles were left, the attacker and the defender, facing each other. From the battlements, the Thebans watched in silence. Eteokles and Polyneikes circled: grim, narrow-eyed, intent on each others' death. Then, in a single instant, they lunged; their spears smashed shields, burst breasts; they toppled and died. Oedipus' curse was fulfilled.

The fall of Thebes

The throne of Thebes passed to Eteokles' and Polyneikes' uncle Kreon (Jokasta's brother, a descendant of the Sown Man Chthonios) – and it was he who caused the city's final destruction. The suicide of his son Menoikeus (who jumped from the battlements when the Argives first attacked) unhinged his mind and he committed a crime against the dead Argives which outraged the gods and lost Thebes their protection. He decreed that every Theban killed in the fighting was to be buried with honour, but that the Argives were to be left to rot. This decree horrified the Thebans – for unburied dead were barred from the Underworld, and their grieving souls wandered for all eternity – but no one dared disobey except for one girl, Antigone, Oedipus' daughter, the sister of Eteokles and Polyneikes. Telling no one except her sister Ismene what she planned, she crept out of the city, sprinkled Polyneikes' body with dust, laid a coin under his tongue and said prayers to ensure him safe passage to the Underworld. Kreon's men caught her in the act, and Kreon walled her in a cave to starve to death – and so committed a crime against the living to equal his crime against the dead.*

Kreon's treatment of the dead Argives caused outrage all over Greece. Adrastos went to Athens and asked King Theseus for help. Theseus marched on Thebes, captured Kreon and insisted that the dead be given decent burial. Funeral-pyres blazed, and when all the remains had been burned the dead men's families carried their ashes home in urns for burial. (Only one stranger's tomb remained. Fiery Kapaneus had already been charred to ash by Zeus' thunderbolt, and his wife Euadne threw herself on to the funeral-pyre in his place, and was buried on the spot where his body fell.) Theseus executed Kreon, saw that he too was buried with reverence, and went home to Athens.

The children of the dead Argive heroes, however, were still not satisfied. They wanted to see every last Theban dead and the city sacked. Alkmaion,* Amphiaraos' son, gathered a second army (including the Epigonoi or Second Champions, the sons of the original seven) and marched on Thebes. They surround the city just as their fathers had done, and fought a pitched battle. This time the Thebans drove them off with only a single death (that of Aigialeus, son of Adrastos). But that night, inside Thebes, Teiresias prophesied that the city's end was near. The gods had cursed Thebes after Kreon's ill-treatment of the Argive dead; they were allowing it to survive only as long as Adrastos, last of the original seven champions, remained alive, and he would kill himself as soon as he heard of his son Aigialos' death. The Thebans decided that their only hope of staying alive was to slip away into exile that same night and abandon the city before it was attacked. They packed their belongings and crept away. Next morning, the Argives found Thebes' gates swinging open, the streets empty and the houses deserted. They plundered the city, smashed the walls, ploughed the rubble and sowed salt so that nothing would ever grow there again.

So Thebes fell. It had lasted for only seven mortal generations, one of the most ill-fated cities in the whole of Greece. Its people (the ones who fled in the night) founded a new settlement at Hestiaia, not far away; but it never grew to be as famous, or as unlucky, as the original city begun by Kadmos and the Sown Men two hundred years before.†

17

THE · TROJAN · WAR

How the war began

No one knows who founded Troy, or when. Settlers went there from the Black Sea, from Crete (led by Scamander, after whom the river of Troy was named) and from Athens (led by Dardanos). Dardanos' son Ilos chose a site for the city: like Kadmos in Thebes, he drove a cow across the plain until it collapsed exhausted, and built the city where it fell. That same night, the wooden statue of a goddess, a metre high, fell from Olympos and embedded itself in the ground at the new city's heart. This statue was the Palladion, and as long as it stayed in the city, Troy could never fall.

Two gods, Poseidon and Apollo, built the city walls. In the earliest days of Olympos they rebelled against Zeus, and their punishment was to serve a mortal man for one year. Their master was King Laomedon (Ilos's son), and he ordered them to build a fortress no enemy could ever storm. Unwilling to give any mortal a city so powerful, the gods asked Zeus' half-mortal son Aiakos to help them build: his section of the walls was weaker than the rest, the one place vulnerable to attack.

When the walls were finished the gods asked Laomedon for their wages. For answer, he skipped inside his new walls and snapped his fingers. 'Attack if you dare!' he crowed. Poseidon and Apollo went back to Olympos, furious – and in due course they had their revenge, when Laomedon, trusting in walls he thought unbreakable, broke a promise to Herakles. Herakles battered his way into Troy (through the section of the wall mortal Aiakos had built), killed Laomedon and left Troy sacked and sorry under the kingship of Laomedon's son Priam, a helpless baby.

When Priam grew up, however, he proved to be not so helpless after all. By conquest, trade and alliances he made Troy a glittering royal capital; he had two wives, Arisbe* and Hekabe (or Hecuba), and a dozen royal mistresses; he had twelve daughters and fifty sons.*

The Age of Bronze, the heroic age of mortals, was at its peak. When the gods went walking in the world, or looked down on it from Olympos, they saw that it had changed. Instead of quiet countryside with a scattering of market towns, it was now bustling with armies, traders, travellers and the pomp of ten thousand kings. The human race was thriving, but it was also beginning to squabble and argue – and the cause was the gods' own half-mortal children, the heroes. They swaggered and lorded it over lesser men, strong, fearless, always in search of challenges and happy, if none were found, to make them by fighting wars.

Zeus decided to cut down the heroes' numbers by setting up the fiercest war mortals had ever seen. It would be fought by princes from every state. They would lock skill with skill and cunning with cunning; courage and daring would meet, match – and kill. When it was all over and the most arrogant heroes were dead and gone, the world would return to its former peace.

Once war was decided, it was easy to arrange a cause. At the wedding of Peleus and Thetis, Eris, goddess of quarrels, rolled a golden apple between Hera, Athene and Aphrodite. On it was written 'For the fairest', and the three goddesses asked Zeus to choose which of them was meant. He refused. He said that only a mortal could make an unbiased choice, and that the man to do it was Paris, prince of Troy.* Hermes took the goddesses to Mount Ida near Troy, where Paris was tending cattle. At first Paris refused to judge: he suggested that the goddesses divide the apple equally between them. But Hermes threatened him with a thunderbolt, and he agreed to judge. One by one the goddesses appeared before him – and each offered him a bribe to place her first. Hera offered royal power; Athene offered wisdom; Aphrodite offered Queen Helen of Sparta, the most beautiful woman in the world. Paris chose Aphrodite, and Hera and Athene flew back to Olympos in a rage and began to plan trouble for Paris and doom for Troy.

Paris went to his father Priam and asked for a fast ship. Aphrodite gave him safe journey to Sparta, and Eros buried an arrow of love for him deep in Helen's heart. She eloped with Paris;* to prevent pursuit they avoided the direct route home and instead reached Troy by way of Egypt, Phoenicia and Cyprus, a voyage which lasted several months.

The Greek fleet sails

Many Greek princes – Aias, Diomedes, Idomeneus, Machaon, Nestor, Palamedes – were eager to join the warfleet and sail for Troy. Others were reluctant. The oracle told Odysseus that if he went to war he would be twenty years away and would return a beggar. When the kings came recruiting, therefore, he pretended madness by wearing a silly hat, yoking an ass and an ox to the same plough and sowing his fields with salt. But the kings dropped his baby son Telemachos in front of the plough; Odysseus stopped to prevent him being trampled to death (something no lunatic would have done), and so was proved sane and had to agree to go. King Kinyras of Cyprus agreed to provide fifty ships, but later changed his mind and sent clay models (for which Apollo shot him dead). Achilles' mother Thetis* (who knew that he was fated to die if he went to Troy) dressed him as a woman and hid him among the palace women on the island of Skyros. The recruiting kings foiled her by blowing a trumpet and sounding the alarm: Achilles was the only one of the palace women to throw off his veil and run to fight.

When the recruiting was done, the Greek fleet gathered at Aulis, and the kings sacrificed for victory. The prophet Kalchas led them: he was a Trojan, but his master Apollo sent him to join the Greeks, with orders to stay and interpret the gods' will to them until the war was won. (He had told them about Achilles' hiding place on Skyros; now, at Aulis, he explained the omen of the snake and nine sparrows turned to stone (see page 84), and when Artemis held back the winds (see page 201) he ordered, and made, the sacrifice of Iphigeneia.)

Piloting the huge Greek fleet – some say there were more than eleven hundred ships, each with a crew and a band of fighting men – was perilous.* Once they left Aulis they had to cross a hundred kilometres of treacherous open water, the stormy heart of the Aegean Sea. They landed in Mysia, mistaking it for Troy, and fought a fierce battle with the inhabitants.* They landed on Lesbos for water; King Philomeleides refused to let them sail until they found a champion to wrestle him, and Odysseus took him on, wrestled him to the ground and forced him to release the ships. They tried to land at Tenedos, but were pelted with rocks by its people, led by their king Tenes. Achilles swam ashore and killed Tenes, and the Greeks sacked the island. They crossed to the holy island of Chryse to make a thanksgiving sacrifice; Philoktetes (who owned Herakles' unerring bow and arrows) landed first, and trod on a sacred snake which bit his foot. In the days that followed the foot festered, until the Greeks could stand no more of its stench or Philoktetes' groans. They left him on the barren sea-coast of Lemnos, to live or die at the gods' mercy.*

At last the Greeks reached Troy. They landed at the mouth of the river Scamander – and were met by a defence-party pelting them with spears and stones. Protesilaos, the first Greek to step on Trojan soil, was first to die* – and when the others hesitated to follow him Achilles jumped overboard, killed the Trojan leader Kyknos and ran straight at the points of the Trojan spears. The Trojans fell back in alarm: they knew nothing of his immortal skin, and took his confidence for a god's madness. Still he advanced, and they dropped their weapons and scuttled for the city walls.* Quickly, before they could pluck up courage again, the Greeks beached their ships and set up an armed camp.

Skirmishes

There was no chance of finishing the Trojan war in one short siege. Power between Greeks and Trojans was exactly balanced. Each Greek hero was matched by a Trojan; the armies were equal; even the gods' support was divided, with Hera and Athene (thanks to their anger at Paris) leading the gods who helped the Greeks, and Ares and Apollo (who hated Achilles) leading those who favoured Troy. Nor was Troy a single city, to be captured in one energetic afternoon: it was the heart of a web of alliances which stretched north to the Black Sea, east into Persia and Assyria, south to Phoenicia and even as far as Ethiopia in Africa.* The allies sent supplies, and men and ships to harass the Greeks. The Greeks had their own supply-lines and allies, and far from concentrating their forces on Troy itself, spent most of the war making expeditions and fighting battles in a dozen far-off areas at once. Aias, for example, sacked Teuthrania in Thrace and took Princess Tekmessa as his war-prize; Achilles plundered a dozen mainland towns and the islands of Lesbos and Sminthos (whose princess Chryseis he presented as booty to Agamemnon).

After each raid the Greek heroes returned to camp to divide the spoils, rest and harass the enemy. Often raiding-parties or foragers came out from Troy and fought groups of Greeks hand-to-hand. In one of these skirmishes Achilles killed Troilos, chasing him into Apollo's sanctuary and spattering the altar with his blood; in another he captured Lykaon and sold him as a slave to King Euneus of Lemnos (who promptly sold him back to the Trojans for twice the price). Sometimes the gods took part in these adventures: once Aphrodite went raiding with her son Aeneas, and Diomedes smashed Aeneas' hip and wounded Aphrodite's wrist when she tried to protect him, so that Apollo had to hurry from Olympos to rescue the pair of them.

By the tenth year the war was stalemate. Every skirmish ended in a small victory for one side or the other; but there was no overall advantage, and no sign that the fighting would ever end. In the end Agamemnon called in all his scattered forces, and the Greeks began to concentrate their efforts on sacking Troy itself.

Achilles' anger

So long as the Greek leaders had been able to come and go as they pleased, each in undisputed charge of his own men, there was little argument. But once they were cooped up in the same camp, under the authority of Agamemnon (which many of them disputed), wrangles and disagreements began. Sometimes these were petty, but often they led to death. Once Palamedes boasted, in front of every Greek in camp, that he was a better leader than Odysseus because when he went foraging he filled his cargo-ships whereas Odysseus brought back nothing but glory. For answer, Odysseus hid a sack of gold (stolen from Troy) in Palamedes' tent and then accused him of taking bribes to betray the Greeks. The tent was searched; the gold was found; Palamedes was declared guilty and stoned to death.

The most serious quarrel of all was between Agamemnon and Achilles. Both heroes had mistresses, prizes chosen from the noblest prisoners-of-war. Achilles had even found Agamemnon's mistress for him: Chryseis, daughter of Apollo's priest Chryses on the island of Sminthos. Achilles' mistress was Briseis, Kalchas' daughter. Chryses sailed to the Greek camp and demanded his daughter back, and when Agamemnon refused to hand her over, cursed the Greeks with plague. Hundreds of Agamemnon's soldiers died and lay rotting in the shallows; finally (as he had done before, over the sacrifice of Iphigeneia at Aulis) Agamemnon gave way to the other leaders, handed Chryseis back to her father – and in exchange took Briseis from Achilles. At once Achilles pulled his soldiers out of the fighting, retired to his tent and refused to have anything more to do with the war.

Achilles' sulk delighted the Trojans. They began massing their forces for the final assault that would rout the Greeks and smash their ships. Hastily Agamemnon sent messengers suggesting that they decide the war by single combat instead of pitched battle. Paris and Menelaos both claimed Helen, he said; let them fight for her, and let the result decide the war. The Trojans agreed, and the two heroes armed. But the gods had no intention of ending the war this way. Aphrodite gathered Paris up in a cloud and spirited him back inside Troy,* while the Greeks jeered that he was too besotted with Helen ever to want to leave her bedroom. Athene made Pandaros fire an arrow at Menelaos; Diomedes killed Pandaros; Glaukos attacked Diomedes – and the fighting flared. It went on till dark; then both sides drew back to wait for daylight and the next attack.

Under cover of darkness, Chryses brought his daughter back. She had refused to go home to Sminthos; she was perfectly happy with Agamemnon, pregnant with his child, and eager to go with him to Mycenae as soon as the war was over. Agamemnon sent Odysseus, Aias and other leaders to Achilles to return Briseis and beg him to come back and fight. Achilles refused. He said that it was a matter of honour and insult, not of Briseis;* he was sailing home next morning, and the Greeks would have to win the war without him. The Greek leaders went back to their tents, checked their armour and weapons, and waited for day.

Dawn broke, and the battle began. At first the fighting went the Trojans' way. Led by Hektor, they sliced their way through the Greek lines, scattering the soldiers as wolves scatter sheep. They wounded Agamemnon, Diomedes, Eurypylos, Machaon and Odysseus; for a time Idomeneus and Aias held them at bay, but then they broke through and reached the Greek ships.

In Olympos, the gods decided to take a hand. Hera borrowed Aphrodite's golden belt (which made its wearer irresistible) and charmed Zeus into bed with her while Poseidon helped the Greeks. Poseidon saw Aias hurling a boulder at the oncoming Trojans, and guided its flight so that it crushed Hektor. The Trojans fell back – and their howl of dismay was so loud that it reached Zeus in Olympos. He leapt out of bed, shouted angrily to Poseidon to stop interfering, revived Hektor and sent him limping back to Troy.

From their tents in the Greek camp Achilles, Patroklos and their Myrmidon soldiers watched the fighting ebb and flow. When the Trojans burst through the Greek lines they groaned; when Aias felled Hektor they cheered; when Zeus helped Hektor up they groaned again. But when they saw the first feathers of smoke from the burning ships, Achilles gave Patroklos his own armour and told him to take the Myrmidons and protect the ships. Dressed in Achilles' armour, Patroklos rode out in his war-chariot. He swept up to the ships, killed the Trojan leaders Pyraichmos and Sarpedon, wheeled on the Trojans and drove them back. Thinking he was Achilles, the Greeks rallied round him, and the Trojans ran. The Greeks poured after them as a wave pours up the shore, and Patroklos rode at their head to the walls of Troy.

The Trojans scrambled inside and slammed the gates. Hektor buckled his armour over bruised limbs and limped to the defence. He found Patroklos and his men seething round the walls, ramming and burrowing; then they set up ladders and began to climb. Patroklos swarmed up first, his helmet-plumes nodding and his armour – Achilles' armour – glinting in the sun. The Trojans showered him with arrows, harmless as twigs; he was a step from the top, and if he once jumped down into Troy then Troy would fall. Desperately Hektor prayed for help – and Apollo swirled round Patroklos' head like mist and knocked him from the ladder. Patroklos crashed to the ground; Achilles' helmet flew from his head, baring his neck and face. As soon as they saw that he was not Achilles, the Greeks fell back; the Trojans surged out of the city, and Hektor stabbed Patroklos dead and stripped him. He carried the armour back into Troy, and Menelaos and Aias lugged Patroklos back through the dust to Achilles' tent.

Achilles and Hektor

Patroklos' death brought Achilles back into the fighting: he swore not to rest until Hektor lay dead at his feet. His mother Thetis gave him new armour, made by Hephaistos: helmet, breastplate, greaves and a bronze shield decorated with silver-gilt.* He strode out, glittering, death-dealing, and the Trojans ran. He challenged Hektor to single combat, and all fighting stopped as Greeks and Trojans alike lowered their weapons, awe-struck, to watch.

Achilles and Hektor were equally matched. A god, favouring one or the other, could have settled the duel; but Zeus forbade interference. The loser, therefore, would be the hero who tired first and dropped his guard. Hektor realised this, and began running away from Achilles, round the plain outside the walls, taunting him. He hoped that Achilles, weighed down by Hephaistos' armour, would exhaust himself and lay himself open to the death-blow. But Achilles had the strength of a goddess' son, redoubled by fury: he kept pace easily with Hektor, chased him three times round the walls, and finally caught him and stabbed him dead. He stripped the corpse, cut holes in its heels and threaded through them a purple belt which Aias had given Hektor the day before. Then he fastened the belt to his chariot and drove three times round the walls of Troy, dragging Hektor's body mercilessly through the dust. The Trojans peered out in terror. Achilles' savagery tore the fight from them: no one dared challenge him. Every morning that followed he harnessed his chariot and dragged Hektor's body three times round Patroklos' grave.

At last Zeus sent Priam, Hektor's aged father, to the Greek camp to beg for his son's body. Achilles demanded, as a ransom, Hektor's full weight in treasure. Scales were brought and the gruesome weighing began. On one side were heaped gold, jewels and bales of cloth; on the other was Hektor's tattered, decomposing corpse. When the weighing was done, Achilles took his treasure and Priam carried Hektor's body back to Troy.* He gave it a prince's burial – and the mingled noise of tears from Troy and celebration from the Greeks was so loud that birds fell stunned from the sky like stones.

Hektor's death broke the Trojan's spirits, and left the Greeks cock-a-hoop. Achilles stalked the plain like a lion; heroic madness was on him, and the Trojans quailed before him or fought and died.

But the Fates were spinning the end of Achilles' thread: his death was near. The gods sent Prince Memnon of Ethiopia to join the fight.* He was a friend of the gods, the nephew of their cupbearer Ganymede; like Achilles, he wore armour hand-made by Hephaistos. He harvested the Greeks as a scythe cuts corn; he killed leader after leader; once more the Trojan army poised itself to burn the Greek ships. Then Memnon killed Antiochos, Achilles' favourite since Patroklos' death, and Achilles stormed after him and cut off his head with a single stroke.

Now the gods took action. While Achilles was bent over Memnon, stripping his armour, Poseidon sent the Trojans swarming after him. Achilles drove them back to the city gates – and there Apollo guided Paris' hand as he set poisoned arrow to bow and shot Achilles in the only vulnerable part of his body, the heel. Achilles twisted with pain, and died. There was a fierce battle for his body, which ended only when Zeus sent a thunderstorm to pelt the combatants. The Trojans retreated into the city, and Odysseus and Aias carried Achilles' corpse across the sodden plain to the Greek camp.* For seventeen days the Greeks held funeral games; Thetis and her sea-nymphs wept for Achilles, and the Muses sang songs of grief. On the eighteenth day they burned him and buried his ashes (with Patroklos') in a golden urn made by Hephaistos. His soul took its place in the Underworld, where he married Medea and lived an honoured life in the Elysian Fields.

The Palladion

After Achilles' death the Greek leaders were convinced that the gods had turned against them and would never let them take Troy. Several, already restless after ten years away from home, suggested abandoning the siege altogether. But Kalchas the prophet reassured them. Troy's end was near, he said. Its fall was fated, and the cause would be one of Herakles' unerring arrows. All the Greeks had to do was persuade Philoktetes (who now owned Herakles' bow) back from exile on Lemnos, and he would fire the shot which would begin Troy's end.

Odysseus and Diomedes sailed to Lemnos to fetch Philoktetes. They found him in a cave by the shore, in squalor: his clothes were tattered, his body was caked with filth, and his wits were wild. At first he spat at them, furious and disdainful; but they persisted and persuaded, and at last he agreed to go back with them to Troy.*

So Philoktetes returned. The doctors Machaon and Podaleirios laid him in Apollo's sanctuary, and drugged him asleep while they cleaned his wounded foot and poulticed it. The gods – who were as anxious as the Greeks to end the war – saw to it that the medicine worked at once, and when Philoktetes awoke next day he found both his health and his wits restored. He sprang straight to the walls of Troy and challenged Paris to a duel: bow against bow. Paris shot first, and missed. Then Philoktetes set one of Herakles' poisoned arrows, sticky with Hydra's blood, to his unerring bow and fired. The arrow hit Paris in the ankle (exactly where he had fatally wounded Achilles); the poison poured into his body and he screamed in pain. The Trojans beat Philoktetes back, dragged Paris inside the city and slammed the gates. That night they took Paris to Mount Ida, and begged Oinone, the mountain-nymph who had been his wife before he deserted her for Helen, to give them herbs to counteract the poison. She refused, bitterly. 'He preferred Helen to me; let him ask her for help!' So Paris died – and Oinone, frenzied with grief, threw herself on his funeral-pyre, and her angry ghost flew down with his to the Underworld.

As soon as Paris was dead, Priam's other sons began squabbling over Helen. She wanted to marry none of them, and one night hung a rope ladder over the walls and began to climb down. She meant to go to the Greek camp, find Menelaos and beg him to take her back. But when she was half-way down, Priam's son Deiphobos hauled in the ladder and threatened to kill her unless she married him. They were married next morning – and Deiphobos' brothers Helenos and Antenor, furious with jealousy, at once began looking for ways to betray Troy to the Greeks. Helenos (a prophet of Apollo) told Odysseus the gods' three conditions for the fall of Troy: Pelops' ivory shoulder-bone must be fetched from Pisa, Achilles' son Neoptolemos must be brought to Troy to avenge his father's death, and the Palladion (the sacred statue which fell from the sky at Troy's foundation) must be stolen from the citadel.

The first two conditions were easy. The Greeks sent fast ships to Pisa to fetch Pelops' shoulder-bone and to Achilles' kingdom of Skyros to bring back twelve-year-old Neoptolemos. Stealing the Palladion, however, was another matter. It was the life of Troy; it was locked in a temple in the centre of the city, protected by armed guards and by a witch-priestess whose magic withered anyone who dared approach. Odysseus and Diomedes made all kinds of plans to

176

get into Troy; but they could find no way to steal the Palladion without inside help.

Then that help came: Helenos' brother Antenor promised to make stealing the Palladion easy if in return the Greeks banished Priam and made him, Antenor, king of Troy. He showed Odysseus and Diomedes a secret way into the city – not up ladders or past guarded gates, but through a muddy drain at the river's edge. They crept through the dark streets, and found the temple guards drugged asleep or killed and the witch-priestess (bribed by Antenor) holding out the Palladion to them, wrapped like a baby in a cloth. Carefully they carried it to the wall; Odysseus stood on Diomedes' shoulders, pulled himself up, then hauled Diomedes and the Palladion after him. They jumped down and ran back to the Greek camp. Diomedes perched the Palladion on his shoulders: in the shadows it looked as if the statue was running from Troy on its own two legs.*

The wooden horse

In the end it was neither gods nor magic statues that toppled Troy, but the efforts of a coward and a trickster. The coward was Epeios. When Odysseus suggested that one way to get inside Troy and open the gates was by hiding men in a hollow wooden horse, Epeios offered to build it so long as he was never asked to ride in it. He made it of pine-planks, pegged like ship's timbers; it rode on solid wooden wheels and its belly was large enough to hold two dozen men. On its side Epeios carved the words 'Offered to Athene, to grant the Greeks safe voyage home'. In one of the legs he built a trapdoor, carefully concealed – and he was so carried away by his own craftsmanship that he made a fastening which no one but himself could work. Unfortunately for him, this meant that the Greeks had to forget their promises and take him with them after all: late in the evening, when twenty-four hand-picked heroes hid in the horse's belly, Odysseus forced Epeios up the ladder and made him sit, grey with fear, beside the trapdoor to let them out again.

When the heroes were in place and the trapdoor was shut, the rest of the Greeks launched their ships. But instead of loading them with tents, huts, animal-pens, and all the other paraphernalia of a ten-year camp, they piled everything together and set fire to it. Then, taking nothing but their weapons, they embarked and sailed away.

They moored the fleet on the far side of the island of Tenedos, out of sight of Troy, and waited. There was nothing left on the plain but smouldering wreckage, the wooden horse pregnant with armed men, and the second of the two men whose skill was to topple Troy, Sinon the actor (grandson of the famous trickster Autolykos).

All night the Trojans had been looking out in bewilderment at the fires blazing on the plain. As soon as dawn broke they poured out to see what was happening. They found no Greeks: only ashes, rubble and the huge horse with its dedication to Athene. The townspeople ran about their own plain like tourists, exploring all the places they had been barred from for ten long years: here Diomedes had pitched his tent; here was the camp-site of Achilles and the Myrmidons; this had been Odysseus' hut; over there was the council area where the Greek leaders had gathered to plan Troy's fall. While they seethed about like ants, their leaders stood anxiously discussing what to do with the horse. Some said that since it was dedicated to Athene it should be taken to her temple inside the city and offered to her there. Others said that horses were sacred to Poseidon, and that it should be rolled down to the beach and burned there in his honour. The argument see-sawed back and forth: Priam and his warrior-sons thought the horse harmless, but others, led by the prophet Laokoön, were convinced that it would bring Troy's doom. 'I fear the Greeks – especially when they bring gifts', said Laokoön, and flung his spear hard at the horse's side. The blade jarred into the wood, and there was a boom and a ring of weapons from inside. But even this omen failed to persuade Priam, and Laokoön went angrily down to the shore, with his sons, to sacrifice to Poseidon and ask his help. He built the altar, and was just beginning the sacrifice when two sea-snakes, shark-toothed, slid shorewards, coiled round his sons and began feeding on their flesh. Laokoön tore at the scaly coils, and the snakes turned on him and devoured him too. Then they slipped back into the sea and disappeared, leaving the altar naked on its patch of blood-soaked sand.

Now there was no doubt in the Trojans' terrified minds. Poseidon was angry; the horse should be dragged to the beach and burnt to appease him. They brought ropes and levers, and gathered mules and men to pull. Priam was just lifting his hand to signal them to start when soldiers ran up with a Greek prisoner. It was Sinon: he had waited, with an actor's perfect timing, for the exact moment to let himself be captured. He begged Priam to spare his life. He said that the Greeks had planned to leave Troy months before, but had been held up by lack of winds, just as they were ten years before at Aulis. As then, so now: Kalchas the priest had demanded human sacrifice – and he, Sinon, was chosen as victim. In the nick of time a breeze had come along and the Greeks had forgotten him, leapt on board ship and sailed. Now he had no future: he was a scapegoat, doomed to die if he ever went back to Greece, and surrounded by enemies if he stayed in Troy.

The purpose of these lies was to persuade Priam that Sinon hated the Greeks and could therefore be trusted. It worked: Priam eagerly asked him about the horse. Why had it been built, and why was it so huge? Sinon answered with his second prepared speech, the one that would win the war for Greece. He said that the horse was built to placate Athene after the stealing of the Palladion; so long as it stood on the plain the Greeks would be safe from her anger, but if it was ever dragged into Troy and placed in her temple, every man in the Greek fleet would drown. That was why the horse was so huge: to make it impossible for the Trojans to pull it into Troy.

When they heard this, the Trojans forgot Laokoön. Excited as children, they turned the horse to face the city, laid hold of the ropes and began to pull. Three times the horse stuck on the rough ground, and spears and arrows rattled from inside – but the gods made the Trojans deaf. They were so eager that when they found the horse too big for the gates, they knocked down a wide section of the wall (the part built, long ago, by mortal Aiakos) and hauled the horse across the gap and through the streets to Athene's temple. Kassandra the prophetess ran wildly round them, screaming that the horse was full of armed men and would be the end of Troy – but who ever listened to Kassandra? They set the horse in Athene's courtyard, decorated it with flowers, and spent the day in an orgy of celebration for the end of war.*

The fall of Troy

That night, no guards were posted – what need was there, now that the Greeks had gone? Drunk with liberation, the Trojans slept. In Athene's dark temple, Epeios opened the trapdoor in the horse's flank and let his cramped companions down on ropes. They scattered: some to the gates, some to the guard-posts. Odysseus signalled to Helen, and she lit a beacon to alert the Greeks waiting at Tenedos. They rowed back to shore and ran to the city, eager to begin their butcher's work. The sleeping Trojans woke to find their houses swarming with armed men; throats were slit, women and children dragged to slavery, treasures looted and houses burnt. A few Trojans, blurry with sleep, fumbled for their weapons; others, like Aeneas, saw that the city was doomed, gathered what valuables they could and slipped away to exile. One by one, those who stayed were cut down and died: the ordinary townsfolk, the heroes, Priam's sons and finally Priam himself, killed at his palace altar by Neoptolemos, Achilles' son. The survivors, women and children mostly (including Queen Hekabe and her daughter Kassandra) were herded to Athene's temple and kept there under guard with piles of furniture, treasure and weapons looted from the houses. Around them in the darkness the city blazed: the red glow of dawn mingled with orange flames and the crimson of blood-soaked streets.

It had taken five mortal generations to build Troy, and ten weary years for the Greeks to get into the city; it took just one night to topple it.* When the killing was done, the division of spoils began. Agamemnon took Kassandra, Odysseus took Hekabe, and Neoptolemos took Hektor's wife Andromache and baby son Astyanax. (But Kalchas prophesied that if Astyanax lived a new, greater Troy would rise from the ashes – and Neoptolemos took the baby by the feet, swung him round his head and flung him over the battlements to death. Hekabe's suffering drove her mad, and her shrieking and cursing plagued Odysseus so much that he killed her – whereupon her spirit became one of the black dogs of the Underworld and ever afterwards haunted the place of her death, howling and snapping at sailors' heels. Agamemnon took Kassandra home with him, to death, in Mycenae.*)

The Greeks loaded prisoners and spoils till their ships wallowed at the waterline. They broke down the buildings and walls of Troy – now that the city was fallen, its god-built walls crumbled into ruin of their own accord – and sowed its fields with salt. They left Priam's last surviving son,* Antenor (who had helped Odysseus and Diomedes steal the Palladion), to rule the few farmers whose lives they spared: human rubble to match Troy's shattered stones. Then they prayed to the gods for fair weather, climbed on board ship and sailed for home.*

18
ODYSSEUS

Ithaka

An oracle told Odysseus that if he sailed for Troy he would be away for twenty years, and would come home to trouble in his house. At first, therefore, he tried to trick his way out of going to Troy at all; then, when he had no choice, he made arrangements to keep his kingdom Ithaka loyal throughout the twenty years he would be away. He left the throne in the charge of his father Laertes* and his wife Penelope, and made all the local chieftains swear oaths of loyalty.

But twenty years is half a lifetime. Laertes grew old and tired of kingship; he retired to his hillside farm and left Penelope to govern in Odysseus' place. A new generation grew up in Ithaka: young men the age of Odysseus' own son Telemachos, who had been a tiny child when his father sailed for Troy. These princes laughed at their fathers' loyalty-oaths: few of them had ever seen Odysseus, and none remembered him. They insisted that Penelope choose a new husband and make him king in Odysseus' place. They thronged the palace, feasting and dancing at Penelope's expense while she made up her mind, and neither she nor Telemachos could stop them. For a long time she held them with a trick: she was weaving a rich grave-cloth to have ready when her father-in-law Laertes died, and said that as soon as it was finished she would choose one of the suitors and marry him. Every day, she wove – and every night she sat up by lamplight and unpicked the threads. This went on for three whole years, until the suitors began to grow suspicious, and one night burst into her room and discovered the trick. They forced Penelope to finish the weaving; when it was nearly done she sent Telemachos to

Sparta to see if Menelaos had any news of Odysseus; while he was away all she could do was weave as slowly as she could, and wait.

Odysseus' wanderings

Poseidon's anger was the cause of Odysseus' wanderings. When the Greeks left Troy in their booty-laden ships, they offended the gods by forgetting to make proper thanksgiving sacrifices for victory; they arrogantly took all the credit for themselves, and the gods sent storms which scattered the fleet, drowned the crews and made many leaders' homecomings bitter and long-delayed.* Odysseus and his men were driven for nine days at the winds' whim, all the way south to Africa, where they landed to fill their water-skins. Odysseus sent three men inland to find out where they were. But this was the land of the Lotos-eaters, whose favourite food the lotos-fruit destroys memory; Odysseus' men ate lotos-fruits, forgot who they were and sat with glazed eyes asking nothing more than to live with the Lotos-eaters forever. When Odysseus rescued them they cried bitterly, held out their hands to their new companions and begged him to leave them where they were. Hurriedly he flung them on board and sailed before any other crewmen could taste the drug.

The ships next beached on a fertile island bustling with sheep and goats. This time Odysseus himself went foraging, with twelve armed men. They found a cave filled with sheep-pens, baskets of cheese and tubs of milk. They made a meal and sat down to wait for the cave's owner. At evening he came: Polyphemos, Poseidon's son, a giant Cyclops with a single eye in the centre of his forehead. He drove his sheep into the cave, and blocked the entrance with a stone so huge it would have taken a dozen teams of men to move it. He milked the ewes, made the fire for his evening meal — and saw Odysseus and his men. Odysseus asked him politely for hospitality; for answer Polyphemos snatched two of the men, cracked their heads on the floor like eggs and devoured them raw. Next morning he ate two more for breakfast, drove his sheep out of the cave to pasture and stoppered the entrance with the gigantic stone. That day, while Polyphemos was away, Odysseus sharpened a green olive-branch and hardened it in the fire. Then he took beside him some skins of sweet wine he had brought from the ship, and waited. At evening Polyphemos returned, milked his ewes, stirred up the fire and killed

182

two more men for supper. Odysseus politely offered him one of the wine-skins. Polyphemos drank it dry and demanded another, and another. He offered Odysseus a present in return, if he told him his name. 'My name is — Nobody' said Odysseus. 'Good!' answered Polyphemos. 'Of all your men, I'll eat Nobody last. That'll be your present.' And he fell on the floor in a drunken sleep. Odysseus and his surviving crewmen heated the olive-pole red-hot and ground it into Polyphemos' single eye, which bubbled and sizzled till all its sight was gone. Polyphemos howled and groped for them, but he was too fuddled with drink to catch them. His screams brought the other Cyclopes running. 'What's the matter, Polyphemos?' they shouted from outside the cave. 'Nobody's here. Nobody's hurt me!' wailed Polyphemos. 'Well, if nobody's there, go back to sleep. You're drunk!' they answered and went away. Polyphemos lay groaning on the floor till dawn. Then he lifted the stone to let his sheep out to pasture. He sat by the cave-mouth, feeling them as they passed to make sure that they were sheep not men. But Odysseus fastened each of his men to three fleecy sheep and covered them with wool, so that as the sheep jostled out of the cave-mouth Polyphemos felt nothing but matted fleece. Odysseus himself went last, clinging under the belly of Polyphemos' fattest ram.* Once he was back on board ship, instead of slipping quietly away, he could not resist shouting back to Polyphemos, taunting him and boasting that the Nobody who had tricked him was really Odysseus king of Ithaka, greatest of heroes. For answer Polyphemos hurled a house-sized rock after the ships, lifted his arms and prayed to his father Poseidon to drown Odysseus and all his men, or if their death was forbidden to make Odysseus' journey home the most dangerous any mortal had ever made. This was the prayer Poseidon heard – and he answered it by keeping Odysseus from Ithaka for ten interminable years, and by putting him at the mercy of monsters and savages who stripped him of his treasure and killed every man who sailed with him.

Poseidon's weapons against Odysseus were not always waves or storms. Sometimes he made use of Odysseus' own mortal failings, or of his crew's foolishness and greed. After they left Polyphemos' is-land, Odysseus' ships visited Lipara, the floating kingdom of Aiolos the wind-lord. Aiolos was pleased to see visitors, especially when they brought news of such an exciting event as the Trojan war. He entertained Odysseus and his men for a month, and when they left promised them smooth sailing home to Ithaka. He drove all the

winds into a bulging leather sack and knotted the top tightly shut.
Flat calm fell on the world: every wave, every cloud hung still. Only
the warm west wind was left, to fill Odysseus' sails and blow his
ships peacefully to Ithaka. Aiolos gave Odysseus the wind-sack and
showed him the secret of the knot. If he needed to change direction,
all he had to do was unfasten the sack and let one wind out at a time.
All through the voyage that followed, Odysseus' crewmen grumbled.
Why had no one else been given a present? What treasure was Odysseus guarding so carefully in the sack? Their greed and curiosity
itched; but Odysseus was always there, protecting the sack with
sharp words and a sharper sword. At last, when they were so close
to Ithaka that they could see fields, farms and fingers of smoke from
cooking-fires, he let himself sleep for a moment – and his men
snatched the sword, cut the knot and freed the winds. The ships
were sucked, helpless as corks in a whirlpool, all the way back to
Lipara. Aiolos gave them no second welcome. The gods hated them,
he said; they would get no more winds from him; they could row
home to Ithaka, to Hades or anywhere else they pleased.

Laboriously, the ships' crews rowed for seven weary days. At last
they came in sight of land: a sheltered bay backed by fields and
woods. Odysseus distrusted it, but the other ships' captains beached
their ships and sent men inland to look for food and for signs of
human inhabitants. Only Odysseus' ship was moored in deep water,
beside a headland clear of the shore. This saved his crew's lives: for
the country was Laistrygonia and its people were cannibals. They
killed the foragers, fell on the beached ships and began butchering the
crewmen and carrying them off to make their feast. They outmatched
the Greeks as foxes outmatch chickens: there was no defence. Odysseus hacked through his mooring-rope and shouted to his crew to
row. The blades bent as they heaved the sea aside; not till they were
out of sight of land did they relax, put up their sail and let the winds
carry them east, weeping bitter tears for their slaughtered companions and their own helplessness.

They came to another floating kingdom: Aiaia, home of the Sun's
daughter Kirke. Remembering the Laistrygonian cannibals, Odysseus
urged his men to fill their water-skins and leave at once. But again he
was outvoted: twenty-four men set off inland, led by Eurylochos.
Hours later Eurylochos stumbled back, alone and sobbing. He said
they had found a golden palace, led to it by beautiful singing from

184

inside. Kirke was weaving at her loom. She welcomed them with honeyed words and sat them down to a feast – but when they had eaten she tapped them with a magic wand, turned them into pigs and locked them in sties with dozens of other pig-men. They had snouts, bristles and tails; but they kept human minds and memories, and snuffled about the sties weeping for their own stupidity. Only he, Eurylochos, had been suspicious of Kirke, avoided the magic wand and so escaped. Odysseus left him sobbing by the ship, buckled on his sword and set off to rescue his men. On the way, in a forest clearing, Hermes (Odysseus' guardian, the god of trickery) appeared to him, gave him a sprig of the magic plant moly* and told him how to protect himself against Kirke's spells. Odysseus followed the sound of singing to the palace and found Kirke at her loom, just as Eurylochos had described. She welcomed him, offered him food – and then tapped him with the wand and told him to go and wallow with the other pigs. But the moly cancelled her magic; Odysseus drew his sword and threatened to kill her unless she promised to set free the bewitched pig-men. Kirke was a goddess, and no mortal's sword could kill her; but she knew that Odysseus' coming was the will of Zeus, and that she must give way to him. She set the pig-men free, and sent to the beach for the rest of Odysseus' crew. She entertained them at a real banquet, without spells – except that what took one night for a goddess lasted several mortal months, and when the men woke next morning they found their nails and hair grown and their faces covered with flowing beards.*

Like all the Sun's children, Kirke had the gift of prophecy. She told Odysseus that he must go to the dismal land of the Kimmerians on the borders of the Underworld. Here, at the intersection of the Rivers of Fire and Weeping, he should dig a trench, sacrifice to the spirits of Hades and talk with the ghost of the prophet Teiresias, which would tell him what adventures lay ahead. None of Odysseus' crew wanted to leave Kirke's island, especially on such a dangerous journey; but he forced them on board, and the north wind drove them to the Kimmerians' icy land. Odysseus moored the ship, left his men trembling on the rowing-benches, and took a black ewe and a ram down on to the corpse-cold mud. He dug a trench, said prayers to the spirits of Hades, and slit the victims' throats. Their blood steamed in the trench, and its smell enticed the ghosts from the Underworld and brought them fluttering up like bats. Chittering and squeaking, they jostled round the trench, eager to sip life-giving blood. But Odysseus, for all that he was grey with terror, kept a tight grip on his sword and held them at bay until at last he saw Teiresias' ghost and beckoned it forward to taste bright blood. As the ghost drank, two spots of red glowed in its pale cheeks, and instead of squeaking it began to speak clear words, like the whisper of leaves in the wind. It told Odysseus what adventures lay ahead for him, and warned him in particular not to lay hands on the cattle of the Sun, for whoever touched them would immediately be scorched to ash. It prophesied his returned to Ithaka and the battle he would fight there; it told him of Poseidon's anger, and how his death would one day come from the sea. When its prophecies were done it drew back, and the other ghosts flocked forward to sip the blood. First came Odysseus' cabin-boy Elpenor – to Odysseus' astonishment, for he thought Elpenor was alive and waiting on board ship.* Then Odysseus saw his mother Antikleia, whom he had left alive and well when he sailed for Troy, and many of his companions and friends from the Trojan war. He would have stayed, to talk to the spirits of heroes from earlier times; but the jostling ghosts, fluttering and beckoning with hollow hands, suddenly filled him with panic and he ran for the ship and shouted to his men to row.

They first went back to Kirke's island and buried Elpenor's body under a cairn of stones, planting his oar on top to mark the grave. Then they set sail for Ithaka. Odysseus took the shortest route, even though it meant steering past the Sirens' island and through the narrow gulf between Scylla and Charybdis. The Sirens were bird-daughters of the river-god Acheloös, and their singing was so beautiful that any sailor who heard it was irresistibly bewitched – he forgot home, wife and children; he forgot to eat or drink, and sat smiling, listening to the Sirens' song till the flesh withered from his bones and he became one more in their mouldering audience of skeletons. Odysseus told his men that whatever they saw they were to row on past the island – and the more he signed to them to stop, the harder they were to row. Then he plugged their ears with wax and had himself tied hand and foot to the mast. (He left his own ears unplugged: he meant to be the only man to hear the Sirens' song and live.) Soon, in the distance, he heard the Sirens' lovely singing. 'Odysseus,' they sang, 'beach your ship; land and listen; we will tell you the secrets of the gods, and ease your soul with song.' Filled with longing, he struggled with the ropes and shouted himself hoarse trying to make his men untie his fastenings. But the more he roared the faster they rowed, and only when the Sirens' island was far out of earshot did they unplug their ears and cut him free.

Now they saw needle cliffs ahead, smoky with spray, and heard the roar of surf on rocks. The sea narrowed to a funnel of water between high, sheer cliffs. On the sea-bed to the left, Charybdis lay ravenous. Three times each day she swallowed the water above her, filtering out mouthfuls of fish and men before spewing back the empty sea in a whirlpool which hissed and seethed like water in a pan. Scylla perched high on the other side; she snatched any bird, fish or human being that came too close, and made it her meat. As Odysseus and his crew reached the narrow gap between the cliffs, they could hear rumbling and gurgling from Charybdis' depths – and then, in a single moment, she opened her gullet and drank the sea. Odysseus shouted to his helmsman; but the helmsman and the rest of the crew were peering into the depths like men transfixed – and while they gazed Scylla leaned down from behind and snatched up six of them as easily as an angler flicks his prey to land. They hung in her clutches, pitifully piping Odysseus' name; then Scylla drew them into her lair and crunched their bones. As Odysseus and his crew sat stunned, Charybdis' backwash began and the whirlpool's edges tugged the ship. The men flung themselves on the oars and hauled themselves clear.

Their escape left them shocked and mutinous, and when Odysseus tried to steer them past the island of the Sun, they refused to obey him and insisted on landing. The fields were full of the Sun's tawny cattle, placidly cropping the grass beside long-haired, shaggy sheep. Odysseus, mindful of Teiresias' warning that to touch a single animal meant death, ordered his men to eat nothing but the provisions in the ship and any fish or seabirds they could catch. So long as their stocks lasted, they obeyed him. But Poseidon sent thirty days of gales: it was impossible to sail, and stocks ran low. The crew quartered the island for game, picking their way through the Sun's fat flocks to bring back a bedraggled pigeon or a pair of scrawny hares. They were hungry and sullen, and only kept their hands from the Sun's cattle because Odysseus stayed wide awake to warn them off. But at last even his eyelids closed, and Eurylochos (the fool who had earlier insisted on exploring Kirke's island) seized his chance. He told the men to promise the Sun a brand-new temple as soon as they set foot in Ithaka; then he led them into the herd with knives. They had been deaf to warnings; now they were blind to omens: the cattle were no sooner skinned than the hides festered, and the meat writhed and groaned as they skewered it. But they carried on blithely, and Odysseus woke to the smell of steak. 'Fools!' he shouted. 'Get on board, fast, before the Sun gets to hear of this!'* He pushed the sailors on board and forced the ship out to sea; but they were too late. The sky whitened as the Sun's fury seared the clouds; the ship's sail flared and the timbers began to split and smoke. The mast splintered, and smashed down on the helmsman's skull; Zeus threw a thunderbolt which shattered the ship and left the men bobbing like gulls among the wreckage. One by one they sank and drowned, until only Odysseus was left. He lashed himself to two jagged timbers, the remains of the mast and keel, and gave himself up to the sea's fury. He was carried back in a wide sweep towards Charybdis; just as she gulped the sea he grabbed the fig-tree growing from the rock above her lair and clung like a bat. Charybdis swallowed his timbers and spewed them back, scoured white; he jumped astride and held them close. For nine days, in a delirium of storm, sun and thirst, he floated at Poseidon's mercy. Then he was thrown up on the shore of Ogygia, the island home of the goddess Kalypso, and she welcomed him, washed his sea-battered body and gave him food and rest.

Kalypso's welcome extended to seven years. She was as pleased with her mortal lover as a child is with a pet; she meant to keep him as Dawn kept Tithonos, or even to marry him as Thetis married Peleus; she planned to give him immortality and a seat in the councils of the gods. But Odysseus wanted none of it. For seven years he endured Kalypso's kindness, but he was forever slipping away to gaze out to sea and weep for Ithaka and the mortal wife and son he thought he would never see again. At last the gods took pity, and Zeus ordered Kalypso to set him free. As furious as she was, she dared not oppose Zeus' will: she had to help Odysseus build a raft, provision it and load it with gifts, then stand on the beach and tearfully watch him sail away. For a time he travelled safely on towards Ithaka – for Athene, his guardian, had delayed his voyage until Poseidon was far out of the way, on a visit to the Ethiopians who live at the end of the world. But as soon as Poseidon returned and saw the mortal he hated skimming blithely over safe, smooth seas, he darkened the sky with storms and swamped Odysseus' raft. The winds made a game of tossing the timbers in the air and dropping them flat in the tumbling waves. Odysseus lost his provisions, his treasure, his raft and even his clothes; he would have lost his life as well if the seagull-goddess Ino had not given him her veil, which he tied round his waist for protection as he swam through the crashing sea. He swam for two days and nights, and finally, exhausted, salt-caked and naked, waded ashore in the kingdom of Phaiakia. Here Princess Nausikaa found him – she and her maids came to the shore to do the laundry, and Odysseus covered his nakedness with a leafy branch and appeared to them as a mountain-lion, desperate with hunger, comes down on a lowland farm. Nausikaa took him home, and her father King Alkinoös warmly welcomed him. The Phaiakians crowded to hear his account of the fall of Troy and his long wanderings. Then, after nine days' feasting, they loaded him with presents and gave him a ship and crew to take him home to Ithaka.

Odysseus in Ithaka

As soon as Odysseus stepped on board the Phaiakian ship the gods poured over him a sweet, deep sleep which eased from his mind all the care and anxiety of his ten years' wandering. He was still asleep when the Phaiakians landed him in Ithaka and sailed away, and at first when he awoke he was alarmed to find himself alone on a misty beach, in an unknown country which might for all he knew be the home of thieves, cannibals or giants who feared neither mortals nor gods.* But Athene appeared, disguised as a shepherd boy, cleared the mist and showed him Ithaka. He fell on his knees and kissed the ground he had not seen for twenty years. Then, with the goddess' help, he stacked in a secret cave all the treasure the Phaiakians had given him, and began to plan the downfall of the suitors who infested his palace and lorded it over his wife and son. Athene changed his appearance: she wrinkled his smooth skin, clouded his eyes, snowed his hair white and bent his back. She dressed him in rags and gave him a stick to lean on and a worn leather knapsack of the sort beggars use to carry scraps. So disguised, Odysseus made his way to the hut of his old swineherd Eumaios. Eumaios welcomed him, not yet knowing who he was, and poured out bitter tales of the suitors eating his absent master out of house and home. 'If only Odysseus would come back!' he said. 'He'd send them packing! He'd give them a wedding day they'd not forget!' Odysseus said nothing;

but his heart leapt to find that there were men in Ithaka still loyal to him.

The gods brought Odysseus' son Telemachos to Eumaios' hut. At first he was no more than polite to Eumaios' beggar-guest, but then Athene showed him the true man beneath the disguise, and father and son ran into each other's arms. Odysseus told Telemachos to go back to the palace, say nothing to Penelope or the suitors, but gather what loyal servants there were and make preparations. In particular, he was to take down all the weapons from the palace walls and lock them away. Then he was to wait quietly until Odysseus revealed himself and the work of vengeance began.

Later that day Eumaios set off to the palace, driving some fat pigs down for the suitors' evening meal. Beggar-Odysseus walked beside him, bent and leaning on his stick. On the way they met a goat-herd named Melanthios. He jeered at Eumaios' loyalty to his long-lost master and his friendship with every tattered rogue who came to Ithaka. 'Who's this prize specimen?' he said. 'Give him to me: I'll find him some honest work and make him earn his keep!' So saying he kicked Odysseus and sent him sprawling. Odysseus wondered whether to kill him then and there; but it was still not time to reveal himself, and he let Melanthios go laughing on his way, picked himself up and hobbled down to the palace with Eumaios.*

They found the suitors' servants in the courtyard butchering meat for the evening's feast. Inside the palace hall the suitors lolled at their ease, listening to music from the minstrel Phemios and drinking wine. Odysseus took his place humbly at the door, as a beggar should, and waited to be invited in. At once he was challenged by another beggar, Iros, a lazy boaster who had fattened for years on scraps from the suitors' feasts. 'Get up, old man,' he snarled. 'That's my place. Clear off or I'll box your ears!' His noise attracted the suitors' attention. They were bored, always eager for new entertainment, and Antinoös their leader suggested that the two beggars fight for their dinner. The loser would be sent packing, and the winner would have a stool and a side-table of his own, and a fat sheep's haggis to feed on when the feast began. Odysseus and Iros stripped to fight – and Iros saw Odysseus' muscular arms and thighs and panicked. But the suitors (who were taking bets on him) pushed him forward, and Odysseus gave him a punch which smashed him to the ground and left him dazed, spitting blood and teeth. Odysseus hauled him to his feet and sent him scuttling to the gate to keep pigs and dogs away. In this way, without revealing himself, he cleared Iros out of the palace and so saved his miserable life; he pulled on his rags and the suitors gleefully led him into the palace hall.

If the suitors had taken any heed of omens, they would have seen Odysseus' fight with Iros as a clear warning from the gods. But their fate was to die, and no omens could prevent it. They began their feast, laughing, shouting, banging their winecups on the tables and cramming themselves with bread and meat. They had a gaggle of maids to serve them, giggling girls who looked after their every need and shared their beds. These girls crowded round making fun of Odysseus, until he raised his head and gave them a look which sent them scurrying.

So the feast went on. Darkness fell, and the servants brought three huge firebaskets to light the hall. In the red glow the suitors drank, laughed and sang all evening long. They were carefree and confident; they knew nothing of the death-clouds clustering overhead.

The gods now put it into Queen Penelope's mind to propose a contest. Accompanied by two of her maids, she came down the stairs from the women's part of the palace and stood quietly by a pillar until the suitors saw her and stopped their row. Then she said that she meant to find a husband that very night. She made them clear the floor and plant twelve axe-heads in the ground with their handle-holes all facing the same way in a straight line. Then she fetched from the store-room Odysseus' magnificent war-bow, tall as a man, and said that the first man to string it and shoot an arrow through all twelve axe-heads would be her husband.

One by one, the suitors tried to string the bow. Some used force, others prayers; they warmed tallow at the fire and greased the wood to make it supple; they argued and jeered and cursed. Even Telemachos failed: he could easily have strung the bow, but a look from Odysseus warned him and he laid it aside and sighed. Then Odysseus politely asked if he too might try the bow. 'What?' jeered the suitors. 'You? How can you succeed when princes fail?' But Odysseus persisted, and Telemachos told Eumaios to hand him the bow. He balanced it in his hands, turning it about to see if worms had nibbled it in its owner's absence. The suitors sneered. 'Just look at the expert!' they said. 'He must be a collector – or perhaps he wants

191

to set up a bowmaking business. Just look how he handles it!'

Odysseus ignored them. He finished his examination and then, as easily as a musician slips a new string round the pegs of his lyre,he strung the bow and plucked the string to test it. The string gave a mellow twang like a swallow's cry, and Zeus marked the moment with a thunderclap which made Odysseus' heart leap with joy. He took an arrow, aimed carefully (still sitting on his stool), and fired unerringly through all twelve axe-heads. Then he jumped to his feet and said 'Telemachos, the stranger in your hall has passed the test. I am no beggar; I am Odysseus king of Ithaka, returned. Now it's time to make these gentlemen pay for their supper, and to begin the dancing which crowns the feast.'

So saying he shot a second arrow, straight through Antinoös' neck. The suitors leapt to the walls for weapons and found them bare; they ran to the door and found it locked. Telemachos, Eumaios and a handful of loyal servants stood at Odysseus' side, and the slaughter began. The suitors were like a shoal of tunny caught in a net. All round them the fishermen stab and kill; blood pours; there is no escape. So died the suitors, and those of Odysseus' servants like Melanthios who had fawned on them. When all was done, Odysseus sent for the trembling maids – no giggling now, only whimpering and tears – and made them haul the bodies into the courtyard, sponge the hall clean of blood and fumigate it. Then he and Telemachos took the maids outside and hanged them in a row. They flapped for a while, like washing on a line; but they were dancing the dance of death, and soon grew still.

So Odysseus cleared his palace. But he still had to prove to the suitors' relatives that he was their rightful king returned – and he had to prove to Penelope that he was no crafty adventurer but the husband she had waited for so faithfully for twenty years. He bathed and dressed in new, royal clothes, and Athene stripped his disguise as a cook strips an onion-skin, leaving him tall and handsome as an immortal god. Even so, Penelope tested him: if he was truly Odysseus, he would know the secret of their bedroom, the secret no visiting adventurer could possibly guess. 'Nurse!' she called. 'Pull the big bed out from our bedroom, and make it up on the landing with clean sheets and blankets for our visitor.'

'Impossible!' said Odysseus. 'I made that bed myself, and I know its secret. I built it out from the trunk of an olive-tree, a living pillar growing up to support the roof. No one could move that bed unless he sawed through the tree-trunk and brought the whole bedroom crashing down.'

These words thawed Penelope's suspicious heart: she wept, and fell into her beloved husband's arms. When shipwrecked sailors struggle through the sea to land, their muscles bent with cramp and their bodies caked with salt, and finally reach safety on the shore, the joy in their hearts is like Penelope's joy then, as she hugged Odysseus close. Dawn would have surprised them at their tears; but Athene held the long night lingering, and kept Dawn waiting in the east until King Odysseus and Queen Penelope were reconciled at last.

There was still the matter of the suitors' relatives. There was hardly a noble family in Ithaka which had not lost sons, brothers or nephews. They gathered spears and swords, and massed to attack Odysseus and Telemachos,who had taken refuge on the hill-farm of Odysseus' old father Laertes. But the gods had long decided that it was time for war to cease, and Zeus sent Athene to part the combatants and end the fighting. In obedience to heaven's will, the suitors' relatives put down their weapons, bowed to Odysseus and accepted him once more as king.*†

19

THE · SERPENT · SON

Pelops

Pelops' father Tantalos* served him up as a meal for the gods. No one knows why – some say he had no other food, others that he was testing the gods – but whatever the reason, he invited them to a banquet and served them stew made from Pelops' chopped-up flesh. Demeter, whose mind was clouded with grief for lost Persephone, ate a piece of meat; but the other gods pushed back their plates in horror, and Zeus hurled Tantalos to the depths of Tartaros, where he was punished for all eternity. Hermes gathered the pieces of Pelops' flesh, and boiled them in the cauldron of rebirth. Then the Fate Klotho reassembled them into human form, and Demeter brought an ivory shoulder (carved by Hephaistos) to replace what she had eaten. Rhea breathed life into Pelops, and he was reborn. Poseidon took him to Olympos and gave him a team of winged horses and a chariot so light that it could skim the sea dry-wheeled.

Pelops grew up in Olympos, until it was time for him to find a mortal kingdom and a wife. He chose Hippodameia, daughter of King Oinomaos of Pisa. Oinomaos was a son of Ares, but even so an oracle had foretold that he would one day die, killed by his own son-in-law. To prevent this he determined that Hippodameia would never marry, and put all her suitors to a test they were bound to fail. He challenged each of them to a chariot-race, all the way from Pisa to the Isthmus of Corinth. The would-be husband took Hippodameia as his driver, and was given half an hour's start; then Oinomaos and his driver Myrtilos set out after him in a war-chariot. If the suitor reached the Isthmus first, he would marry Hippodameia; if Oinomaos won, the suitor would die. Oinomaos always won: his chariot-horses were a gift from his father Ares, and could outrun the winds. Twelve suitors risked the race, and their heads rotted on poles at Oinomaos' palace gates. Oinomaos boasted that one day there would be enough skulls to build Ares a temple – and this boast disgusted the gods and earned him death.

Pelops could have won the race simply by using Poseidon's wing-ed horses and chariot. But he decided to make sure of it by treachery. He discovered that Myrtilos, Oinomaos' charioteer, was in love with Hippodameia, but was too frightened of Oinomaos to challenge his master to a race. Pelops bribed Myrtilos: if he made sure Pelops won the race, he could sleep with Hippodameia on the wedding night. Myrtilos eagerly agreed, and when he was harnessing Oinomaos' chariot for the race replaced the metal axle-pins with pins of wax. The race began; Pelops and Hippodameia streamed away in Poseidon's chariot; half an hour later Oinomaos galloped after them. The friction began to melt the wax axle-pins, and just as the wheels spun away from Oinomaos' chariot Myrtilos jumped clear and left his master to crash and be killed. So Pelops won the race and Hippodameia's hand – and Zeus shattered Oinomaos' palace with a thunderbolt and so buried the remains of the twelve murdered suitors as they deserved.

Pelops, Hippodameia and Myrtilos set out in Poseidon's chariot on a victory-ride. They galloped across the country (which Pelops renamed Peloponnese, 'Pelops' island', after himself), and then turned out to sea, skimming the waves. Pelops waited until they were out of reach of land, then kicked Myrtilos into the sea and ho-vered overhead to watch him drown. Myrtilos choked and sank – and with his last breath cursed Pelops and all his descendants.*

Atreus and Thyestes

Pelops and Hippodameia rode to the edge of the world, to an altar on Ocean's brink. They prayed to be cleansed of guilt for Myrtilos' death (on the grounds that he had deserved to die for killing his master Oinomaos); Hephaistos, whose favourite Pelops had been ever since the carving of the ivory shoulder which allowed him life, granted their prayer. Pelops and Hippodameia rode back to the Peloponnese and settled as king and queen of Pisa. They had six daughters and sixteen sons, and their children and grandchildren ruled most of the great cities round about.

At this same time, Zeus was trying to provide mortals with a champion, Herakles, to protect them and rescue them from evil. But Herakles was never able to harness his immortal power in his mortal body, and the conflict led to bouts of madness which defeated Zeus' purpose. The gods devised another way of ending mortal squabbling and the evil it caused: they decided to unite the mortal world under a single king, as Olympos was united under Zeus. They chose Pelops, the mortal they had themselves re-made, to be this king. Hephaistos made a royal sceptre, the gods' gift of authority, and Zeus gave it to Pelops and his descendants, hoping that they would rule the whole world evermore in peace.

But human nature has two sides, good and bad, and although the gods had the power to guide people as they chose between them – and to punish those who chose evil – they had no power to change a choice once it was made. Perhaps Pelops' descendants were tainted by Myrtilos' drowning curse; perhaps they inherited evil from Tantalos, the founder of their race; but whatever the cause, every time they were faced with the choice between good and evil, they chose evil. An example is Pelops' son Atreus. He promised one day to give the finest sheep in his flocks to Artemis, and to test him Artemis put among his sheep a ram with a glittering golden fleece. Greed drove promises from Atreus' mind. He sacrificed the ram and gave Artemis the meat and bones. But he kept the fleece for himself, locked in a wooden box.

Atreus and his brother Thyestes were joint rulers of Midea, a town near Mycenae where Eurystheus (Hera's favourite) was king. After Eurystheus' death the Delphic oracle told the Myceneans to place a son of Pelops on the throne, and the Myceneans asked Atreus and Thyestes to choose for themselves which of them it should be. Thyestes suggested that it should be whichever brother owned Artemis' golden fleece – and Atreus (who thought the fleece was his) enthusiastically agreed. Then Thyestes, quick as a conjurer, opened a wooden box and produced the fleece. (It was no conjuring trick. Unknown to anyone, he had been having an affair with Atreus' wife Airope, and she had stolen him the fleece as a love-gift.) The Myceneans prepared to make Thyestes king. But now the gods, seeing that a wrong choice was about to be made, sent guidance. Helios wheeled his sun-chariot round and rode back across the sky; the stars reversed their courses; the earth roared. Thyestes was terrified, and

197

confessed that Atreus was the rightful mortal owner of the fleece; the Myceneans made Atreus king, and he banished Thyestes from Mycenae on pain of death.

So Atreus punished the man who stole the fleece from him. But he had himself stolen it, and now its true owner Artemis took *her* revenge. She sent Atreus insane, and he committed a hideous crime, an unwitting imitation of his grandfather Tantalos' crime against the gods. He sent messengers to tell Thyestes that he was forgiven and could come home from exile. He welcomed Thyestes, gave him the seat of honour at a banqueting-table, and with his own hands served him a dish of stew. Ravenous, Thyestes ate every morsel and sucked the bones – and then Atreus brought in a dish containing the heads and feet of Thyestes' children. He had butchered them to make their father's feast. Thyestes fell back retching, kicked the table from him and called on the gods to destroy Atreus and all his children. Then he ran from Mycenae and went to Sikyon, where his only surviving daughter Pelopeia (who had left Mycenae years before, and so escaped butchery) was a priestess of Athene. King Thesprotos gave him sanctuary.

Thyestes asked the oracle how his dead children were to be avenged, and the oracle told him to make love to Pelopeia: their incestuous child would take revenge. Thyestes hid in a grove of trees beside the temple. Pelopeia was dancing in the goddess' honour, and happened to slip and stain her dress in the spilled blood of a sacrifice. She went to a pool among the trees and took off her dress to wash it – and Thyestes jumped out of hiding, masking his face in his cloak, raped her and fled. Pelopeia had no clue about her attacker except for his sword, which fell from his belt in the struggle.

Pelopeia's baby was born, and she gave him to goatherds to bring up. (He was given the name Aigisthos, 'Strength-of-goats', because he was nursed on goat's-milk.) Years passed. In Mycenae, Atreus' sons Agamemnon and Menelaos grew to manhood. Their mother Airope died, and Atreus took as his new wife his niece Pelopeia. The child Aigisthos (whose father no one knew) was rescued from the goatherds and taken to Mycenae to grow up as a bastard prince.

But however many mortal years the gods wait, they leave no mortal crime unpunished forever. They sent a plague on Mycenae, and when Agamemnon and Menelaos went to Delphi to ask how it should end the oracle answered 'By the death of a son of Pelops'. On their way home they found their uncle Thyestes begging by the roadside, and took him eagerly back to Mycenae, thinking that he was the sacrifice Apollo meant. Atreus threw Thyestes into prison; then, to prevent the taint of killing a blood-relative falling on himself or on his sons, he ordered Pelopeia's bastard child Aigisthos to murder him. Aigisthos lifted his sword, and Thyestes recognised it as the one he had dropped years before by the pool in Sikyon. He embraced Aigisthos as his son, told him how Atreus had butchered his brothers and sisters, and begged him to avenge their deaths. Aigisthos ran to Atreus' bedroom and stabbed him dead. Thyestes seized power; Agamemnon and Menelaos were hustled from their beds: it was their turn for exile now.

Agamemnon took into exile with him the gods' sceptre, the sign of the true king's authority. He and Menelaos went to the court of King Tyndareos of Sparta, and in due course married his twin daughters: Agamemnon married Klytemnestra and Menelaos married Helen. Tyndareos raised an army and attacked Mycenae; but before there was any fighting Thyestes (by now an old man) agreed to give up the throne and begged for mercy. Agamemnon banished him once again, sent Aigisthos, too, into exile, and established himself as king of Mycenae. He built a fortress inside a ring of walls crowned by the Lion Gate, constructed a huge beehive-shaped tomb outside the citadel, and there buried the remains of his father Atreus with a wealth of chariots, weapons and treasure of every kind.

Klytemnestra

For a time it seemed as if Pelops' descendants had escaped at last from darkness into light. Unlike his father, grandfather and uncle, Agamemnon had won his throne fairly, without crime; he seemed the ideal king to carry the sceptre of the gods and unite the mortal world. When Paris of Troy stole Helen and the Greeks assembled an army to fetch her back, they chose Agamemnon as commander not because he was the brother of Helen's husband Menelaos, but because he was the one leader every other prince in Greece agreed to follow.

But even though no one remembered it, there still hovered over Agamemnon the curse of Myrtilos, the charioteer his grandfather Pelops drowned. The curse worked on Agamemnon as it had on his father Atreus, and led him to anger Artemis. This happened at Aulis,

where the Greek fleet gathered to sail for Troy. Agamemnon and the other leaders were planning a sacrifice to ensure fair winds for Troy, and were discussing what the best offering might be. 'The best offering is the most beautiful,' said Agamemnon – and even as he spoke he saw a beautiful fawn in the trees by the shore, lifted his bow and shot it dead. At once, instead of favourable winds, a storm arose. It blew for nine days, hurling the ships against the land, splintering masts and disabling men. Flat calm followed: endless, wearisome, the sea like glass. The sailors grew mutinous; the kings anxiously discussed how to bring back the winds.

Then Kalchas the prophet spoke. The delay was Agamemnon's fault. He had killed Artemis' sacred fawn, in Artemis' sacred grove; it was for this that she was holding back the winds. The only way to pacify her was for Agamemnon truly to sacrifice 'the most beautiful': his daughter Iphigeneia. Only her death would unlock the winds.

Agamemnon angrily refused. Sooner than kill his own child, the lamb of his heart, he threatened to disband the army and abandon the Trojan war. The other kings argued and threatened: he was the leader, the calm was his fault and it was his duty to his followers to end it. At last, bitterly, Agamemnon gave way. He sat apart, head bent, while Odysseus galloped with messengers to Mycenae. They told Queen Klytemnestra that Agamemnon had given Iphigeneia in marriage to Achilles, the noblest of the Greek heroes, and had sent them to fetch her for her wedding at Aulis right away. Overjoyed, Klytemnestra dressed Iphigeneia in wedding clothes and went with her and the messengers to Aulis. The Greek army stood in ranks on the shore; beside the altar Kalchas whetted his sacrificial knife. Agamemnon looked into Iphigeneia's eyes; then he covered his face and gave the sign for death. While Klytemnestra screamed, Iphigeneia was seized, tied and killed; at once fair winds gusted and the Greeks could set sail for Troy.*

So the Trojan expedition began with treachery and human sacrifice – and the gods punished the Greeks by keeping them ten years at Troy and causing the deaths of many of the kings and princes who had connived at Iphigeneia's death. For her father Agamemnon they reserved the most terrible punishment of all: death at his own wife's hands. After the fleet sailed, Klytemnestra was left on the beach at Aulis, alone with Iphigeneia's gaping corpse. She laid the body in a chariot, took it back to Mycenae and buried it with prayers to Zeus lord of relationships and to Hekate queen of night. Her love for

Agamemnon blistered into hate. She fetched home from exile Aigisthos, Agamemnon's cousin (and, after herself, his bitterest enemy) and flaunted him in Mycenae as her lover. She sent her son Orestes, Agamemnon's child, to exile in Phokis, and when her daughters Elektra and Chrysothemis refused to bow down to Aigisthos, she disowned them and treated them as slaves. (Chrysothemis was still a child; but Elektra was a grown woman, and to prevent her bearing a son who might grow up to claim the throne, Klytemnestra married her to a poor peasant, too aged to father children.)

Day and night, Klytemnestra stationed guards on the battlements of Mycenae to watch for the chain of beacon-fires that would announce the fall of Troy and the Greeks' return. She had to wait ten years, and the waiting hardened her heart to stone.* Then, one night, the watchman saw in the darkness the distant beacons' glow and ran to tell Klytemnestra. She set in motion her long-planned welcome for Agamemnon.* As his chariot swept up the royal road to the Lion Gate, she made a speech of loyal welcome, and unrolled a crimson carpet before him, a path fit only for conquerors to walk. The townspeople embraced their sons and brothers back at last from weary war (and also celebrated in their hearts the end of cruel Aigisthos' reign, now that their true king Agamemnon was returned). Klytemnestra took Agamemnon to the bath-house, and slaves washed him and massaged away his weariness with scented oil. Agamemnon stepped from the bath, and Klytemnestra held out a crimson robe. As he tried to put it on she tangled him in the folds as a fish is tangled in a net, and Aigisthos stepped from the shadows and felled him with an axe as heartlessly as a forester fells a tree.

Orestes

So Iphigeneia's death was avenged. But for the Mycenean people, tyranny still was king. For the next seven years, while Orestes grew up in Phokis, Klytemnestra and Aigisthos lorded it in Mycenae, squandering Agamemnon's riches and ill-treating his subjects, proud as cockerels. They feared no man's vengeance: they had killed Agamemnon, the gods' appointed champion – how could any mortal do them harm?

On his eighteenth birthday Orestes visited the Delphic oracle with his friend Pylades (son of King Strophios of Phokis). He asked Apollo

to foretell his future, and the oracle replied that he was destined to bring to an end the curse of Myrtilos and the chain of treachery and death in the dynasty of Pelops. He was the gods' chosen avenger: he was to go to Mycenae and kill Klytemnestra. The Furies would swarm after him with torments, and for a year he would wander the world, mad, in search of purification. But in the end Apollo would help him find peace and sanity, and he would inherit his father's throne. This prophecy filled Orestes with horror – how could any man bring himself to kill his own mother? But Apollo told him the penalty if he disobeyed: leprosy lichening his flesh, mushrooming in his brain until he died. Orestes gathered his courage and went with Pylades to Mycenae.

Before they climbed to the citadel and entered the Lion Gate, Orestes and Pylades went to Agamemnon's tomb. Orestes cut a lock of hair and laid it on his father's grave, a token of grief and of vengeance soon to come. Then he heard women's voices, singing songs of grief. He and Pylades drew back into the shadows, as a procession of black-robed slave-women came to the graveside, led by Orestes' sister Elektra. They sang songs of sorrow for Agamemnon, and laid funeral offerings on his grave. To her amazement – for no one but slaves ever visited the tomb – Elektra found on the grave Orestes' lock of hair. Its colour and texture were identical to hers, like no one else's in Mycenae. Then, in the dust, she found footprints, the exact match for her own. Her heart fluttered with hope – and Orestes himself stepped from the shadows, like a ghost returning to life, and she fell into the arms of the brother she had thought she would never see again.

That same night Queen Klytemnestra dreamed a terrifying, prophetic dream. She was suckling her baby son at her breast; all at once he changed into a serpent, stabbed her with his fangs, and as she died lapped up her milk curdled with blood. She ran screaming for her priests to interpret the omen. But her slaves knew already what it meant: the serpent son was Orestes and the dream foretold Klytemnestra's death.

Next morning Orestes and Pylades entered Mycenae disguised. They wore Phokian clothes, spoke with Phokian accents, and told Klytemnestra they were messengers from King Strophios. Their news, they said, would sadden her: Orestes was dead, and they had brought her his ashes in a bronze pot. They were to ask whether she wanted to bury them in Mycenae, or if they were to take them back for burial in Phokis. At the words 'Orestes is dead' joy flared in Klytemnestra's heart, and she barely managed to hide it with a pretence of mother's tears. She sent a slave, Kilissa, Orestes' old nurse, to fetch King Aigisthos so that he, too, could share the news – and Kilissa (who knew who Orestes really was) added to the message and told Aigisthos that he had no need of guards or weapons, since Orestes, the only man he had to fear, was dead. Aigisthos ran in hotfoot and unarmed, and Orestes stabbed him dead. Now Klytemnestra recognised Orestes; now she understood her dream of the serpent son. She spoke cunningly. 'My son, my dear son, can *you* kill *me* – your own mother? I gave you life; will you now give me death?'

So she spoke, wheedling him. But Orestes' loyalty was to Apollo: he lifted his sword and stabbed her, and her blood mingled with Aigisthos' in the dust. Orestes covered them with the same crimson robe as they had used to trap Agamemnon. He summoned the people and proclaimed that the tyrants were dead and the king avenged. But already the Furies, whose task it is to torment those who murder their kinsmen, were swarming up from Tartaros and teeming in his mind. His brain teetered into madness; like a hunted animal he ran from the palace, scattering the people, and scrambled out of Mycenae to begin his punishment.

The Age of Iron

The Furies tracked Orestes as hunting-dogs track prey. Their aim was to bring him down, rip out his throat, tear the flesh from his bones and gulp his blood. His only hope was to outrun them; his only chance of rest was to find a priest willing to sprinkle him with running water or spilled pig's blood which would hold the Furies at bay long enough for him to catch his breath. If he survived a whole year's running, his prize would be life; if the Furies tripped him, their prize would be his death. There was one moment, on the road near Messene, when they thought they had him; but in desperation he bit off his own finger and tossed it to them. They fought over it – those who accepted the offering turned from black to white, those who scorned it stayed remorseless black – and while they bickered he slipped away.

When his year was up, Orestes ran to the sanctuary at Delphi, where Apollo had long ago promised help, and dropped with exhaustion. The Furies crowded after him, yapping and slavering. But so long as he stayed on holy ground he was immune from them; they tumbled into sleep on the sanctuary floor, whimpering and snuffling in their dreams, their eyes oozing and their mouths and noses bubbling snot. While they slept, Apollo appeared to Orestes. 'Go to Athens, to Athene's temple. Clutch her image for protection. There your case will be tried, and I will speak for you.' Wearily Orestes picked himself up and ran.

Now, in the midst of the sleeping Furies, Klytemnestra's ghost billowed up from the underworld. The sword-wound hung open in her breast; she blazed for vengeance; her eyes spat hate. 'Get up! Up! While you sleep, your quarry slips away!' She kicked the Furies awake, and they shook themselves, sniffed out Orestes' trail and yelped after him. They caught up with him in Athens, and found him in Athene's temple on the Acropolis, clutching the statue for protection. They crouched on guard: if he once let go, even for an instant, he was dead meat.

Then Athene appeared, and put an end to it. She established a court to try Orestes' case, and appointed a jury of citizens to judge the evidence. The Furies demanded Orestes: he had killed his own mother; the age-old law was death for death; he was theirs. Apollo spoke for Orestes: it was time for justice to replace age-old laws; Klytemnestra's murder of Agamemnon had earned her death; Orestes had acted on the orders and with the agreement of the gods. When the speeches were done, the jury voted: equal votes on either side. It was for Athene, president of the court, to give the casting vote. She cast it for justice, for reason, and set Orestes free. To pacify the Furies, she gave them new powers, to bless instead of blight, and a temple of honour in caves below the Acropolis. They became the Eumenides, the Kindly Ones, and their jobs were to help in childbirth and at harvest, to bring prosperity and to banish civil war.

So Orestes, the Serpent Son, stopped the seesaw of retribution and violence which had rocked generations of the house of Tantalos. He married Hermione, Helen's daughter, and when she died took as queen his half-sister Erigone, daughter of Aigisthos and Klytemnestra: the warring families of Atreus and Thyestes were reconciled at last. He wielded the sceptre of the gods, and led Greece in a fifty-year period of peace based on firm alliances and the rule of law. It seemed as if the gods' ambitions for a united humankind were at last fulfilled.

But human memory is short. Orestes died (at seventy, from snakebite)*, and the gods' sceptre passed to his son Tisamenos. Elektra's sons immediately claimed it; it was fought over, stolen, lost – and finally turned up in the tiny town of Chaironeia in Boeotia, whose dull inhabitants had so little idea of its true meaning that they stuck it in a temple and sacrificed to it as if it were a god. The fourth age of mortals, the Age of Bronze when true gods and heroes still walked the earth, came to an end, and the savage fifth age, the Age of Iron in which we still now live, began.†

SHORTER · MYTHS
ALTERNATIVE · VERSIONS
AND · NOTES

OTHER CREATION-MYTHS:
EURYNOME AND NIGHT (*page 1*)

In another creation-myth, the first being made from Chaos was not Gaia or Ouranos, but Eurynome (Wide-wandering). Needing a surface to dance across, she made the sea, and above it the sky. As she danced she caught hold of the breeze stirred up by her movement (the North Wind Boreas) and moulded it into a giant serpent, Ophion (Snake). She changed her shape into that of a dove, and laid the first egg; Ophion coiled seven times round it to incubate it. When the egg hatched all created things were born: the sun, moon and stars, and the earth and everything that grows and lives on it. Eurynome and Ophion ruled on Mount Olympos; but they quarrelled and she banished him to Tartaros. She made the Titans to rule the planets, and the first man Pelasgos (Age-old/Voyager) to enjoy the fruits of the earth and sail the sea.

In another creation-myth, the first being was Night. From a silver egg laid in the womb of dark, Eros (Sexual Love) was born, and from him came sun, moon, stars, sky, earth and all created things. He lived in a sacred cave with his mother Night. Each had three forms. He was Eros, Erikapaios (Heather-browser) and Protogenos Phaëthon (Firstborn/

Shining One); she was the triple goddess Night, Order and Justice, and for a time her oracles and prophecies guided the world. In time the power of these first beings declined, and Ouranos, father of Kronos, became ruler of the universe.

THE TITANS AND THE PLANETS
(*page 3*)

Some versions of the creation myth link the Titans with heavenly bodies in the solar system. (In these versions there are fourteen Titans: the names of Iapetos and Mnemosyne disappear and are replaced by Atlas (Daring/Sufferer), Dione (Honoured), Eurymedon (Wide Ruler) and Metis (Cunning).) The Titans and the planets they govern are these (one male and one female Titan to each planet):

Hyperion and Theia:
the Sun (symbol of light)
Atlas and Phoibe:
the Moon (symbol of magic)
Krios and Dione:
Mars (symbol of growth)
Koios and Metis:
Mercury (symbol of wisdom)
Eurymedon and Themis:
Jupiter (symbol of law)
Okeanos and Thetis:

209

Venus (symbol of love)
Kronos and Rhea:
Saturn (symbol of peace)

Earth (the hub of the Greek universe) has no governing Titans; the planets Uranus and Pluto were unknown to the Greeks. Later, in the age of the Olympian gods, most of the Titans' planetary powers were taken over by gods: Helios ruled the Sun, Selene the Moon, Ares Mars, Hermes and Apollo Mercury, Zeus Jupiter and Aphrodite Venus. The only Titan who kept his authority was Kronos (who ruled Saturn).

AMALTHEIA AND CAPRICORN
(*page 6*)

When he became all-powerful, Zeus did not forget Amaltheia, the she-goat who nursed him as a baby. He set her in the sky as the constellation Capricorn, the Goat. From her skin he made the *aigis*, a magic shield that guaranteed its wearer protection against all weapons, and from one of her horns he created the *cornucopia*, or horn of plenty: whoever owned it had only to wish for any kind of food

Constellation Capricorn

and drink, and the horn provided it in abundance.

In the zodiac, Capricorn is the birth-sign of those born between 22 December and 19 January. Their birth-stone is jet, and in character they are practical and patient.

DAKTYLS (*page 6*)

The five Curetes and their five sisters were the Daktyls (Fingers), so called because they grew out of the fingerprints Rhea made when she pressed her hands in the earth to support her when she was giving birth to Zeus. Little is known of the five females, except that one of them, Kelmis, later offended Rhea and was turned into a block of iron. (She is the guardian spirit of the middle left-hand finger, still regarded in Greece as the most insulting finger of all to brandish in someone's face.)

The five male Daktyls, as well as warriors and dancers, were also athletes. When they were visiting Olympia once, the eldest set his brothers to race for a prize consisting of an olive crown – and so (some say) began the Olympic Games.

All the Daktyls remained servants of Rhea and guardians of her sacred Mysteries. The wild, noisy dances they first used to protect baby Zeus became part of the religious ceremonies which honoured Rhea under the name of Cybele; the priests at these ceremonies were called Corybants (Crested dancers).

ATLAS AND ATLANTIS (*page 7*)

Atlas (Daring/Sufferer) was the son of the Titan Iapetos and the ocean-nymph Klymene; his half-brothers were Menoitios (Defiant), Prometheus (Forethought) and Epimetheus (After-thought). He ruled over a huge island kingdom in the Far West, Atlantis. It was as large as Asia and Africa combined; its surrounding ocean was so vast that it made the Mediterranean, by comparison, look like a landlocked harbour. This myth follows the story of the creation of humankind not by Prometheus (see page 15) but as the children of Gaia (see 'The Five Ages', page 212): accordingly, Atlas' kingdom had a large and prosperous human population. They built bridges, roads and cities; they had spreading orchards and fertile farms and mined gold and silver in abundance. At first they were honest and god-fearing, but soon turned to wickedness and cruelty. Seeing this, the gods sent a flood which destroyed them and swallowed their continent; where it used to be there is now a stormy ocean covering half the world.

Atlas himself escaped the flood; it was in revenge for the destruction of his people that he led the Titans against the gods. He was punished by being condemned to support the sky; later, the hero Perseus (see page 237) showed him the Gorgon's head and turned him to stone (the Atlas Mountains in northwest Africa).

Atlas' children were the seven Pleiades (see page 215), the five rain-nymphs the Hyades and the three Hesperides (mountain-nymphs who looked after a miraculous golden-apple tree, Gaia's wedding present to Hera when she married Zeus. See the story of Herakles, page 133.)

THE ISLANDS OF THE BLESSED
(*page 9*)

In some versions of the creation myth, Zeus showed mercy to all the Titans, not merely to those who helped him in the war. On condition that they never troubled the world again, he gave them a beautiful kingdom, the Islands of the Blessed in the Far West. Here they lived in peace and contentment like the first happiness when the world was newly made. If any mortals or immortals were particularly favoured, they might be allowed to join them when their time on earth was over.

THE OMPHALOS AT DELPHI (*page 9*)

After he became all-powerful, Zeus sent out two of his eagles, carrying in their talons the stone his mother Rhea gave Kronos to swallow in his place. The eagles flew to the exact mid-point of the earth, Delphi in Greece, and there dropped the stone. Later, people called it the *omphalos* or navel-stone of the world, and Delphi became the site of a famous oracle, supervised by Apollo god of prophecy and visited by throngs of enquirers every year. Although prophecies are rare in 20th-century tourist Delphi, the navel-stone still has pride of place in the Museum there.

ZEUS' CHILDREN (1): DIVINE CHILDREN (*page 13*)

The beings in this group, having immortal mothers as well as an immortal father, are themselves immortal: gods, goddesses and other divine beings.

Zeus' children by Hera: **Ares** (Warrior), **Eris** (Strife), **Hephaistos** (Day-bright), **Eileithuia** (Helper-in-Childbirth), **Hebe** (Youth).

Zeus' child by Metis: **Athene** (Heaven-queen)

Zeus' child by Demeter: **Persephone** (Death-bringer)

211

Zeus' children by Leto: **Apollo** (Destroyer), **Artemis** (Water-spring)

Zeus' child by Maia: **Hermes** (Upright pillar)

Zeus' children by Eurynome: the three Charites (Graces): **Pasithea** (Goddess-to-all), **Kale** (Beautiful), **Euphrosyne** (Cheerfulness). (NB. Some versions give their father as Dionysos, others their mother as Aphrodite. They were beautiful girls, the constant companions and servants of Aphrodite, goddess of beauty and of her son Eros (that is, Cupid).)

Zeus' children by Themis:
(a) the three Horai (Seasons): **Eunomia** (Law and Order), **Dike** (Justice), **Eirene** (Peace). They looked after three of the seasons of the world's year (Eunomia, Spring; Dike, Summer; Eirene, Winter) and also opened the gates of Olympos to visitors. (NB. In some versions there are two seasons only, and their names are **Thallo** (Growth) and **Karpo** (Withering).)
(b) the three Moirai (Fates): **Klotho** (Spinner), **Lachesis** (Allotter), **Atropos** (Unbending). They took the form of old women robed in white, spinning the threads of life. Klotho held the distaff (and sang songs of the present); Lachesis spun the thread (and sang songs of the future); Atropos cut the thread to end a life (and sang songs of the past). (NB. In some versions the Fates are the daughters of Night (and have no father), and Zeus himself is subject to their laws.)

Zeus' children by Mnemosyne: the nine Mousai (Muses): **Kalliope** (epic poetry), **Klio** (history), **Euterpe** (flute-playing), **Melpomene** (tragedy), **Terpsichore** (dancing), **Erato** (lyre-playing), **Polyhymnia** (sacred music), **Ourania** (astronomy), **Thalia** (comedy). Their homes were Pieria and Mount Helikon, and for this reason they are sometimes called Pierian or Heliconian. They also spent much time making music with Apollo on Mount Parnassos; anyone who drank from the Castalian Spring at the foot of the mountain would be filled with their inspiration. (Some say that the name Pierides comes not from Pieria, but because the Muses were 'daughters of Pieros'; but Pieros' nine daughters were in fact mortals who challenged the Muses to a contest of song, lost, and were changed into magpies.)

For Zeus' other children, see page 234.

PROMETHEUS' CLAYPIT (*page 15*)

The place where Prometheus found clay to make his mortal dolls was thought to be Panopeia, not far from the town of Chaironeia in Boeotia, Greece. The ground there is mainly thick, brown clay, and it is often baked by the sun into distorted shapes like half-completed modern sculptures. There are also many stones, human-size, scattered about: these were said to be the petrified lumps of clay discarded by Prometheus as he shaped humankind.

ZAGREUS; THE FIVE AGES (*page 15*)

There are several other myths of the creation of humankind. In one, Zeus and Persephone were parents of a son. His name was Zagreus (Restored to Life). Hera, jealous of Zeus' love-affair, persuaded some of the Titans to attack Zagreus, tear him to pieces and eat him. Only his heart was saved, and Athene took it to Zeus. He smashed the Titans to pieces with thunderbolts, and from their broken bodies human beings were born, part divine (because of the divine child the Titans had eaten) and part wicked (because of the Titans' evil natures). Zeus himself ate Zagreus' heart, and this

212

enabled him to create the child again, this time in the form of Dionysos (whose mother was the mortal Semele). See page 37.

In another myth, men and women sprang up naturally from Mother Earth, created by her like all the other plants and animals. From this beginning to the present day, the myth continues, there have been Five Ages:

The Age of Gold: In the Golden Age, when Kronos ruled the universe, mortals were happy, untroubled and joyful. They fed on fruits, nuts and wild honey; they never grew old; they suffered no pain and were not afraid of death. That age passed away, but its memory remains a dream of happiness to haunt our mortal minds.

The Age of Silver: The people of this age were ignorant and quarrelsome, and cared nothing for the gods. As well as eating fruit and honey, they were able to bake bread. Their only good quality was that they never made war; apart from that they knew nothing and created nothing, and Zeus put an end to them.

The first Age of Bronze: The people of this age were armed with bronze weapons: they killed and ate animals, and lived for battle and death. In time they destroyed each other totally.

The second Age of Bronze: The people of this age were the great heroes of the world, the sons of gods and mortal women. This was the time of Agamemnon, Achilles and Odysseus, the age of the Trojan War and the expedition to find the Golden Fleece. Many of the myths in this book are about heroes of this age.

The Age of Iron: This is our present age. Its people are pallid shadows of the heroes of the fourth age; cruel, quarrelsome, greedy and treacherous, they destroy more than they create. One day, disgusted by our wickedness, the gods will sweep us away and usher in the Sixth Age – perhaps a second Golden Age.

PROMETHEUS SET FREE (*page 21*)

Prometheus suffered on Mount Caucasus for thirty thousand mortal years. Then, in gratitude for the secret of Thetis (see page 60), Zeus agreed to free him from his punishment as soon as another immortal being could be found willing to give up his immortality and die. At first this seemed unlikely; but then Cheiron the centaur was accidentally wounded by one of Herakles' arrows (see page 246), and begged Zeus for death in place of eternal agony. Zeus turned Cheiron into a constellation of stars, and sent Herakles to kill Prometheus' vulture and set him free.

SURVIVORS (*page 23*)

Perhaps jealous of the story of Deucalion and Pyrrha, other areas of Greece invented flood-survivor stories of their own. Megaros, the son of Zeus and a mortal mother, was sleeping when the flood began, but his father sent a flock of cranes to waken him and carry him to the peak of Mount Gerania (Crane Mountain) out of the water's reach. Kerambos, a favourite of the water-nymphs, was changed by them into a water-beetle and flew to safety on Mount Parnassos. The people of the town of Parnassos itself claim that they were wakened by howling wolves, saw the water rising and hastily climbed to the mountaintop. (These same people later migrated to Wolf Mountain in Arcadia and began human sacrifice, killing a boy to honour Zeus each year and eating his flesh. Whoever ate the boy's guts became a werewolf and had to live among wolves for eight years. If in that time he ate no more human flesh, he was restored to human shape; if he ate, he remained a wolf forever.)

GIANTS' REMAINS; OTOS AND EPHIALTES (*page 27*)

The wreckage caused by the battle of gods and Earthborn was scattered widely across the whole Greek world. The stone-pile of the Earthborn was hurled down and its huge blocks are now the rock formations of Meteora in Thessaly; giant bones, said by some to be from dinosaurs, can still be seen in the museum at Trapezos, where the last battle was fought; the volcanoes under which many of the Earthborn were buried still occasionally shudder and smoke – for example, Mount Etna in Sicily, grave of Enkelados, or the volcanic island Nisyros, grave of Polyboutes.

In another version of this myth, only two giants attacked Olympos: Otos and Ephialtes, the sons of Aloios. First they imprisoned Ares in a bronze jar (from which he was rescued thirteen months later by Hermes). Then, instead of building a pile of stones, they piled Mount Pelion on top of Mount Ossa to reach Olympos. In the end they were defeated by a trick of Artemis. She agreed to sleep with Otos if he lifted the siege; this made Ephialtes jealous, and the giants quarrelled and killed each other.

THE END OF TYPHON (*page 28*)

In one version of the myth, Typhon was tamed by Zeus and lived on in Tartaros, where he fathered a number of monsters including Cerberus (the hideous dog who guards the Underworld) and a family of destructive winds called typhoons. In another version, he was imprisoned under Mount Etna, where his breath provided fire for the Cyclopes' furnaces.

APOLLO, ADMETOS AND ALKESTIS (*page 33*)

When Apollo was sent as cowherd to King Admetos, he found him a kindly, honourable man, and decided to help him. The Fates told him that Admetos was doomed soon to die. Apollo gave them wine to drink, and while their brains were fuddled and their hearts softened, persuaded them to let Admetos live if he could find someone else to die in his place. Back on earth, the only volunteer was Queen Alkestis. She was laid in her tomb and Admetos duly began to mourn for his beloved wife. Just then Herakles arrived at the palace, and sooner than turn away a guest, Admetos pretended that all was well and offered him the courtesies due to visitors. None the less, Herakles discovered the true situation, and when Thanatos (the soldier of the Underworld) came to the tomb to fetch Alkestis to the Underworld, he wrestled with him, drove him off and saved her life.

This story is the basis of one of the most famous of Euripides' plays, *Alcestis*.

KALLISTO (*page 34*)

Zeus seduced Kallisto, one of Artemis' prettiest nymphs. (To prevent her running away, he first appeared to her disguised as Artemis herself.) The next time Artemis bathed naked with her nymphs, she saw that Kallisto was pregnant. At once she changed her into a bear and sent hunting-dogs to tear her to pieces. Zeus snatched Kallisto up in the nick of time, and after her child was born set her in the sky as the constellation Ursa Major (The Great Bear). Her son was Arcas, ancestor of the people of Arcadia. When he died, he became the constellation Arctophylax (Guardian of the Bear), sometimes known as Boötes (Herdsman)

ORION AND THE PLEIADES (page 34)

Another version of the death of Orion tells of his pursuit of the Pleiades. They were seven nymphs, daughters of Atlas and Pleione and followers of Artemis. Orion the huntsman fell in love with them and tried to catch them, but Artemis saved them by placing them as a

Constellation Ursa Major (The Great Bear)

Star Cluster The Pleiades

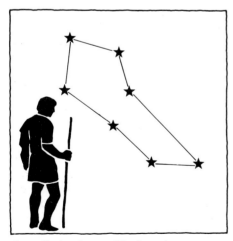

Constellation Boötes (Herdsman)

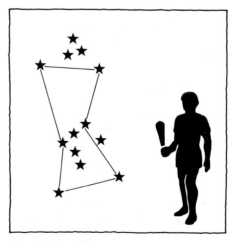

Constellation Orion

star cluster in the sky. She made Orion into a constellation – and still, in his rising and setting, he pursues the seven Pleiades across the sky.

(For another myth about how Orion met his death, see page 44.)

THE CONSTELLATION SCORPIO
(*page 34*)

The scorpion which stung Orion to death on Chios gave its name and shape to the constellation Scorpio. In the Zodiac, this is the star-sign of those born between 23 October and 21 November. Their birth-stone is topaz, and in character they are confident, passionate and determined.

Constellation Scorpio

PALLAS ATHENE (*page 34*)

It is not clear how Athene got the name Pallas. Some say it is simply an honorary title: the word *pallas* means 'youthful' (and refers to her beauty) or 'brandisher' (and refers to her carrying a spear). Others connect it with her childhood

playmate, Pallas: she killed her by accident and took her name in memory. Others say that it comes from the giant Pallas. He was one of the Earthborn who attacked Olympos (see page 25). Athene struck him down in the battle, and later used his skin to make her aegis-shield.

POSEIDON'S WELL (*page 35*)

The place where Poseidon struck water from the rock of the Acropolis can still be seen, just inside the porch of the small temple called the Erechtheum. There are clear marks in the ground, as if the stone has been wrenched apart by a huge blow from above. On still nights you can hear the bubble and rumble of running water deep in the stone beneath your feet.

Poseidon's gift of water was never forgotten. He was worshipped by the Athenians as a benefactor and protector of their city, second only to Athene herself.

AGLAUROS, HERSE AND HERMES
(*page 35*)

In another version of the myth of Aglauros, she met her death not by disobeying Athene (see page 35), but because of another piece of foolishness. Hermes was in love with Aglauros' sister Herse; Aglauros was jealous and when Hermes came calling she barred his way. 'I'll never move from here,' she said. 'That's right, you won't,' replied Hermes – and turned her to stone. Herse and Hermes later had two children, Kephalos (see the story of Eos, page 44) and Keryx (Herald), who became a priest of the mysteries at Eleusis.

In yet another version, Aglauros died not foolishly but bravely. An enemy army was attacking Athens, and an

216

oracle declared that victory would only follow human self-sacrifice; Aglauros, hearing this, jumped to her death from the Acropolis wall and saved the city.

PAN'S DEATH (page 37)

In the time of the Roman Emperor Tiberius (who lived at the time of Jesus Christ and was a collector of curious myths and legends of every kind), an Egyptian ship's pilot was guiding a boat through the channel between two Greek islands, Paxos and Propaxos. Suddenly the ship was becalmed and he heard voices calling his name and crying 'When you reach harbour, tell them great Pan is dead'. When the pilot reached harbour he shouted this message to the people, and the woods and fields near the shore were filled with lamenting. Tiberius' scholars were puzzled by this story – apart from anything else, how can an immortal god die? They decided that the voices must have meant a different Pan entirely, a local forest-spirit, and that what the Egyptian overheard was the wailing chant from some religious ceremony. The story was written down by Plutarch in his book *The Dying Out of Oracles*, and has been part of books of Greek myths and legends ever since. Some early Christian writers claimed that what was heard was an announcement of Christ's coming to earth: the old gods were passing away and the true god was being born.

SEMELE (page 38)

In another version of the myth of Dionysos' birth, Semele was not destroyed by Hera's jealousy and the unbearable sight of Zeus' divinity (see page 38). Instead, her father Kadmos discovered her pregnancy, locked her in a wooden box and threw it into the sea. It floated south, and was washed up on the beach at Prasiai in Lakonia. When the villagers opened it they found Semele dead and beside her the newly-born Dionysos. Semele was taken back to Thebes and given a royal funeral; Dionysos was given to Ino and Athamas to rear as their own son.

THE HYADES (page 38)

The nymphs of Mount Nysa who looked after Dionysos were called Makris, Nysa, Erato, Bromie and Bacche. Each of them was in charge of a particular area of the mountain and gave her name to it. Later, Dionysos himself was sometimes called by two of their names, Bromios (Roaring) and Bacchos (Raging). When Dionysos was safely reared, Zeus rewarded the nymphs by placing them as a star cluster in the sky. They were called the Hyades (Rainy Ones), because if they rise at the same time as the sun, wet weather is sure to follow.

Star Cluster Hyades (Rainy Ones)

IKARIOS (*page 40*)

One of the saddest stories connected with Dionysos is the myth of Ikarios of Attica. He welcomed the god, and in return Dionysos gave him a gift of wine. But when the local people drank wine for the first time in their lives, they thought that Ikarios had poisoned them. They turned on him, killed him and hid his body. His daughter Erigone searched for her father everywhere, accompanied by her faithful dog Maira. At last she found the body, and was so grief-stricken that she hanged herself. At once, to punish the people, Apollo sent plague; when they asked how it could be cured he told them to accept Dionysos and to hold an annual festival in honour of Ikarios and Erigone. They did so; this is the origin of the custom of hanging little statues from tree-branches at local festivals (in memory of Erigone's death). The dog Maira was placed in the sky as one of the servant-dogs of the dog-star Sirius, companion of Orion the Huntsman.

GANYMEDE, EOS AND TITHONOS (*page 42*)

In another version of the myth of Ganymede, it was not Zeus who snatched Ganymede up to heaven but Eos, goddess of the dawn. She was in love with both Ganymede and his brother Tithonos. When Zeus took Ganymede away from Eos to be the gods' cupbearer, he offered in return to let Eos marry Tithonos, and to grant any wish she cared to make for him. Eos asked that Tithonos be made immortal, and it was done. But she had forgotten also to ask for eternal youth for him, and so although Tithonos lived forever he grew older and more shrivelled until finally he turned into a cicada. Ever afterwards, cicadas are silent at night and begin to sing only when dawn comes and warms them into life. As for Ganymede, Zeus was so proud of him that he named a constellation after him: Aquarius the water-bearer.

Constellation Aquarius (The Water-bearer)

In the Zodiac, Aquarius is the star-sign of those born between 20 January and 18 February. Their birth-stone is amethyst, and by nature they are artistic, creative and absent-minded.

THEIA (*page 42*)

As well as the Titan Theia, mother of the Sun, Moon and Dawn, there was another Theia, daughter of the centaur Cheiron. Unlike her father (who, like all centaurs, was half man half horse), this Theia had a wholly human form; but in her nature she was as wild and headstrong as an unbroken colt. Because of her speed and grace she became one of Artemis' hunting-nymphs, and swore an oath of chastity. But she broke her oath and slept with Aiolos, grandfather of the

218

Aiolos who later ruled the winds. She was terrified of telling her father she was pregnant, and knew that her mistress, Artemis, would punish her. Fortunately Poseidon (who is god of horses as well as of the sea) helped her by turning her into a mare until her child was born. The baby was called Melanippe (Black Mare) while she was a foal and Arne (Ewe-lamb) when she became a human girl. As soon as the child was born, Poseidon turned her mother Theia into a constellation of stars: Equuleus (the Little Horse). Arne grew up to be the unhappy mother of Boiotos and Aiolos.

Constellation Equuleus (The Little Horse)

SELENE AND ENDYMION (page 42)

The moon-goddess Selene was sailing through the sky one night when she passed over Mount Latmos in Karia. There, sleeping on the mountainside, she saw the handsome shepherd Endymion and fell in love with him. To keep him for herself, she gently kissed his eyes. From then onwards he was never seen again by mortals but stayed forever in a deep, dreamless sleep, never changing or ageing, and waking up only at night when Selene visited him. They had fifty daughters, star-children still visible in the evening sky.

HEPHAISTOS (page 45)

Hephaistos (Dayshine) was the son of Zeus and Hera. He was such an ugly baby that Hera, in disgust, threw him headlong out of Olympos. He fell into the sea, and the goddesses Eurynome and Thetis rescued him and looked after him for nine years. He set up his first workshop under the sea, and made necklaces and ornaments so beautiful that Hera was charmed and welcomed him back to Olympos to create beauty there as well.

Although the things he made were beautiful, Hephaistos himself was still ugly and deformed. The gods treated him as a joke as he limped and shuffled round Olympos. He helped Zeus in the matter of the birth of Athene (see page 12); but then angered him by complaining of his treatment of Hera. Enraged, Zeus threw him down from Olympos for the second time. Hephaistos fell on Lemnos, and broke both legs. When Zeus allowed him back into Olympos, Hephaistos was even lamer than before, and had to walk with the help of golden leg-irons.

Hephaistos was the god of fire, particularly of the natural fires that issue from the ground. His servants were the Cyclopes, and his workshops were found under volcanoes over all the earth. Apart from beautiful objects (and useful ones like robots or self-moving tables), he made magnificent armour and weapons, both for the gods and for those mortal heroes they chose to honour.

ELYSIUM; TARTAROS: THE FIELDS OF ASPHODEL (*page 50*)

Elysium lay in the far west of the world. It was a kingdom ruled by Rhadamanthys or (some say) by Kronos. It was a land of perpetual sunshine, never cold or wet, and its people lived contented lives among rolling fields and orchards. They could spend eternity there, enjoying banquets, sports, music, dancing and conversation; or, if they chose, they could be born again in the upper world. Those who had returned twice to the upper world, and lived three noble and blameless lives, were rewarded by being made inhabitants of the Islands of the Blessed (see page 211).

Tartaros was the place of punishment for evil-doers, and especially for those who challenged or mocked the gods. Tityos was there (the giant who had tried to rape Leto – see page 32): pegged to the ground, he suffered from two vultures forever ripping at his liver. Tantalos (see page 269) was tormented by food and water he could never reach, and by the threat of an overhanging rock.

Sisyphos (who betrayed Zeus' love-affair with Aigina to her father Asopos – see page 102) spent all eternity rolling a boulder up a hill; every time he reached the top the stone slipped and rolled back down again. Ixion (who tried to rape Hera – see page 75) was bound in Tartaros to a wheel of fire; the Danaids (see page 92) were set to empty a lake with sieves; Oknos, the fool, plaited a reed rope which his ass, behind him, endlessly ate. There were countless other sufferers; their gaolers and tormentors were led by the three Furies, armed with goads and whips.

The Fields of Asphodel lay between the White Rock and the palace of Hades in Erebos (Deep Darkness). They were covered with pale, lily-like asphodel flowers, and thronged with dead souls, flitting in the dark like bats. The souls could drink from two pools: Lethe (Forgetfulness), whose water banished all memory of past mortal life, or the Pool of Memory, which coloured grey eternity with the memory of past happiness, so providing comfort and pain in one.

THE FURIES (*page 50*)

The three Erinnyes or Furies, Allekto (Endless), Tisiphone (Punishment) and Megaira (Jealous Rage), were the daughters of Night or, some say, of Mother Earth and Skotos (Darkness). They were aged women with bats' wings, coal-black skin, dogs' heads, grey rags of clothes and writhing snakes for hair. They stank; their eyes, mouths and noses oozed foulness; their voices were half-way between a cackle and a bark. Creatures of nightmare, they haunted mortal dreams; only the honest and the good were safe. The Furies' home was in Erebos, and they saw to the punishments in Tartaros. But they also appeared in the upper world, to hunt down mortals who had murdered blood-relatives. (See the story of Orestes, page 205.) They were spirits of justice and revenge. Mortals, fearing them, gave them the flattering name Eumenides (Kindly Ones), hoping to keep their rage at bay and prevent them from blighting crops and bringing plague.

STORIES OF DEMETER (*page 52*)

When Demeter first reached Eleusis, she was worn out with her wanderings and with grief for Persephone. She sat down in the dust outside the house of a woman called Misme. Misme gave her a drink of water flavoured with penny-royal, and Demeter sprinkled it with bar-ley-corns and drank – so thirstily that she spilled some of the drink on her clothes. Misme's son Askalabos made fun of this, and Demeter threw the rest of the drink in his face and turned him into a kind of gecko (a lizard still called *askalabos* in Greek, and covered with blotches shaped like barley-corns). The drink became her sacred drink, used at the Eleusinian Mysteries.

When the Mysteries were first estab-lished she made Eumolpos (the brother of Iambe and Demophoön) their High Priest. She taught Triptolemos, another brother, the skills of farming, gave him a bag of seed-corn and a plough, and sent him all over the world in a dragon-chariot to teach men agriculture (a skill until then unknown).

On another occasion, at the wedding-party of Kadmos and Harmonia, De-meter slept with Iasion, making love with him in a field. Unfortunately for Ia-sion, Zeus mistakenly thought he was raping Demeter, and struck him dead with a thunderbolt. Demeter later gave birth to Ploutos, who grew up to become the blind god of Wealth, a companion of the fickle goddess Tyche (Good Luck). To compensate for the loss of Iasion, Zeus allowed Pandareos the Cretan to steal his pet golden dog and give it to Demeter. (She rewarded Pandareos by freeing him forever from indigestion.)

In Thessaly once, Erysichthon wanted wood to build a banqueting hall. He began chopping down trees in De-meter's sacred grove. She warned him, but he persisted – and finally one of the trees fell and killed Nikippe, Demeter's serving-nymph. Her revenge was slow and cruel: she allowed Erysichthon to finish his banqueting-hall, but after-wards nothing would satisfy his hunger. He ate ravenously, day and night, until

he had eaten himself out of house and home and was forced to beg for a living in the streets, growing ever thinner and more wasted until he died.

THE ELEUSINIAN MYSTERIES
(*page 52*)

At first when Demeter came to Eleusis, disguised as an old woman, she was heartbroken at the loss of Persephone. Gradually, however, the jokes and pranks of the king's lame daughter Iambe made her smile, and she agreed to stay. She was given the job of looking after Demophoön, the young son of Queen Metaneira. Because she had no experience of mortal child-rearing, she treated Demophoön like a baby god: she rubbed his limbs with ambrosia to give them strength, and laid him on the blaz-ing fire to burn away his mortality. Un-fortunately the baby's mother Metaneira came in just as this was going on, screamed and broke the spell. Demeter snatched the baby from the fire, but he was dead. At once she changed her shape and appeared before Metaneira in divine majesty. She told her to build a holy shrine in Eleusis, and promised to teach her, in payment for Demophoön's death, the sacred Mysteries of Demeter.

The shrine was built, and Metaneira was the first priestess. Every year there-after, the festival of the Eleusinian Mys-teries was one of the most important in the Athenian religious year, with proces-sions to and from Eleusis, and days and nights of sacred ritual in the shrine. No one, on pain of death, was allowed to re-veal Demeter's mysteries to outsiders; but it seems likely that just as the proces-sions included joking and jollity (in memory of cheerful Iambe?), so the Mystery-ceremonies may have included a fire-ritual to bring about eternal life (in memory of burnt Demophoön). The sacred drink at the Mysteries was barley-water given a minty flavour with the herb pennyroyal.

The Mystery shrine at Eleusis can still be seen today. It includes a large underground chamber, where the most secret rituals took place, and also a cave called 'Pluto's eye', said to be one of the entrances to the underworld.

ARISTAIOS (*page 54*)

Aristaios, who caused Eurydice's death, was the son of Apollo and the nymph Cyrene. He was brought up by myrtle-nymphs, who taught him the skills of cheese-making, hunting, olive-growing and above all keeping bees. He travelled widely in the world, teaching these skills and helping and healing people (he possessed some of the healing power of his father Apollo). It was on one of these journeys that he tried to rape Eurydice.

Soon after he left Thrace, filled with guilt for her death, his bees all died. Proteus, the old man of the sea, told him that the only way to start a new hive was to sacrifice four bulls and four heifers in honour of Eurydice and her sister Dryads. He did so, and nine days later found bees swarming on the rotting carcasses, caught them and used them to begin new hives. (For years afterwards, people thought that bees grew miraculously from rotting meat.)

ORPHEUS' DEATH; ORPHISM (*page 56*)

In another version of the myth of Orpheus he was changed by his grief for Eurydice from a gentle singer into a cruel savage. He taught his Thracian subjects black magic and human sacrifice, and worshipped the sun in bloodthirsty cere-monies. It was because of this that Dionysos decided to end his life, and sent Bacchants to the sun-temple to tear Orpheus apart.

Long afterwards, Orpheus became the centre of a religious cult, Orphism. No one knows what happened at its Mysteries; but they may have involved music, a kind of play about descending to the underworld and returning, animal sacrifice and a mock death. Several poems survived which were claimed to be by Orpheus himself: 28 religious poems, a poem about the Argonauts and two poems on scientific subjects, *About Stones* and *About Earthquakes*. (Since Orpheus was a mythological character, these poems were almost certainly made up by later authors, perhaps priests or followers of the Orphic religion.)

LINOS (*page 57*)

Orpheus' brother Linos, son of the same father and mother, was also a notable musician. He invented a way of teaching mortals the music of the gods (though, being mortal, even at their finest they could never manage more than a pale echo of Olympian harmony). He was beloved all over the world, and was so honoured for his music that Apollo killed him in a fit of jealousy. Thereafter, at shrines in Greece, Asia Minor and Egypt, mystery-cults sprang up in his honour, and a particular kind of lament, called the Dirge for Linos, was sung at their religious festivals.

POSEIDON AND THE RAM (*page 60*)

As well as horses (for grace and speed) and bulls (for savage strength), rams were also sacred to Poseidon. Two myths give reasons. In the first,

Poseidon was not eaten by his father Kronos as soon as he was born (see page 5): instead, his mother Rhea hid him among a flock of sheep and gave Kronos a foal to devour instead, claiming it was her son.

In the second myth, Poseidon fell in love with the beautiful mortal princess Theophane. He snatched her from her father's palace and carried her to a remote island. When her father and a group of her mortal suitors came looking for her, Poseidon changed her into a ewe, himself into a ram, and all the islanders into sheep, so that the pursuers found nothing on the island but placid, grazing flocks. The suitors were changed into wolves (who ever afterwards hunt sheep unmercifully, and howl for Theophane by moonlight every night); the offspring of ewe-Theophane and ram-Poseidon was the ram with the Golden Fleece which Jason and the Argonauts were later sent to fetch (see page 112).

THE NEREIDS (*page 60*)

Nereus (Wetness), father of the Nereids, was an ancient god of the sea from days long before Poseidon became its ruler. When Aphrodite was born in the foam from Ouranos' penis (see page 4), Nereus carried her to safety in Paphos, Cyprus. He led a peaceful life calming storms, soothing the waves and helping mortals with prophecies and good advice. His children were the fifty sea-nymphs known as Nereids. Like their father, they could change their shapes at will, and no mortal, seeing them, could ever be sure how many (or even who) they were. So they had many names and many forms; they were the sea-equivalent of mountain- or forest-nymphs on land, and figured in many a traveller's tale. The two most famous were Amphitrite (Encircling Sea), who married Poseidon, and Thetis (Disposer), who married Peleus.

PISCES (*page 60*)

Dolphins were Poseidon's favourite sea-servants. They carried messages, brought him news of events from the far corners of his kingdom, and often acted as guides and helpers to sailors lost at sea. In their honour, he set a constellation in the sky: Delphinus (The Dolphin).

Constellation Delphinus (The Dolphin)

ARION (*page 61*)

Poseidon's son Arion was a singer and lyre-player who lived in Corinth. He sailed to Sicily to take part in a musical competition – and won so many valuable prizes that the sailors on the ship home decided to throw him overboard and keep the money. Arion begged to be allowed to sing and play just once more before he died. The sailors agreed; he went up on to the ship's prow, sang and played, then jumped into the sea. Thinking he was sure to drown, the sailors went cheerfully on their way. But Arion's singing had attracted one of his father Poseidon's dolphin-servants, and it carried Arion on its back all the way home to Corinth. When the sailors reached Corinth with their tale prepared about Arion falling overboard and drowning, they found him waiting on the quay with soldiers.

Later, Apollo named a lyre-shaped constellation of stars in honour of Arion.

Constellation Lyra

THE TRITONS; RHODOS (*page 61*)

The Tritons, Poseidon's mermen-children, were boisterous and riotous, like the half-human, half-goat Satyrs on dry land. They loved noisy music, brawling and strong drink. They raced across the sea playing trumpets made of conch-shells. (Once, the mortal trumpeter Misenos rashly challenged a Triton to a musical contest, lost and was swept out to sea and drowned.) They were fond of stealing up on mortal women bathing in the sea, and raping them. (However, one Triton who tried this, off the coast of Tanagra in Greece, regretted it. His victim cried for help to Dionysos; Dionysos made the Triton drunk, and the towns-people netted him and sliced off his head. His body was dried in the sun, like that of any other fish, and was placed as a thank-offering in Dionysos' temple.)

Poseidon's daughter Rhodos (Rose) lived on an underwater mountain. When Zeus and the other gods were choosing parts of the earth to rule – it was the time when Poseidon quarrelled with Athene over Athens (see page 35) – the sun-god Helios arrived late and found nowhere left. Zeus offered to start the distribution again, but Helios asked instead to be given the next piece of land to appear from empty sea. The gods agreed; Rhodos' mountain duly rose from the sea (and became the island of Rhodes); Helios married Rhodos and together they governed Rhodes in happiness and prosperity.

THE TELCHINES (*page 61*)

The Telchines (Enchanters) were nine of the earliest and most elusive sea-monsters of all. They were Pontos' children, the first creatures ever able to breathe both on land and in the sea. They had dogs' heads and flippered, stumpy arms like sea-lions'; they were skilful craftsmen, who made (some said) the sickle used by Kronos to attack Ouranos, and who invented the art of sculpture. They settled in Rhodes (or, some say, Crete), where they were forever annoying Zeus by interfering with the weather. They also had the evil eye, the ability if they were angered to flash a poisonous mist from their eyes.

Like many of the older gods, the Telchines cared little for the Olympians. Once when Aphrodite visited Rhodes they made such fun of her that she lost her temper and sent them mad, so that they rioted across the island, fouling and breaking everything in sight. In the end Poseidon decided to rid his kingdom of them forever. He sent a flood to swallow them; but they scattered and escaped. No one knows what became of them. Some say that they led the pack of hunting-dogs which killed Aktaion (see page 34). Sailors often claimed to have been attacked by them, in the shape of sea-demons surging on the wings of the bleak East Wind.

MEDUSA (*page 61*)

Medusa, the youngest of the three Gorgons, was once beautiful. But one night she made love to Poseidon in a temple sacred to Athene. Outraged, Athene cursed Medusa with hideous ugliness, and also with mortality: she could be killed and go down to the underworld. To make sure this happened, Athene told Perseus (see page 94) how to fight Medusa without being turned to stone. He killed Medusa, and cut off her head. From her dead body her two children by Poseidon arose: Chrysaor (Goldsword), a hero, and Pegasos (Water-spirit), a winged horse. Perseus gave Medusa's head to Athene. Some say that she fastened it on her shield, others that she threw it into the sky, where it became the face we see on the moon. Medusa's body drifts in the sea to this day, in the form of a venomous jellyfish.

LAMIA (*page 62*)

Lamia (Greedy), who some say was the mother of Scylla, was a beautiful sea-nymph, a grand-daughter of Poseidon. Zeus fell in love with her and often visited her cave-palace in Libya. He gave her an unusual love-gift: she could take out her eyes while she slept and leave them wide-awake beside the bed. No amount of watchfulness, however, helped Lamia against Hera's jealousy – because instead of attacking her, Hera attacked the children she had borne to Zeus. She killed every one of them but Scylla – and only spared her because Hera, goddess of prophecy, knew every detail of her future suffering.

Losing her children turned Lamia from a serene princess to a vengeful, furious monster. She swooped about the world at night, looking for other people's children to devour. If a child died without cause or warning, it was said to be Lamia's doing; nurses often terrified naughty children by telling them that unless they behaved Lamia would come and eat them up. Grown-ups were not safe from Lamia, either: in her uncontrollable lust for children she would fall on sleeping men, trying to make love to them, and the ferocity of her passion would wither the life from them.

If she was cornered, Lamia changed her shape, wriggling and twisting into a thousand unexpected forms, until she broke free. (But if you held on until she was exhausted, you could force her to disgorge your swallowed child.) Her most repulsive form was an Empousa (Pusher-In), a jumble of cow, mule, woman and snarling bitch, with a blazing fire for face and feet shod with brass. She often put on this uncouth form to haunt children's dreams.

PELEUS (*page 64*)

Peleus, one of the unluckiest men who ever lived, was the son of King Aiakos of Aigina, and his brothers were Telamon and Phokos. Phokos was a handsome, gifted prince, and his brothers were jealous of him. They challenged him to an athletics match, and in the course of it Phokos was killed. Spectators argued about how exactly he had died: some said Telamon threw a discus at his head, others that Peleus smashed his skull with an axe. But whichever brother actually killed him, the two were equally guilty, and King Aiakos banished them from Aigina. Telamon settled on the nearby island of Salamis, where he married the king's daughter and duly succeeded to the throne. (His children included the heroes Teucer and Aias: see page 249.)

Peleus went to Phthia, married the king's daughter and was given a third of the kingdom. Now his bad luck began. First he killed a fellow-prince in a hunting accident; then one of the palace noblewomen, Cretheis, angry because he refused to sleep with her, told his wife and her own husband a lying tale about how he had seduced her. Peleus' unhappy wife hanged herself. Cretheis' husband challenged Peleus to a trial-by-hunting on Mount Pelion: if he killed more game than anyone else, it would prove his innocence. The gods gave Peleus a magic sword, and with it he killed a huge pile of game. But he celebrated by holding a lavish feast, ate and drank too much, and fell into a gluttonous sleep. The others stole the game, hid his magic sword and left him on the mountain as prey for the wild centaurs who lived there.

Peleus was rescued by Cheiron, king of the centaurs. He showed him great kindness, and later when the gods chose Peleus to be Thetis' husband, explained what he had to do to win her hand (see page 65). After the disastrous outcome of the marriage (the business with the seven children: see page 66), Peleus went back to Phthia; Zeus gave him an army of ants which grew into men (called Myrmidons or Antmen), and with this he defeated his enemies and made himself king. He ruled the kingdom until he was an old man, protected by the immortal weapons the gods had given him as wedding-presents. But when his son Achilles sailed for Troy, he gave him the weapons, and his enemies at once rose up and banished him.

At this point, Thetis took pity on her unlucky husband. She promised that if he would wait for her in the cave where they had first made love, she would take him down to her sea-kingdom and make him immortal. Unfortunately for Peleus, however, his bad luck still held. While he was waiting in the cave, he heard news that Troy had fallen and that his grandson Neoptolemos, Achilles' child, was travelling home. He set out to meet Neoptolemos, but died on the journey and so was denied the immortality Thetis had offered him. His life was a chapter of bad luck; he was a man fated to be given superb chances which always turned sour; his only claims to greatness, in the end, were to have been the husband of a goddess and the father of Achilles.

ACHILLES AND THE STYX (*page 66*)

In another version of the story of Achilles' birth, Thetis tried to make him immortal not by burning and boiling, but by dipping him into the river Styx. The effect was the same: the whole of his body was protected by the magic except for one heel (the one she held him by).

226

Achilles' heel remained vulnerable to mortal weapons, and ensured that however godlike he seemed he still remained a mortal, doomed to die.

THE MYTH OF TEREUS (*page 69*)

Tereus' story was told in several different forms. In one, it was Prokne whose tongue was cut out, not Philomela: Tereus then made her a slave, told her father she was dead and married Philomela. (The rest of the story, the embroidered cloth, the murder of Itys, the transformation into birds, was the same.) In other versions, the birds were different: Tereus became a hawk, Philomela the nightingale and Prokne the swallow. In some accounts, Dryas (Tereus' brother) was turned into an oaktree and baby Itys into a pheasant. From the day of the murder onwards, no swallows were ever known to nest in Daulis.

SILENOS' CONVERSATION (*page 69*)

There are two different accounts of the conversation Midas had with Silenos while he entertained him in his palace. In the first, Silenos was still suffering from the effects of too much drink, and said nothing except for one glum remark which became a proverb: 'What's the best thing in life? Not to be born. What's the next best thing? As soon as you're born, to die.' In the second, he told Midas a version of the myth of Atlantis, a magic continent beyond the edge of Ocean. Atlantis was the land of the Hyperboreans (People Beyond the North Wind), and was guarded by a whirlpool and a grove of trees bearing the Fruit of Weeping and the Fruit of Youth – one of which made you die of grief, and the other made you grow backwards from age to infancy until you disappeared. If you escaped these dangers you came to a fertile kingdom with thriving cities, rolling countryside and happy people. Unfortunately, no traveller who found this kingdom ever came back, so there were no guides to tell new travellers the way.

KING GORDIOS AND THE GORDIAN KNOT (*page 69*)

Gordios, the Phrygian king who shared his kingdom with Midas, started his life not as a king but as a poor farmer. One day he was driving to market when he was surrounded by an excited, cheering crowd. The oracle had just declared that they were to make king the next man they found driving an ox-cart along the road that led to the temple of Zeus.

So Gordios became king. He placed the ox-cart in Zeus' temple as a thank-offering. He fastened the pole to the cart with a uniquely complicated knot – the ends of the leather thongs were hidden deep inside – and a story grew that anyone who could solve the riddle and unfasten the knot would rule all Asia. For several centuries no one succeeded. Then Alexander the Great, on his journey of conquest through Asia, came to the temple, heard the prophecy, and unfastened the Gordian knot – not by untying it, but by slicing through it with his sword.

LAPITHS AND CENTAURS (*page 70*)

The battle between Lapiths and Centaurs in Kaineus' reign was not their only encounter. They were old enemies, descended from two warring brothers, Lapithos and Centauros. (It was also natural for there to be hostility between horse-tamers and a race of beings half man, half horse.) On another occasion, the Lapiths held a feast to celebrate the wedding of their prince Peirithoös to Hippodameia, and invited the Centaurs. Many of the gods, and Theseus the hero (see page 151), were also guests; but Peirithoös sent no invitation to Ares or to Eris, remembering the trouble Eris had caused at the wedding of Peleus and Thetis (see page 66). To punish him, Ares gave the Centaurs wine, something they had never tasted before, and when they were drunk put it into their heads to rape all the Lapith women, beginning with Hippodameia, the bride. There was a pitched battle; finally, with Theseus' help, the Lapiths won.

This battle – a favourite subject for later Greek sculptors, including those who made the Parthenon frieze – began a feud between Lapiths and Centaurs which lasted for many years.

EUROPE (page 72)

Some people believe that Europa gave her name to the continent of Europe. But Europa herself never set foot in Europe. The continent is more likely to have been named either from a Greek word meaning 'wide' – compared to mainland Greece itself, it covered a huge area, equalled in the known Greek world only by Asia and Africa – or from the ancient Asian word 'oo-rap', which means 'to the west of us'.

TAURUS THE BULL (page 72)

In honour of Zeus' bull-disguise, the people of Crete ever afterwards worshipped bulls, and made the sport of bull-leaping part of their religious ceremonies. (See the story of Theseus, page

143.) To celebrate his love for Europa, Zeus set the constellation Taurus (the Bull) in the sky.

Constellation Taurus (The Bull)

In the zodiac, Taurus is the birth-sign of those born between 21 April and 20 May. Their birth-stone is emerald, and in character they are placid, reliable and self-controlled.

TRAVELLERS (page 72)

After Europa disappeared into the sea on the bull's back, her father sent her brothers in ships to look for her. Each brother took a different direction. Phoinix sailed to North Africa and founded the city of Carthage; Cilix travelled to a mountainous part of Asia Minor later called Cilicia after him; Phineus sailed to the Black Sea; Thasos went first to Olympia in Greece, then settled on the island that took his name. (For the journey, and the later adventures, of Europa's last brother Kadmos, see page 155.)

When Europa's three sons grew up they quarrelled over a handsome boy called Miletos. He favoured the youngest brother Sarpedon, and as a result was banished from Crete by the eldest, Minos. (He sailed north to Asia Minor, where he founded the city of Miletos.) Sarpedon hated Minos for this, and when their father died he fought Minos for the throne of Crete, lost, and was banished. He settled in Cilicia in Asia Minor (the rocky country named after his uncle Cilix), and became its king. Later, he was one of the Trojan allies in the Trojan War, and was killed in single combat by Patroklos (see page 173).

Minos, the eldest brother, travelled nowhere: he stayed in Crete and founded a dynasty of kings, all known as Minos (a ceremonial title like the name Pharaoh in Egypt). With the third brother, Rhadamanthys, he was after his death appointed one of the judges of the Underworld.

KARYA (page 74)

The story of Phyllis (Leafy) was probably made up to explain how the almond-festival began. A similar story tells of the Spartan princess Karya (Nut-tree), who was turned by her lover Dionysos into a walnut-tree. Karyatids, the girl-statues which support the roofs of buildings, were named either after her, or after the girls who danced at her walnut-festivals.

DEMOPHON (page 74)

By coincidence, Akamas' brother Demophon also fell in love with a woman called Phyllis, a Thracian priestess not connected with the Phyllis who became an almond-tree. He stayed with her for a few months, then tired of her and prepared to abandon her. But instead of telling her the truth, he swore falsely that in a year's time he would return and marry her. She gave him a locked box, and told him to open it only when he knew for certain he would never see her again. Demophon went on his way, delighted to be free of her. The year passed, and Phyllis, knowing that he would never return, took poison and died. At that exact moment Demophon opened the box – and the sight of whatever was inside it filled him with terror. He leapt on to his horse and galloped away – and he was shaking so much with panic that his sword flew out of its scabbard and stuck point-upwards in the ground. At that precise moment, his horse threw him. He landed on the sword-point and was stabbed to death.

PHLEGYAS (page 75)

Ixion's father Phlegyas was the son of Ares and a mortal woman. He inherited Ares' violent nature, and spent his life as a marauding bandit chief, stealing cattle, pillaging cities and raping women. As well as his son Ixion, he had a beautiful daughter called Koronis. Apollo fell in love with her and stole her away to Delphi – and Phlegyas, furious that anyone at all, even an immortal god, should treat him as he treated everyone else, led an army to Delphi and pillaged the sacred shrine. For this he was punished by being pegged out in the Underworld below a huge overhanging rock, which forever tilted and shifted, sending down showers of rubble and threatening to crash on top of him.

CENTAUROS (page 76)

The result of Ixion's love-making in Olympos with the cloud-goddess Nephele was a son, Centauros. He inherited the rough nature of his father and grandfather, and roamed the countryside raping and pillaging just as they had done. One day he saw a herd of mares grazing in a field at the foot of Mount Pelion, and was filled with uncontrollable lust. He made love to them all, and from this mating of man and horse the race of Centaurs was created. They combined the wildness of their father with their mothers' gentleness: sometimes they were placid and peaceloving, fond of music and skilled in the arts of prophecy and healing; at other times, for no reason, they fell into wild fits and galloped crazily across the countryside. (It was at these times particularly that they welcomed war with their neighbours the Lapiths, the descendants of Centauros' half-brother Lapithos. See page 70.)

KASTOR AND POLYDEUKES (page 76)

The twins Kastor and Polydeukes, although known as 'Zeus' sons' (Dioskouroi), lived their lives as mortal men. They were athletes and huntsmen, princes envied by everyone for beauty and strength. They took part eagerly in any kind of adventure, and in sporting events such as the Olympic Games: Polydeukes was outstanding at boxing, and Kastor at riding and taming wild horses. They sailed with Jason and the Argonauts (see page 112), and throughout the voyage their fiercest rivals were another pair of twins, the princes Idas and Lynkeus. This rivalry began in a friendly way, but led at last to blows and death. Kastor and Polydeukes stole cattle (some say girls) from Idas and Lynkeus, and the princes came after them with soldiers. There was a battle, and Idas, Lynkeus and Kastor were killed. (Clearly

Kastor, after all, was mortal and therefore Tyndareos' son, just as the palace priests had said.) Polydeukes, griefstricken at the loss of his twin, begged his father Zeus to let him share his own immortality with Kastor. Zeus agreed, and ever afterwards they took turn and turn about, spending one day each in Olympos and the Underworld.

As part of their heavenly duties, Kastor and Polydeukes looked after sailors lost at sea. They appeared to them as will-o'-the-wisps, lights flickering across the waves or dancing at the mast-tip to guide their sails. (Even so, these lights were often unreliable: the twins' immortal sister Helen also played will-o'-thewisp – and she used her light to lead men astray.) They can be seen in the sky as the constellation Gemini (the Twins).

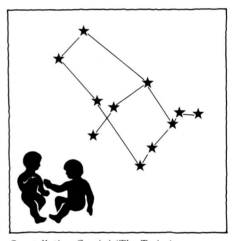

Constellation Gemini (The Twins)

In the zodiac, Gemini is the star-sign of those born between 21 May and 20 June. Their birthstone is jade, and in character they are a mixture of quickwittedness and good sense on the one hand, and rashness and boasting on the other.

230

IDAS AND LYNKEUS (*page 76*)

Idas and Lynkeus, twin sons of King Aphareus of Messene and his queen Arene, were cousins and rivals of the Spartan twins Kastor and Polydeukes. Idas was a skilful athlete, and Lynkeus had eyes so powerful that he could see clearly even in pitch darkness.

Idas fell in love with Marpessa, daughter of King Euenos. Like his half-brother Oinomaos (see page 195), Euenos made all his daughters' would-be suitors race him in a chariot, and be-headed those who lost. Idas borrowed a team of horses from Poseidon, won the race easily and claimed Marpessa. He had to fight for her with Apollo, who also loved her; but Zeus stopped the fight and asked Marpessa to choose for herself. Marpessa knew that Apollo was never faithful to the mortals he married, and chose Idas.

Idas and Lynkeus were among the heroes who hunted the Kalydonian boar (see page 87), and they also joined Jason's expedition to fetch the Golden Fleece (see page 112). They were forever squabbling with their rivals Kastor and Polydeukes, who one day stole cattle from them and started a fight. (For what happened next, see page 230.)

THE CASTALIAN SPRING (*page 77*)

Castalia was a water-nymph, daughter of the river-god Acheloös who fought with Herakles (see page 138). She was beautiful and pure, a follower of the vir-gin goddess Artemis. Apollo saw her and fell in love with her; she ran from him in panic, plunged into a spring on Mount Parnassos (see page 77) and was drowned. The spring was named the Castalian Spring after her; its water was some of the purest in Greece. The water appeared from underground, and ran down the hillside to the river Pleistos on the valley floor. There was a story that all the rivers for kilometres around were in love with the Castalian Spring, and sent presents: if you threw honey-cakes into the waters of the river Kephissos, for example, they would disappear underground and reappear days later in Castalia.

To make amends for causing Casta-lia's death, Apollo gave the water of the spring power to inspire prophecy and poetry. At first it was reserved for the priests of the oracle, and especially for the Pythonesses, the prophetesses; but visitors too were later allowed to drink it and even to bathe in it.

ION (*page 78*)

An example of the way in which the Del-phic oracle guided mortal affairs was the story of Ion. He was the son of Kreousa, an Athenian princess, wife of Xouthos. Apollo made love to her, and when their child Ion was born (secretly, in a cave on the Acropolis) he carried him to Delphi, where the boy grew up as one of the temple priests.

Back in Athens, Xouthos and Kreousa remained childless for several years. In the end Xouthos went to the Delphic Oracle to ask how to get a son. The oracle told him that his son would be the first person he met on his way out of the sanctuary. This turned out to be Ion.

Xouthos assumed that Ion's mother must have been a mountain-nymph he had met years before, in a Dionysos-dance on Mount Parnassos. He intro-duced the young man to Kreousa as his son and heir. Kreousa, furious that

Xouthos should so favour a bastard child, plotted to poison Ion. But Ion discovered the plot, and Kreousa fled to the priestess at Delphi. When Ion arrived, the priestess stopped him from killing Kreousa. She explained their real relationship, and told them to keep it secret from Xouthos. Ion went back to Athens as prince, and when his grandfather King Erechtheus died, he succeeded to the royal throne.

APHRODITE AND ADONIS (*page 79*)

The parents of Priapos (the scarecrow-god who killed Dionysos' donkey) were Aphrodite and her mortal lover Adonis. The story of their love-affair began with a foolish Assyrian king who boasted that his daughter Smyrna was more beautiful than Aphrodite herself. To punish him, Aphrodite made him fall in love with his own daughter, and he took Smyrna to bed and made love to her. When he realised that she was pregnant, he tried to kill her; but Aphrodite rescued her and changed her into a myrrh-tree. This tree splits its trunk in spring to allow new growth, and when Smyrna's trunk split, baby Adonis was found inside.

Aphrodite fell in love with Adonis, and planned to make him her lover as soon as he was old enough. In the meantime she hid him in a box, and gave it to Persephone to guard. Persephone opened the box, fell in love with Adonis too, and refused to give him up when the time came. The case was tried by the Muse Kalliope. She decreed that Adonis' time should be divided: he should spend one third of each year with Persephone, one third with Aphrodite and one third with anyone he chose.

So it was decided. But at the end of Aphrodite's four months she charmed Adonis with her girdle of desire until he declared that he would stay with her forever. Furious at being tricked, Persephone went to Ares, god of war (who was still smarting after his humiliating love-affair with Aphrodite: see page 45), and told him he had a mortal rival. Ares disguised himself as a wild boar, and the next time Adonis went hunting, gored him in the thigh and killed him. At this, since the whole matter was getting out of hand, Zeus intervened and decreed that Adonis should spend half of the year with Aphrodite and half (the half she spent as queen of the Underworld) with Persephone.

Where drops of Adonis' blood fell on the ground, wild wood-anemones sprang up, and their descendants grow in woodland to this day. Aphrodite had three children with Adonis, two mortal and beautiful (Golgos and Beroe), the third immortal, misshapen and hideous (Priapos). Priapos was so ugly, and so full of shamelessness and lust, that the gods refused to keep him in Olympos. He became a companion of Pan and the satyrs, a spirit of fertility and growth.

PRIAPOS AND THE DONKEY
(*page 79*)

Priapos' quarrel with Dionysos' donkey (see page 79) went back to an earlier occasion, one of several events which caused the gods to ban him from Olympos. The goddess Hestia, Zeus' sister, had sworn never to marry or to have children, and for this she was greatly respected by the gods. She was serene and beautiful, and Priapos (who had no respect for anyone) was attracted by her and decided to take the first chance he could to make love to her. He thought his chance had come after a banquet held one day on earth. All the gods, full of mortal food and wine, had fallen asleep in the sunshine in the grassy fields. Priapos thought that he was the only one awake, and crept up on Hestia to make love to her. But Dionysos' donkey, resting in the shade at the fields' edge, saw what was happening and brayed so suddenly and so loudly that all the gods woke up with a start. Priapos was sent packing – and from that day on vowed vengeance on Dionysos' donkey and the whole donkey race.

AGAMEDES' DEATH (*page 81*)

In another myth, Agamedes and Trophonios (see page 80) met a far more scandalous end than being favoured by Apollo. They were asked by King Hyrieus of Boeotia to build a stone treasury so secure that it would deter all robbers. They did so, but built into the wall a movable stone whose secret they alone knew. Every night they went back to the treasury, moved the stone, wriggled inside and stole as much of the king's gold as they could carry. One night Agamedes greedily tried to take out too much. He stuck in the tunnel, and could move neither forwards nor backwards – exactly the fate later visitors to Trophonios' cave-oracle most feared. To prevent Agamedes being recognised, Trophonios cut off and hid his head. In punishment for this, the earth opened and swallowed him – at exactly the place where the oracle was later found.

THE CROW-MESSENGER (*page 81*)

Why are crows black? One myth explaining this is the story of Aglauros (see page 36). Another tells how a snow-white crow told Apollo of the love-affair between Koronis (whose name also means crow) and Ischys; to punish it for bring-

ing bad news Apollo turned it and its descendants crow-black for evermore.

ASKLEPIOS AND EPIDAUROS; ASKLEPIOS' CHILDREN (*page 81*)

Another version of Asklepios' myth (see page 81) explains his connection with Epidauros. This story says nothing of Koronis' unfaithfulness to Apollo. She went with her father Phlegyras on a raiding expedition to Argolis, and while she was there gave birth to Apollo's child on the mountainside at Epidauros. Phlegyras, furious with Apollo for raping his daughter, left baby Asklepios on the hillside to die and stormed off to Delphi to destroy Apollo's temple (see page 75). The baby lay peacefully on the hillside, where he was suckled by a sheepdog-bitch and a she-goat. Their owner, a shepherd, found the baby and would have taken him home as his own son. But Apollo surrounded Asklepios with a flickering, dazzling light, and so warned the shepherd not to interfere with what concerned the gods. The child was miraculously carried away to Mount Pelion, and given to Cheiron to educate.

Asklepios had four immortal children: Iaso (Healing), Panakeia (Cure-all), Hygeia (Health) and Telesphoros (Accomplisher). His mortal sons were Podaleirios (He-who-wards-off-death) and Machaon (Scalpel); they went as doctors with the Greeks to Troy.

PROITOS' DAUGHTERS (*page 83*)

In another version of the myth about Proitos' daughters they were driven insane not by Hera but by Dionysos – their madness on the mountain was like the orgies of the Theban women on Mount Kithairon (see page 39), and was caused by the same failure to recognise Diony-sos as a god. Melampous cured them not by driving them into a holy spring or a cave, but by feeding them on the plant hellebore. (Hellebore afterwards became a commonly-used cure for lunacy.)

THESTOR AND HIS DAUGHTERS
(*page 84*)

Thestor, the father of the prophet Kal-chas, also had two daughters, Theonoë and Leukippe. Theonoë was stolen by pirates as a child, and her father set sail to look for her. After many years with-out news, the second daughter, Leukip-pe, asked the Delphic oracle how to find her father and sister. The oracle told her to disguise herself as a priest and go to the court of King Ikaros of Karia. Leukip-pe disguised herself as a priest – a young man with flowing robes and shaved head – and the disguise was so convinc-ing that when she came to Karia, Ikaros' queen fell in love with her and tried to rape her. Leukippe indignantly broke free, and the queen threw her into pris-on and planned her death. But killing Apollo's priest brings down Apollo's an-ger, so instead of murdering the 'young man' herself, the queen told her soldiers to pick a prisoner from the jail and make him do it. The soldiers chose Thestor, by now an old man who had lain in jail for years. He went to Leukippe's cell to kill her, but in the nick of time Leukippe rec-ognised him and told him who she really was. Father and daughter now went to kill the wicked queen – and Thestor found to his amazement that she was his other long-lost daughter, Theonoë.

This myth, with its pirates, girl-disguised-as-boy and wicked queen who turns out good, is just like a made-up fairy tale. (Why did Thestor and Queen Theonoë not meet and recognise each other earlier?) It is also one of the very few Greek myths in which everyone lives happily ever afterwards.

TEIRESIAS, APHRODITE AND ATHENE (*page 85*)

In another version of the story of Teire-sias (see page 85), his change of sex was caused by Aphrodite. She was arguing with the three Graces about which of them was most beautiful, and asked Teiresias to judge. He chose the Grace Kale (Lovely), and Aphrodite punished him by changing him into an old woman. Even after he turned back into a man (thanks to Zeus' help after the argu-ment with Hera – see page 86) he still kept wrinkled old woman's breasts.

In still another version, the argument between Zeus and Hera never hap-pened. Teiresias lost his sight because one day on Mount Helicon he saw Athene bathing in the spring called Hip-pokrene. The punishment for any mortal who saw a goddess naked was blind-ness, and could not be avoided. But Athene compensated Teiresias by giving him second sight instead, and also a stick made of cornel-wood which had the power of guiding his steps as clearly as if he could see. (In this myth, Teire-sias' mother Chariklo was one of Athene's servant-nymphs, and it was her pleading for her son which softened Athene's heart.)

ZEUS' CHILDREN (2):
HALF–MORTAL CHILDREN
(*page 87*)

There is no way of telling how many children Zeus had with mortal mothers such as human beings or nymphs, or what their names were. It was common practice for women to claim that gods had fathered their children, and over the whole of Greece, in the whole of Greek history, Zeus was credited with hundreds of offspring. Some of the most important, with their mothers, are these:

Aiakos (son of the river-nymph Aigina): see page 91

Dionysos (son of the mortal Semele): see pages 37, 79

Epaphos (son of the river-nymph Io): see page 236

Helen; Polydeukes (children of the mortal Leda, twins of her mortal children with Tyndareos, Kastor and Klytemnestra): see page 76

Herakles (son of the mortal Alkmene): see page 123

Minos; Rhadamanthys; Sarpedon (sons of the mortal Europa): see page 71

Peirithoös (son of the mortal Dia): see page 151

Perseus (son of the mortal Danaë): see page 94

For Zeus' fully immortal children, see page 211.

ATALANTA AND PARTHENOPAIOS
(page 90)

Atalanta was the daughter of Iasos of Kalydon. But he wanted a son, and when Atalanta was born he left her on a hillside to die. Artemis sent a she-bear to suckle her, and later gave her into the care of the Amazons, her servants, hunting-women who lived in the hills and woods. It was only after the hunting of the Kalydonian boar (see page 87) that Iasos accepted Atalanta as his daughter – and agreed to her marriage in order to win himself, if not a son, at least a son-in-law.

There are several other versions of the myth of Atalanta's race. In some, the man who finally beat her was called Melanion, and the holy place they defiled was a sanctuary of Zeus, not Rhea. In others, Atalanta was not turned into a lion, but disclosed after the race that she was pregnant and that the child's father was either Meleager or Ares, god of war, himself. When the baby – a boy called Parthenopaios – was born, he was exposed on the hillside where baby Atalanta had once been left to die. But he too was saved by Artemis; when he grew up he was one of the seven champions who fought for Thebes (see page 162).

ZEUS AND AIGINA *(page 91)*

Aigina (see page 91) was one of the twenty daughters of the river Asopos. He was a strict father, but not strict enough to prevent several of his daughters having love-affairs with Apollo, Poseidon and Zeus himself. Zeus first tried to keep his love-affair with Aigina secret – both from her river-father and from his own jealous wife Hera – by hiding her in a wood. Only King Sisyphos of Corinth knew where the lovers were; Asopos bribed the story out of him (see page 102), and plunged through the trees in spate to drive them out. Zeus changed himself into a huge boulder, against which Asopos' waters pushed in vain. Then he hurled a thunderbolt at Asopos, so hot that it burnt trees to charcoal. Asopos was slowed to a sluggish, zigzag stream, and before he could recover Zeus changed into an eagle and carried Aigina away across the sea (where no river could follow without being swallowed up). He landed on the island of Oinone, and made love to Aigina there.

MYRMIDONS (*page 92*)

The myth of Aiakos is one of several which give an origin for the name Myrmidons (Ant-people). In another, they were named after King Myrmidon of Thessaly, because Zeus took the form of an ant and made love to Myrmidon's daughter Eurymedousa. In another, they were the ant-army given to Aiakos' son Peleus (see page 226). In yet a third, they were descendants of the wood-nymph Myrmex (Ant), who claimed that she, not Athene, had invented the plough and whom Athene punished by turning her into an ant, condemned forever to push loads bigger than herself.

IO (*page 92*)

Libya, the grandmother of Aigyptos and Danaos (see page 92), was herself the grand-daughter of Zeus and the river-nymph Io, whose home was in Argolis. Io first caught Zeus' eye when she was a priestess of Hera, and to save her from Hera's jealousy after he had made love to her, Zeus changed her into a white cow. But Hera knew very well who the cow really was, and asked Zeus to give it to her as a present – an innocent gift he could hardly refuse. Hera's first punishment for Io was to keep her tethered forever, a cow among all the other cows. She left hundred-eyed Argos on guard to stop Zeus rescuing Io. Zeus asked Hermes, god of thieves, to help him. The problem was that because Argos had a hundred eyes, he never relaxed his guard: whenever some of his eyes were asleep, the rest were awake and on the alert. Hermes solved this difficulty by playing Argos a tune on his lyre so sweet that all hundred eyes drooped at the same moment in a doze – whereupon Hermes set Io free and cut off Argos' head to stop him giving the alarm. (Later, Hera used Argos' eyes to decorate the peacock's tail.)

When Hera realised that she had been cheated, she sent a stinging fly to torment Io (as flies in fields have tormented cattle ever since). Maddened with pain, Io ran from the fly all over the surface of the earth. (Her wanderings even took her to lonely Mount Caucasus, where she saw Prometheus hanging in agony as a punishment for stealing fire.) Finally, when her punishment was complete, she came to Egypt and was set free of the fly at last. Zeus also restored her to human shape – and at his touch she conceived and bore a child called Epaphos (Touch). Io and Epaphos later came to be worshipped as gods in Egypt, Io as the goddess Isis, Epaphos as Apis the bull-god.

PYGMALION (*page 94*)

Another of the sons of Belos, Danaos' brother Pygmalion, became king of Cyprus. Disgusted by the behaviour of the women of Amathos (later known as Limmasol), he vowed never to marry and to spend his life carving sculpture instead. But one of the statues he made, an image of the nymph Galatea, was so beautiful that he fell in love with it and begged Aphrodite to free him from his vow. She did better than that: she brought the statue to life and allowed Pygmalion to make it his queen. Pygmalion and Galatea had a son, Paphos, who later built a beautiful city (named Paphos after himself) in Aphrodite's honour. Its temple, and the gardens round about, became her favourite place on earth.

ATLAS AND ANDROMEDA (*page 99*)

On his flight back from the Gorgons' cave, Perseus landed twice. The first time was at the feet of Atlas, who had been condemned by the gods forever to support the sky (see page 9). Atlas snarled at Perseus and refused him hospitality; Perseus' answer was to show him the Gorgon's head and turn him to stone – he became the Atlas Mountains, whose peaks still seem to support the sky.

Later, looking down at the sea-coast of Philistia, Perseus saw a naked girl chained to the rocks. Her name was Andromeda, and she was chained there as food for a sea-monster. (Her mother Cassiopeia had boasted that she and Andromeda were more beautiful than the sea-nymphs, and this was the punishment Poseidon decreed.) Perseus drew his diamond-sickle, plunged into the sea on Pegasos and killed the monster just as it reared up to snatch Andromeda.

Perseus asked to marry Andromeda. But her parents, King Cepheus and Queen Cassiopeia, refused to hear of it and sent soldiers to kill him. Perseus showed them the Gorgon's head and turned them all to stone. He married Andromeda, and when he eventually became King of Mycenae, she was his queen. Their children included a daughter named Gorgophonte (Gorgon-slayer).

Later, constellations of stars were named after Cepheus, Cassiopeia and Andromeda.

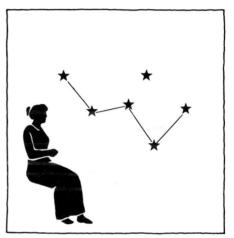

Constellation Cassiopeia

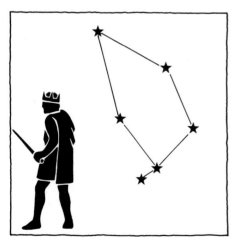

Constellation Cepheus

Constellation Andromeda

PEGASOS (page 100)

After Perseus died, the winged horse Pegasos flew off to Mount Helicon. He found the Muses in despair, for all the streams on the mountain had unaccountably dried up. Pegasos created a spring of fresh water by stamping his hoof in the ground; the Muses named it Hippocrene (Horse-spring). Pegasos often went back to the mountain to browse in the meadows watered by the stream. He visited other springs too, notably Peirene in Corinth – it was while he was drinking there that Bellerophon bridled him to ride him against Chimaira (see page 107).

Pegasos' connection with water-springs suits both his sea-monster ancestry (from Medusa's blood: see page 98) and his name (which means 'Of the wells'). Some later writers, however, explained the myth of a flying horse by saying that it was a landlubber's way of describing the first-ever ships, which carried people on their backs like horses and had sails like wings.

SISYPHOS AND ANTIKLEIA (page 101)

In some versions of the story of Autolykos and the cattle, Sisyphos played another trick. Autolykos' daughter Antikleia was to be married later that day to King Laertes of Ithaka. While Sisyphos' men were arguing with Autolykos about the stolen cattle, Sisyphos slipped into Antikleia's room and made love to her. She conceived a child, who was born in Ithaka as Laertes' son Odysseus – later known as 'the lord of deceit', the most cunning man who ever lived.

SALMONEUS (page 101)

When Sisyphos' brother Salmoneus was banished from Corinth (see page 101), he founded the city of Salmoneia in Elis. Like Sisyphos, he was cruel and arrogant. He announced one day that he was no longer a mortal, but had changed into Zeus himself, and ordered his people to worship him. He drove through the streets in a chariot, dragging a bundle of copper cooking pots: their clattering, he claimed, was how Zeus made thunder in the sky. For thunderbolts he lit oak-branches at a brazier in the chariot and hurled them at his cringing subjects. In the end Zeus threw a real thunderbolt at him and dashed him to the lowest depths of Tartaros.

TYRO (page 101)

Tyro, who bore Sisyphos' sons and killed them (see page 101), was driven mad by guilt. She married Kretheus, another of her uncles; but then she fell in love with a whole river, the Enipeus, and spent all her days lying on its banks and gazing dreamily into its depths. Poseidon disguised himself as the river-god and made love to her. Later, Tyro bore him twin sons, Pelias and Neleus; Kretheus adopted them and brought them up as half-brothers of his own son Aison. (Many years later, an argument between Pelias and Aison's son Jason began the quest for the Golden Fleece: see page 111.)

THE RAM (page 104)

When the golden ram flew north from Boeotia, it passed above the narrow sleeve of water which divides Europe from Asia. The air was thin and cold; Helle's hands grew numb and she lost her grip on the golden fleece, fell off the ram and was drowned. (The water was later called Hellespont, 'Helle's sea', in her memory.) Phrixos flew on the ram's back to Colchis, on the shore of the Black Sea. There he sacrificed the ram and hung its golden fleece in a temple guarded by a dragon. Zeus placed its image in the sky as the constellation Aries (Ram).

Constellation Aries (The Ram)

In the zodiac, Aries is the star-sign of those born between 21 March and 20 April. Their birth-stone is diamond, and in character they are sometimes generous and passionate, sometimes tactless and hot-tempered.

INO AND MELIKERTES *(page 105)*

When Ino and Melikertes fell into the sea, Aphrodite saved their lives. She turned Ino into a sea-goddess, Leukothea (Runner on White Foam) and gave her the job of helping seafarers in distress (for example Odysseus: see page 189). Melikertes was washed up on the shore of the Isthmus of Corinth. He became a minor god, and was renamed Palaimon (Wrestler); the Corinthians built him a temple and held the Isthmian Games every two years in his honour.

GLAUKOS *(page 105)*

Bellerophon's father Glaukos, the son of Sisyphos, kept horses for chariot-racing: his ambition was to train thoroughbreds which would outrun every horse in Greece. He began by experimenting with diet: he fed his mares first on different kinds of grass, then on oats, acorns, turnips and other vegetables, and finally on meat – including, to the gods' disgust, human flesh. Then he noticed that his fillies often ran faster than mares which had borne foals. From that time on he kept mares and stallions apart, hoping that if he prevented the older mares from breeding they would keep all the stamina they already had and add to it the speed of younger horses.

Aphrodite (who looked after the breeding of animals as well as human love-affairs) took this training-method as an insult. She fed Glaukos' mares on the herb hippomanes, which drives horses mad. They began prancing and whinnying and kicking their heels in ecstasy – and Glaukos thought that his training-method had worked. He took the mares to the stadium and tried to harness them to a training-chariot. But as soon as the harness touched their skins they reared, trampled Glaukos and repaid him for giving them the taste for flesh by eating him.

Because his body was eaten and not buried, Glaukos' ghost had no coins to pay Charon's fare, and was barred from the underworld. It wandered about the shore of the river Styx, and every two years, when the Isthmian Games were held in Corinth, came up to haunt the stadium while the chariot-races were being run. It materialised in front of the running horses, and its hideous appearance caused many accidents.

CHIMAIRA (page 107)

Chimaira was the daughter of the whirl-wind Typhon and the sea-monster Echidne: her brothers were Cerberus, guard-dog of Hades, and the Nemean Lion (see page 127); her sisters were Hydra (see page 127) and the Sphinx (see page 160). For middle parts she had the legs and head of a gigantic goat, for the lower part the head and body of a snake and for foreparts the mane and head of a fire-breathing lion. The king of Karia kept her for a time as a monstrous, three-headed pet; but she escaped and made her home on a volcanic mountain in Lycia, Iobates' kingdom. The under-growth on the mountain's lower slopes seethed with snakes; the rocks up to the tree-line were home to wild goats; above the trees, in caves just below the peak, lions had their lairs.

After Chimaira's death, her name be-came proverbial for any monster so hideous and so improbable that people thought it must be imaginary.

AIETES (page 111)

Aietes, king of Colchis, was the son of Helios the sun-god and Perseis, daugh-ter of Okeanos. He lived in a golden palace called Aia, which Hephaistos built for Helios in return for saving his life in the battle with the Earthborn (see page 26). It was in this palace that Helios and his sister Eos slept each night, while darkness covered the earth.

Aietes' sisters were Pasiphaë, queen of Crete (see page 141) and Kirke, who lived on the floating island of Aiaia in a golden palace just like Aietes' own (see the story of Odysseus, page 184). His children were Chalkiope who married Phrixos, Medea who helped Jason (see

page 117) and Apsyrtos whom Medea killed (see page 119.)

JASON (page 111)

Jason was the son of Aison and Alkimede. When his uncle Pelias stole the throne and ordered the execution of Aison's children (see page 111), baby Jason was smuggled out of the palace to Mount Pelion, where he was brought up – like many other heroes – by Cheiron, king of the Centaurs. He became a skil-ful hunter – he took part, for example, with other young heroes in the Kalydo-nian boar-hunt (see page 87) – and at last left Cheiron to seek his fortune. He went to Delphi to ask who his parents were; but instead of answering clearly, the oracle advised him to go to Iolkos. On the way he came to the river Enipeus, swollen by flood-water. On the bank he found an old woman, who said that the stream was too fast for her to ford, and asked Jason to carry her across. Jason agreed. But the old woman was Hera in disguise, and Jason had to carry the full weight of an immortal god-dess on his back. With his utmost strength he struggled across the river; his efforts dislodged one sandal, which was lost in the mud. Once they were across, Hera rewarded him by telling him that Pelias had long ago stolen his father's throne, and that she would pro-tect him if he went to Iolkos and deman-ded it back.

In another version of the myth, 'Jason' (Healer) was a nickname given by Cheiron: Jason's real name was Diomedes. He grew up knowing very well whose son he was and how Pelias had stolen his rightful throne. He asked his uncles, King Admetos of Pherai and King Amythaon of Messenia, to help him persuade Pelias to give up the throne; Pelias (who was by now very old) agreed on condition that Jason first went to Colchis and fetched the golden fleece.

THE NAMES OF THE ARGONAUTS
(*page 112*)

Many different lists were made of the 50 Argonauts: each Greek state later liked to claim that one of its ancestors had taken part in the expedition – just as they all claimed to have sent warriors to Troy. Apart from Jason, the expedition-leader, the Argonauts most commonly listed included 16 sons of gods (Ankaios of Tegea, Askalaphos, Asklepios, Echion, Herakles, Idmon, Kalais and his brother Zetes, Kastor and his twin Polydeukes, Melampous, Nauplios, Palaimon, Periklymenos and the brothers Phanos and Staphylos); the prophets Amphiaraos and Mopsos; the musician Orpheus; the heroes Akastos, Admetos, Aktor, Ankaios of Samos, Argos, Asterios, Augeias, Boutes, Erginos, Euphemos, Euryalos, Eurydamas, Idas and his twin Lynkeus, Iphikles, Iphitos, Kaineus, Kanthos, Kepheus, Koronos, Laertes, Meleager, Oileus, Peleus, Peneleos, Phaleros, Poias, Polyphemos and Tiphys; one woman, Atalanta, and one boy, Herakles' page Hylas. Most were chosen for their bravery, but some had special skills as well: Echion was a herald, Lynkeus the keenest-eyed man who ever lived, Nauplios a navigator and Periklymenos a magician who could change his shape.

Some of the Argonauts died on the journey. But most returned safely, and their later adventures form the basis for many myths.

THOAS AND HYPSIPYLE (*page 112*)

When the women of Lemnos slaughtered their menfolk, only one man escaped: Thoas, king of the island. His daughter Hypsipyle smuggled him to the beach and put him to sea in a wooden chest. It bobbed to Tauris, and the Taurians welcomed him and made him king. (See the story of Iphigeneia, page 270.) After the Argonauts sailed away, the people of Lemnos turned on Hypsipyle. They said that her saving of her father had brought bad luck and caused the Argonauts to leave, and they punished her by selling her as a slave to King Lykourgos of Nemea (see page 162). Meanwhile, the twin sons she bore to Jason grew up as princes of Lemnos, and eventually one of them, Euneos, became king of the island.

KALAIS AND ZETES (*page 114*)

Long after the voyage of *Argo*, Herakles met up with Kalais and Zetes on the island of Tinos, and took his revenge on them for persuading the Argonauts to abandon him after Hylas' disappearance. He killed them, and set over their graves a V-shaped boulder so finely balanced that it rocked to and fro at the slightest breeze, always threatening to crash down on them, and so preventing them ever being able to sleep easily in their graves.

PHINEUS (*page 114*)

Phineus married Kleopatra, daughter of the North Wind, and they had two children. When Kleopatra died he married a second wife, Idaia. She was jealous of Kleopatra's children and persuaded

Phineus to let her put out their eyes – no blind person could inherit the royal throne. For allowing this atrocity, Phineus was punished by Zeus, who ordered him to choose between death or blindness. He chose blindness. But he also had second sight, and used it to tell the gods' secrets to strangers. When Phrixos landed in his country after Helle fell from the golden ram (see page 238), Phineus told him how to get to Colchis and find the secret palace of the Sun. For this, Helios the sun-god punished him by sending the Harpies to snatch his food and starve him to death.

APSYRTOS' DEATH (page 119)

In another version of the Argonants' escape from Colchis (see page 119), Medea's brother Apsyrtos was not a child but a grown man. Aietes sent him after *Argo* in a warship, and he cornered the Argonauts at the mouth of the river Danube. They took the case to the local king, and asked him to decide who was the rightful owner of the golden fleece. But while the king and his council were still discussing, Medea secretly told Apsyrtos that Jason was planning to sail without her, and asked him to rescue her. Apsyrtos went to the place she named. But the message was a trick: Jason was lying in ambush, and he killed Apsyrtos and mutilated his body. Next morning, instead of guarding the Argonauts, Apsyrtos' men had to gather the pieces of his body for burial in Colchis; while they were doing this, *Argo* escaped.

ARGO'S JOURNEYS (page 121)

There are several other accounts of *Argo*'s journeys home from Colchis. In one, she sailed north-east, crossed into the river of Ocean which girdles the earth and was carried south to the Indian Ocean, from which she laboriously made her way back to the Mediterranean Sea. In another she travelled northwestwards (by way of the river Don or the river Danube), reached Scandinavia, and sailed south in the river of Ocean until she entered the Mediterranean through the Pillars of Herakles. In another she was blown by storms all the way to Africa, and left high and dry in the desert: it was only by the help of the god Triton (who dragged her overland) that she reached the Mediterranean. In some versions Jason and Medea never left *Argo* in Drepanon (see page 119), but sailed her and her crew to Aiaia to be purified by Kirke.

Many Greek cities later claimed that *Argo* visited them on her homeward journey. These places included the islands of Elba (where the Argonauts' drops of sweat turned into wrinkled, skin-covered pebbles on the beach), Anaphe (where, having no animals to sacrifice, they burnt water-offerings on the altar-fire) and Aigina (where they held a footrace carrying water-pots, which later became an annual event). One island even claimed that it owed its birth to an Argonaut. Triton, in Africa, gave a clod of earth to the Argonaut Euphemos, and when Euphemos later threw it into the Aegean Sea, his father Poseidon turned it into the island Kalliste (Most beautiful), later renamed Thera (Hunting-place).

MEDEA'S CAULDRON (page 121)

In some versions of the myth, Jason's father Aison did not die by drinking bull's blood (see page 121). Instead, Medea cut him up and boiled him as a

242

demonstration of her magic power to give people second youth. The spell worked for Aison, who became young and strong again; but when Pelias was cut up and boiled Medea changed the spell and let him die.

Some people explained the idea of a cauldron of rebirth by saying that it was an imitation of the golden vessel which carried the Sun round the world from west to east each evening (see page 42). In some accounts this vessel was a ship, in others a golden cooking-pot. If the Sun could be reborn in a cooking-pot, why should the same miracle not work for human beings?

PELIAS' FUNERAL GAMES (page 121)

At Pelias' funeral games, the Argonauts won many events. Polydeukes won the boxing, Peleus the wrestling, Meleager the javelin, Zetes and Kalais the foot-races, Herakles (who came specially to the games) the unarmed combat and Euphemos the two-horse chariot race. A visitor, Glaukos son of Sisyphos, would have won the four-horse chariot race, but Aphrodite drove his horses mad (see page 239), and they turned on him and ate him, leaving Iolaos the Argonaut to win the race.

MEDEA'S CHILDREN (page 122)

There are several different versions of the fate of Medea's fourteen children. In one, she was determined to make them immortal, and when each child was born she took it to Hera's temple, cut it up and boiled it as she had done with Pelias. It was for this that Jason decided to divorce her and marry Glauke.

In another myth, the Corinthians stoned Medea's children to death in revenge for her murder of Glauke. Shortly afterwards, the children's ghosts began haunting houses in Corinth, infecting them with plague until every Corinthian child was dead. The Corinthians ended the plague by holding magic ceremonies in the temple of Akrocorinth – ceremonies followed for many generations afterwards.

The most famous account of the children's death is in Euripides' play *Medea*. (Some said he made it up as a deliberate piece of propaganda, to prove the Corinthians innocent of the children's deaths, and that the Corinthians paid him 30,000 drachmas, a fortune, for doing so.) In Euripides' version, Medea had only two children, Mermeros and Pheres. They took Glauke the poisoned wedding-gifts (see page 122); after Glauke's death, Medea stabbed them, took their dead bodies and escaped from Jason in a chariot pulled by dragons.

AMPHITRYON AND PTERELAOS (page 123)

Pterelaos, king of the Teleboans, had one immortal hair: unless it was discovered and plucked out of his head, he could not be harmed. Armed with this protection, he raided the cattle of King Elektryon of Mycenae, and killed eight of Elektryon's sons who guarded them. Elektryon planned to raise an army and go to punish the Teleboans leaving Mycenae in the care of his daughter Alkmene and her husband Amphitryon. But Amphitryon argued with him, saying that it was pointless to attack a man who could not be killed. He dashed his stick on the ground to emphasise what he was saying; the stick hit a stone, bounced up and killed Elektryon.

Since this was an accident, Alkmene said that Amphitryon should not be banished for murder. But she refused to have anything more to do with him until he defeated the Teleboans and avenged the deaths of her eight brothers. Amphitryon went to Thebes to ask King Kreon for help. Kreon offered him an army, on condition that Amphitryon rid the Theban countryside of a monstrous fox: it was fated never to be caught or killed, and each month it carried off and ate a Theban child. Amphitryon hunted the fox with the famous dog Lailaps: this was a present given long ago by Zeus to Europa, fated always to catch and kill the animals it chased. So the hound which always caught its prey hunted the fox which could never be caught. In the end, to avoid breaking the laws of fate, Zeus turned the pair of them to stone.

As soon as the fox was dealt with, Kreon gave Amphitryon his army, and Amphitryon went to fight the Teleboans. He was not at all sure how he was going to beat Pterelaos, who was still protected by his immortal hair. Fortunately, the gods made Pterelaos' daughter Komaitho fall in love with Amphitryon. She plucked out her father's immortal hair while he was asleep, and so Amphitryon was able to kill him and defeat the Teleboans. (What happened to Komaitho? She was executed for treachery.) It was while Amphitryon was fighting this battle that Zeus visited Alkmene and made love to her – the love-making which led to the birth of Herakles (see page 123).

HERAKLES' NAME (*page 124*)

Herakles was not actually given the name Herakles until he visited the Delphic oracle after the murder of his children (see page 126). Until then he was called either Alkaios (Strong) or Palaimon (Wrestler).

The reason for Herakles having three quite different names is probably that the story of Herakles we know today was made up from dozens of short myths about different heroes, linked together and connected with Herakles long before Greek myths came to be collected or written down. In some retellings the names were changed; in others the old-fashioned names remained.

Why was 'Herakles' (Glory of Hera) so called, when Hera, throughout his mortal life, was his unbending enemy? It was probably a name given to ward off disaster, just as the grim Furies were often called 'The Kindly Ones,' or the name 'Sea Kind to Strangers' (Pontos Euxeinos) was given to the Black Sea, one of the stormiest oceans known to the Greeks.

ALKATHOÖS (*page 125*)

The people of Megara had their own version of the myth of the cattle-eating lion (see page 125). In their account Herakles is never mentioned. The lion, they said, killed children as well as cattle, until finally it ate the son of King Megareus of Megara. Megareus promised his daughter's hand and half his kingdom to anyone who disposed of the lion – and a man called Alkathoös (Bold Strength), son of Pelops and Hippodameia, accepted the offer and killed the lion.

HERAKLES AT THEBES (*page 126*)

In some accounts, the goddess Athene helped Herakles to defend Thebes. Erginos' soldiers, before demanding tribute, disbanded the outnumbered Theban

244

army and removed every weapon from the city. Athene told Herakles to take down the sacred shields and ceremonial spears from the city temples, and use them to arm the citizens. She promised the Thebans victory if one high-born nobleman sacrificed himself for the city's sake. The noblest Theban of them all, Antipoinos, refused; but his daughters Androkleia and Alkis committed suicide in his place, and the city was saved.

After Herakles defeated Erginos' army, the Boeotian king Pyraichmos, an old ally of Erginos, came with an army to sack Thebes. Herakles defeated this force too, and executed Pyraichmos by tying him to four horses and driving them off in opposite directions. After this, no other allies of Erginos made war on Thebes.

HERAKLES AND HERA (page 126)

In some versions of the story, the tasks were not Herakles' punishment for murdering his wife and children: instead, they were Hera's way of delaying his immortality as long as possible and making it a prize hard to win. In these accounts, his madness came after the twelve tasks, and he was freed from the guilt of murder by spending one year as slave to Queen Omphale (see page 138). (As in the case of Herakles' name (see page 244), these garbled alternative accounts probably result from stories originally about other heroes inserted into the main myth of Herakles.)

HERAKLES AND MOLORCHOS (page 127)

While Herakles was searching for the Nemean lion, he lodged with a shepherd called Molorchos. (Molorchos was the

only man not to have fled the area: the lion had killed his son, and he said that he had nothing more to live for and therefore nothing to fear.) After Herakles killed the lion, he found the bones of Molorchos' son in its cave and gave them pious burial; in gratitude, Molorchos built him a temple in the grove of trees near Nemea, and became its priest. (The Nemean Games were later held there every two years: see page 255. Several of their main events, for example archery, wrestling and chariot-racing, were chosen in honour of Herakles' especial skills.)

LEO (page 127)

After the Nemean lion's death, its mother Selene created the constellation Leo (the Lion) in its honour.

Constellation Leo (The Lion)

In the zodiac, Leo is the birth-sign of those born between 22 July and 21 August. Their birth-stone is amber, and in character they are confident, ambitious and sometimes conceited.

CANCER (*page 127*)

As a memorial to the crab which helped Hydra fight Herakles, Hera set the constellation Cancer (the Crab) in the sky.

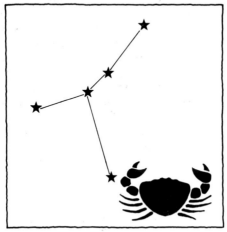

Constellation Cancer (The Crab)

In the zodiac, Cancer is the birth-sign of those born between 21 June and 21 July. Their birth-stone is ruby, and in character they are sometimes gentle and reflective, sometimes sulky and timid.

SAGITTARIUS (*page 128*)

On his way to capture the Erymanthian boar, Herakles was entertained to dinner by the centaur Pholos. Pholos opened a jar of delicious wine, and a gang of wild centaurs, attracted by the smell, trotted up and demanded a share. There was an argument, then a fight, and soon Pholos and Herakles found themselves waging a full-scale battle against rocks, logs and uprooted trees. Nephele, the cloud ancestor of the race of Centaurs (see page 229), made the ground wet and slippery, to slow Herakles down and

favour the centaurs (whose hooves gave them a better grip). This slipperiness proved fatal for Cheiron, king of the centaurs. He came to stop the fight, but lost his footing and slipped into the path of one of Herakles' poisoned arrows. Cheiron was immortal, and could not be killed; but not even his skill in medicine could stop the arrow-wound festering or ease the pain. In the end, he begged Zeus to grant him death and end his misery; Zeus took him into the sky and turned him into the constellation Sagittarius (the Archer).

Constellation Sagittarius (The Archer)

In the zodiac, Sagittarius is the birth-sign of those born between 22 November and 20 December. Their birth-stone is sapphire, and in character they are very like centaurs: generally strong, cheerful and hard-working, but sometimes restless and quick to lose their tempers.

ABDEROS (*page 131*)

In some versions of the myth of Diomedes' man-eating mares, Herakles took a band of heroes to help him steal the horses. Among them was his friend Abderos. The heroes crept into Diomedes' palace, freed the mares from their bronze stables and drove them warily across the plain down to the coast. When Diomedes and his men came riding after them, Herakles left the mares in Abderos' charge and dealt with the pursuers by tearing open an underground sea-channel and flooding the plain. He came back to find that the mares had fallen on Abderos and eaten him. Furious, Herakles ran round the newly-formed lake, seized Diomedes, dragged him back round the lake and fed *him* to the mares as well. He founded the city of Abdera in Abderos' honour, and populated it with the rest of his companions. (Later, in memory of Abderos, an annual athletics festival was held in Abdera: it was like every other athletics festival except that all events involving horses were forbidden.)

THE QUEST FOR
HIPPOLYTE'S BELT (*page 131*)

The parents of the race of Amazons were Ares and Aphrodite: the Amazons were the result of their ill-fated Olympian love-affair (see page 45). Although the Amazons were beautiful women, their chief joy in life was battle. They honoured only girl-children: they crippled boy-babies by breaking their arms and legs, and when they grew up used them as household slaves. They suckled their children with the left breast only; they cut their right breasts off, to make bow-shooting easier. Their clothes were the skins of wild beasts, and they lived rough in the woods, coming out to attack and destroy their neighbours' cities. Their only buildings were temples in honour of Ares, Aphrodite and the hunting-goddess Artemis; they were

feared by every nation round the Black Sea shores.

The adventures of Herakles and his crew on their voyages to and from the Amazons' kingdom (see page 131) were very like those of Jason and the Argonauts. On the outward voyage they landed on the island of Paros, and defeated an army led by the sons of King Minos of Crete; they helped King Lykos of Paphlagonia win a war against his neighbours; they passed through the dangerous channels of the Hellespont and Bosporos. On their homeward journey they stopped again in Paphlagonia and took part in funeral games; Herakles rescued Hesione from a seamonster (see page 249); he was challenged to a wrestling-match by Proteus' sons, and killed them (see page 64).

These adventures are generally sketchy and little-known – and the reason is that, unlike the voyage of *Argo*, Herakles' journey was never made into a long epic poem. Ancient Greek writers preferred some of the other myths about him, and his adventures on the voyage remained local stories, told in detail only in the places concerned.

STRANGE ENCOUNTERS (*page 133*)

Driving Geryon's cattle overland from the Pillars of Herakles to Mycenae was no easy task. There were mountains to cross – the Pyrenees, the Alps – and countless cattle-thieves. Herakles dealt with the mountains by beating out passes and tunnels with his club; but the thieves were more of a problem. In Liguria a whole army of bandits attacked him, and he ran out of arrows before he could drive them off. He begged Zeus to help, and Zeus showered the ground with thousands of stones, which Herakles threw at the Ligurians and killed

247

them all. (The plain where the stones fell is still covered with pebbles: a shingle beach twenty kilometres inland.) In Italy, by the river Tiber, Herakles lay down to rest – and while he slept Kakos, a firebreathing son of Hephaistos and Medusa, stole six cattle and dragged them backwards to his cave. Herakles woke and found the cattle missing, but could see no hoof-prints leading away from the herd. But then his own cattle began to low, and the stolen six answered from Kakos' cave. Herakles ran into the cave, and before Kakos could scorch him with his fiery breath, seized him by the throat and squeezed him dead.

Later, just as he was about to cross into Greece, Hera sent a fly to torment the cattle, and they stampeded north to Thrace. Herakles galloped after them in a chariot. He stopped to rest in Hylaia, and the queen of the area, an earth-spirit half snake half woman, stole his chariot-horses and refused to return them unless he made love to her. (Three sons were born after this encounter; the youngest, Scythes, later founded the kingdom of Scythia.) Herakles reharnessed his mares, found his cattle and began to drive them south. The giant Alkyoneus was lying in wait, and pelted him with rocks the size of carts; Herakles clubbed the biggest rock in mid-air and sent it flying back to crush Alkyoneus. (The rock can still be seen on the Isthmus of Corinth.) After this no other enemies dared attack, and he brought the cattle safely to Mycenae.

HERAKLES AND PROMETHEUS (*page 133*)

In some accounts it was not Proteus who told Herakles where to find the garden of the Hesperides, but Prometheus. In gratitude for this help Herakles shot dead the vulture which feasted on Prometheus' liver, and shortly afterwards Zeus, as he had long ago agreed (see page 213), set Prometheus free.

ANTAIOS; THE PIGMIES (*page 134*)

On his journey home from the Atlas Mountains, Herakles was challenged to a wrestling match by King Antaios of Libya. Antaios was a giant, the son of Mother Earth – and like all Earth's children could never be killed so long as he kept even the smallest part of his body in contact with the ground. Since wrestlers defeat their opponents by pinning them to the ground, he had never been beaten in a contest, and killed everyone he challenged. But Herakles guessed his secret, and instead of pinning him to the ground lifted him high overhead, crushed his ribs and killed him. At once Antaios' half-brothers the Pigmies made war on Herakles with siege-weapons (since to them he was a giant, the size of a fortress). He gathered them up like ants in a fold of his lion-cloak, and took them back to Mycenae as a present for Eurystheus' children.

THE END OF EURYSTHEUS (*page 135*)

After Herakles left the earth for Olympos, Eurystheus of Mycenae continued his cruelty to Herakles' children. But then he made war on their ally Keyx, king of Trachinia – and this proved fatal, since to fight Keyx he had to leave the security of Mycenae, and so lost the gods' protection and was killed by Herakles' son Hyllos. (For the story of the next king of Mycenae, Eurystheus' uncle Atreus, see page 197.)

HERAKLES, TELAMON AND HESIONE (*page 136*)

Herakles and Telamon became friends (see page 136) when Herakles visited Telamon's kingdom, the island of Salamis. Telamon made Herakles guest of honour at a feast to celebrate the birth of his son Aias. In return, Herakles gave baby Aias the gift of heroic strength, by wrapping him in his lion-skin cloak. Wherever the cloak touched Aias' skin, he could not be hurt by mortal weapons; only his neck and armpit (where Herakles' quiver got in the cloak's way) were vulnerable. When Aias grew up, he was one of the greatest heroes who took part in the Trojan War (see page 262).

Hesione, Laomedon's daughter, went back to Salamis with Telamon after the heroes captured Troy (see page 180). She stayed for a year, until their son Teucer, Aias' half-brother, was born. After that, tired of Telamon, she dived into the sea and swam to Miletos in Asia Minor, where she married King Arion.

HERAKLES AND IPHITOS (*page 137*)

In some versions of the myth, Iphitos came to Tiryns not to apologise for his father's treatment of Herakles but to look for twelve stolen horses. These had, in fact, been stolen by the trickster Autolykos, who changed their colour and sold them to Herakles as if they were his own. Iphitos recognised the horses in Herakles' herd – and Herakles, wrongly thinking that Iphitos was about to call him a thief, fell into a madman's fury and threw him from the walls.

HERAKLES, OMPHALE AND PAN (*page 138*)

Some versions of the myth of Herakles and Omphale, thinking it insulting for a hero to wear women's clothes, tell the story a different way. Herakles and Omphale were walking in the hills, when the god Pan ran after Omphale to rape her. Herakles and Omphale hid in a cave and changed clothes. When Pan arrived, he paid no attention to the figure dressed in a lion-skin and carrying a club, but took in his arms the person wearing a woman's dress. His reward was a kick from Herakles that sent him spinning across the countryside for kilometres – and out of spite for this he told everyone he met that Herakles wore women's clothes.

HERAKLES AND THE BANDITS (*page 138*)

Among the bandits Herakles captured or killed for Queen Omphale was Syleus. He used to capture passers-by and force them to hoe his endless rows of vines. Instead of hoeing, Herakles dug the vines up and made them into an enormous fire. On it he roasted Syleus' prize bull, and when the meat was ready he put out the fire by diverting a river through Syleus' farm, ripped the house-door off its hinges to make a table, opened a cask of wine and invited Syleus to join the feast. Syleus ran at him to kill him, and Herakles clubbed him dead before calmly sitting down to his meal.

Another bandit, Lityerses, made passers-by reap his cornfields until they dropped, then planted them in the ground, reaped off their heads and bound their bodies into sheaves with the corn-stalks. Herakles reaped all day, pace for pace with Lityerses, until Lityerses himself dropped with exhaustion. Then Herakles cut off Lityerses' head and threw his body into the river Meander.

After Herakles' year as Omphale's slave, Apollo asked him to deal with the bandit Kyknos (a fierce son of Ares the wargod). Kyknos killed passing travellers and hung their skulls as offerings in his father Ares' temple. Herakles challenged Kyknos to a duel, and their fighting caused an earthquake which shook forests and demolished buildings for kilometres around. Ares came to help Kyknos, just as Herakles killed Kyknos with a blow to the neck. Herakles next wounded Ares in the thigh, and would have brained him then and there if Zeus, disapproving of a fight between god and god, had not thrown a thunderbolt and parted them.

The only bandits who escaped Herakles were the twin brothers Sillos and Triballos, known as the Kerkopes (Those with eyes in their bottoms). Herakles slung them over his shoulder to carry them back to Omphale's palace. When they saw his coal-black bottom – it was scorched when he tamed the fire-breathing Cretan bull – they laughed so much that he put them down and asked them to share the joke. When they told him, he set them free – but he changed them into baboons and gave them bare red bottoms to show that he could enjoy a joke as well.

MINOS AND THE ATHENIANS
(*page 141*)

Minos' enmity with Athens was caused by the death of his son Androgeos. Androgeos was a keen sportsman, and visited Athens to take part in the Panathenaic Games (where he won every event he entered). King Aigeus of Athens, who felt that his throne was in danger from his rebellious brother Pallas, knew that Androgeos was a friend of Pallas' sons, and thought that he had come to Athens not only to compete in the Games but also as a spy. Accordingly, when Androgeos left Athens to go to Thebes, Aigeus' men ambushed him and killed him.

At first Minos tried to avenge this murder by gathering an army to destroy Athens. But he found the Greek cities unwilling to make alliances with Crete, and soon he was himself fighting wars and laying siege to many small towns in Greece. He captured the island of Seriphos by bribing Princess Arne with gold to open the city gates; in punishment the gods changed Arne into a jackdaw, forever stealing anything with the glint of gold. Nisa near Corinth was fated never to fall so long as its king Nisos kept on his head the lock of hair which contained his life; Minos bribed Princess Skylla to slip into her father's bedroom and snip the lock while he slept. So the city fell, and Minos sailed for Crete. Skylla swam desperately after his ship (for he refused to take on board a traitor and a murderer); her father's ghost, in the form of a sea-eagle, swooped on her time and again until she drowned.

Success with a few Greek states was of no help to Minos with the Athenians, and in the end he prayed to his father Zeus to avenge Androgeos' murder. Zeus sent earthquakes and plagues to torment the Athenians. They asked the Delphic oracle how to appease the gods, and the oracle told them to agree to whatever conditions Minos imposed. He demanded that every nine years they should send seven men and seven girls to Crete as slaves. (After the Minotaur was born, these Athenian slaves were trained as bull-leapers, and after they had taken part in the festival were sent into the labyrinth as human sacrifice. This barbarous custom was the one ended by Theseus: see page 148.)

MINOS, PROKRIS AND KEPHALOS
(page 141)

Among the many love-affairs of King Minos which caused his queen Pasiphaë to quarrel with Aphrodite, the one with the most tragic results was with an Athenian princess, Prokris. She was married to Kephalos; but he was seduced by Eos the dawn-goddess, and Prokris sailed in despair to Crete. Here she found that Queen Pasiphaë had put a spell on Minos: whenever he made love to another woman he filled her with venomous insects which stung her dead. Prokris gave Minos a potion to cure this spell, and in gratitude he not only slept with her but gave her two presents: a hunting-spear which never missed its target, and Lailaps the hunting-dog which could run down any prey on earth.

Prokris took these presents and went back to Athens. She disguised herself as a boy, intending to spy on her husband Kephalos and see if he was still carrying on his affair with Eos. Kephalos fell in love with what he thought was a beautiful boy, and it was only when they went to bed that he found that his lover was actually his lawful wife. The gods were disgusted by all this free-and-easy behaviour, and decided to punish both Kephalos and Prokris. It was Kephalos' habit to go hunting early every morning – and the gods whispered to Prokris that he was really slipping away to sleep with Eos, with whom he was still in love. She crept after him, bitter with jealousy; he

heard her feet in the undergrowth, mistook her for prey and killed her with the unerring spear. For this murder he was banished from Athens and went to Crete (where he later loaned Lailaps the hunting-dog to Herakles' father Amphitryon: see page 244). But he could escape neither from Prokris' ghost nor from his own guilt, and one day threw himself into the sea and drowned.

POSEIDON'S BULL *(page 141)*

Minos was one of the three sons of Europa, whom Zeus made love to in the shape of a bull (see page 71). When the three princes grew up, they quarrelled over the throne of Crete, and Minos won. He boasted that the gods would prove that he was the rightful king by sending a second white bull from the sea for sacrifice. Poseidon answered his prayer: a gigantic, fire-breathing bull with a creamy-white hide and bronze hooves splashed ashore and stood by the altar, docilely waiting to be sacrificed. The people gaped; but Minos was so struck by the bull's beauty that he decided not to sacrifice it. He replaced it with another animal, the finest on Crete, and set Poseidon's bull free to wander among his own royal herds. It was to punish this disobedience that Poseidon later allowed the bull to mate with Queen Pasiphaë, so bringing shame and dishonour on Minos and creating the Minotaur. The bull afterwards went mad and rampaged across the island, until Herakles tamed it as one of his twelve tasks (see page 131).

GLAUKOS AND POLYEIDOS *(page 142)*

Before she fell in love with Poseidon's bull, Pasiphaë bore her husband Minos six children: three daughters (Akakallis, Ariadne and Phaidra) and three sons (Katreus, Androgeos and Glaukos).

While Glaukos was still a child the scandal over the Minotaur happened, and Minos had the labyrinth built to hide Pasiphaë and her monster-child. One day Glaukos wandered into the labyrinth and got lost. Minos sent all his servants, priests and prophets to look for him, including Polyeidos, a visiting soothsayer from Argos. Polyeidos found Glaukos' body in one of the store-rooms of the labyrinth. (He had climbed up to take honey from a huge storage-jar, fallen in and drowned.) Polyeidos took the body to Minos – and Minos at once locked him in a dungeon and refused to let him out until he brought Glaukos back to life.

Polyeidos sat in despair. He was no god's son, no Asklepios – how could he bring the dead to life? Then a snake coiled across the boy's body, and he killed it. At once a second snake appeared, holding in its mouth a twig, which it rubbed against the dead snake's body. The dead snake wriggled back to life and the two snakes slid away. Polyeidos snatched the twig and rubbed it on Glaukos, hoping that some of its life-giving power was left. The boy yawned, stretched and rubbed his eyes, waking from death as easily as from sleep.

Glaukos and Polyeidos were set free from the dungeon. But still Minos refused to let Polyeidos leave Crete unless he taught Glaukos all he knew of magic and prophecy. Polyeidos taught the boy; but when the time came for him to leave Crete and sail home to Argos, he told Glaukos to spit in his open mouth, and as soon as Glaukos did so he forgot everything he had learned.

THESEUS' JOURNEY TO ATHENS
(*page 144*)

To the Athenians, Theseus was as important – and as real – a historical character as William Tell later was for the Swiss or King Arthur for the British. Accordingly, their myth-gatherers tried to make Theseus as great a hero as Herakles (who belonged to the rival town of Thebes), and therefore found many adventures for him to rival those of Herakles. In particular, on his journey from Troezen to Athens, they pictured him fighting giants, bandits and ferocious beings of every kind. He began with Periphetes, who used to batter travellers to death with a huge bronze club. Theseus tripped him, snatched the club and beat him to death – so winning a club to match Herakles' olive-tree. Next he tackled Sinis, who tied passers-by to two pine-trees bent to touch the ground, then let the trees spring upright and tear his victims apart. Theseus wrestled him to the ground, tied *him* to two trees and split *him* in two. After that he fought and killed a ferocious wild pig (offspring of the monsters Typhon and Echidne), the giant Skeiron (who made travellers wash his feet, saying this was the payment for letting them pass, and then kicked them over a precipice into the sea), Kerkyon the wrestler, and last of all Prokrustes. Prokrustes used to welcome travellers, feast them and give them a bed for the night. He had only one guest-bed, and if the visitors were too long for it he cut off their legs to make them fit; if they were too short he put them on a rack to lengthen them.

THE SHAPE OF THE LABYRINTH
(*page 148*)

The labyrinth is not usually imagined as

a vertical maze, shaped like a spiral shell – though this fits with Minos' way of discovering Daidalos' hiding-place in Sicily by challenging people to pass a thread through a triton-shell (see page 143). The vertical shape would have been like a system of underground caves, and going into it like modern potholing. (Modern potholers often report hearing strange noises, like monstrous breathing or roaring, from deep underground.)

If we imagine the labyrinth in the usual way, horizontal like a modern maze, it fits the idea of a huge palace filled with branching corridors and many rooms. (This is like the palace excavated by Sir Arthur Evans at Knossos in Crete.) Ariadne's thread, though essential for finding your way out, would be no help to you in going in: if this version of the story is followed, therefore, we must imagine that she knew the way to the Minotaur's lair and either explained it to Theseus (as modern guides explain the 'key' to mazes) or else led his steps herself.

AIGEUS' DEATH (page 149)

In some versions of the myth of Aigeus and Theseus, the sail Theseus forgot to hoist was coloured not purple-red, but white. (But since white was the colour of mourning, this seems a less likely sign of a successful mission than rejoicing red.) In other versions, Aigeus threw himself not from the Acropolis but from cliffs into the sea which was later named after him, the Aegean.

THESEUS AND ANTIOPE (page 150)

There are many confused versions of the myth of Theseus and Antiope. (Some even say that it was not Antiope he mar-

ried at all, but Hippolyte: this is the version followed by Shakespeare in A Midsummer Night's Dream. But it clashes with the story of Hippolyte's death at the hands of Herakles: see page 132.) In some accounts Antiope was Theseus' prisoner-of-war after the expedition with Herakles, and the Amazon attack on Athens was made to win her back; in others she was in love with Theseus from the start, betrayed her fellow-Amazons to help him and was killed in the battle beside the Areiopagos; still others say that she never married Theseus at all, and that Hippolytos was a bastard child.

These different versions of the story may have arisen because details of several different Amazon invasions were run together into one account; or they may be attempts by Athenian myth-writers to cover up a disreputable part of Theseus' story, the abandoning and murder of his legally-married wife.

HIPPOLYTOS AND ARTEMIS
(page 151)

One reason for Hippolytos' horror at the idea of sleeping with his step-mother Phaidra was that he was a follower of the virgin goddess Artemis. He had sworn to have nothing to do with women; his interests were hunting, horse-riding and athletics. (Some versions of the myth say that it was Aphrodite, angry because Hippolytos refused to sleep with her, who made Phaidra fall in love with him.)

After Hippolytos died, Artemis asked the famous healer Asklepios, Apollo's son, to bring Hippolytos back to life. The attempt cost Asklepios his life (see page 81), and caused a serious quarrel between Apollo and Zeus (see page 33).

THE WEDDING OF KADMOS AND HARMONIA (*page 156*)

Kadmos and Harmonia led the wedding procession from Olympos to Boeotia. They rode in a chariot pulled by a lion and a wild boar. (Apollo made the unlikely creatures pull together in friendship, out of respect for Harmonia, who was a goddess of peace and harmony.) The gods followed with presents: a dress woven by Athene and embroidered with stars like the night sky, a golden necklace made by Hephaistos which made its wearer the most beautiful woman in the world, and from Demeter the gift of fruitful harvest. The gods sat on golden thrones set up in the future market-place of Thebes; Zeus himself sat next to Kadmos, as a sign of special honour. While the guests feasted, the Fates sang a wedding-song, one line of which is still remembered as a proverb: 'What is beautiful is forever dear'.

CHRYSIPPOS (*page 158*)

In some versions of the myth, Laios took Chrysippos safely all the way back to Thebes, and set him up in the palace as his lover. Chrysippos' step-mother, queen Hippodameia, saw her chance to get rid of both Laios and Chrysippos, and so remove any chance that they might inherit King Pelops' throne instead of her own sons Atreus and Thyestes. She went secretly with her sons to Thebes, and tried to persuade them to murder Chrysippos by throwing him down a well, and then to blame Laios. They refused, and so she herself crept at night into Chrysippos' bedroom and stabbed him with Laios' sword. She left the sword stuck in the wound to incriminate Laios; but unfortunately for her Chrysippos lived long enough to say

who had really murdered him. Hippodameia fled; Pelops divorced and disowned her, and she committed suicide.

PERIBOIA AND OEDIPUS (*page 159*)

In one version of the story, Oedipus was not left to die on Mount Kithairon. Instead, Laios floated him out to sea in a wooden box. It drifted to land near Corinth, to a beach where Queen Periboia and her slaves were laundering clothes. Periboia picked up the baby, hid behind some bushes, cried and screamed as if giving birth, and then produced Oedipus as her own baby son.

This story is highly unlikely. In the first place, Thebes is nowhere near the coast (it is fifty kilometres inland). Secondly, if Oedipus had spent days or weeks bobbing in the wooden box, why did no one in Corinth notice that he was too old to be Periboia's newborn child? And thirdly, what is the point, if this story is preferred, of his name Oidipous (Swollen-foot)?

THE END OF OEDIPUS
(*page 162*)

The details of Oedipus' life in Thebes (see page 160) are known chiefly from Sophocles' play *King Oedipus*. (In that, Oedipus does not live on in Thebes after he blinds himself, but goes straight into banishment, leaving Jokasta's brother Kreon in charge while his sons Eteokles and Polyneikes grow up.) In Homer's *Odyssey* only Oedipus' wife-mother dies (and she is called Epikaste, not Iokaste or Jokasta); after she hangs herself, although the Furies torment Oedipus for causing both his father's and his mother's deaths, he lives on as king of

Thebes until he dies in battle and is buried with royal honours.

In another play, *Oedipus at Kolonos*, Sophocles tells of the end of Oedipus' life. He wandered about Greece for years, a blind beggar tormented by the Furies and guided by his daughter Antigone. At last he came to Athens, where the Delphic oracle had foretold that his life would end. King Theseus welcomed him in a grove of trees at Kolonos on the outskirts of the city. This place was a crossroads between the upper world and the Underworld, one of the entrances to Hades' kingdom, and here, to the accompaniment of supernatural voices and peals of thunder from below the earth, Oedipus passed at last from mortal sight.

POLYNEIKES AND TYDEUS (*page 162*)

King Adrastos of Argos was eager to help Polyneikes because of an oracle from Delphi. He had two daughters, Aigeia and Deiphyla, and asked the oracle who their husbands were to be. The oracle answered 'A lion and a wild boar'. Adrastos was baffled by this until two strangers arrived at his palace: Polyneikes prince of Thebes and Tydeus prince of Kalydon. Each was the child of an incestuous marriage: Polyneikes' father Oedipus had slept with his own mother; Tydeus' father Oineus had slept with his own daughter. Each had left his native land after a quarrel with his brother (Tydeus in fact had killed his brother Melanippos). Each was a powerful warrior, heir to a great kingdom. On each of their shields was painted the sacred animal of their cities: a lion for Thebes and a wild boar for Kalydon. Adrastos realised that these were the husbands the Delphic oracle meant; he married Aigeia to Polyneikes and Deiphyla to Tydeus, and promised to help each of them win the throne of his native country.

AMPHIARAOS AND ERIPHYLE
(*page 162*)

Amphiaraos was extremely reluctant to take part in the expedition of the Seven against Thebes. He was a prophet, able to foresee the future, and he knew that the expedition would fail and that he himself would not survive. But some time before, he had quarrelled with his brother-in-law Adrastos, and his wife (Adrastos' sister) Eriphyle had prevented them fighting and killing each other. In gratitude each of them had promised, by the gods, to consult her in every matter of life and death and to follow whatever advice she gave.

When Polyneikes heard from Adrastos about this promise, he bribed Eriphyle with Harmonia's golden necklace to say that Amphiaraos should join the expedition – and Amphiaraos, who could not break his promise to the gods, had no choice but to go along. (The reason it was easy to bribe Eriphyle was that she was afraid of growing old and ugly, and one of the benefits of Harmonia's necklace was that it gave its wearer lifelong beauty.)

ARCHEMOROS; THE NEMEAN
GAMES (*page 163*)

Often, to ward off bad luck, people were given nicknames exactly the opposite of what was wanted for them. (For example, if you wanted your child to grow up straight-backed and strong you might nickname him 'Humpback', so that the spirits of bad luck would think him already deformed and pass him by.) For the same reason, after baby Opheltes was killed by the snake, Amphiaraos gave him the nickname Archemoros (Beginner of Death), hoping in this way to make his death the last the expedition would see. (Unfortunately, the gods were not taken in: the expedition was still doomed.)

At the funeral games for Opheltes-Archemoros there were seven events (each won by one of the seven champions): a foot-race, a horse-race, a chariot-race, boxing, wrestling, archery and discus-throwing. These became the chief events of the Nemean Games, held every two years in the place where Opheltes died. They began with a speech in Opheltes' memory; the judges always wore funeral clothes; the winners were given, instead of olive-crowns, wreaths of wild parsley, the herb of death.

ANTIGONE AND HAIMON (*page 164*)

Sophocles based his play *Antigone* on the events in Thebes after the deaths of Eteokles and Polyneikes. He discarded an earlier part of the legend, that Kreon's son Haimon was one of the children killed by the Sphinx (see page 160), and instead imagined him grown-up and about to marry Antigone. When Kreon passed his law forbidding burial of the Argive dead, Haimon stood up to him and begged him to change his mind; but Kreon refused and imprisoned Antigone, who then hanged herself. When Haimon found her dead body, he stabbed himself to death.

In another version of the myth, when Kreon found that Antigone had buried Polyneikes, he ordered Haimon to bury her alive in her brother's grave. Haimon pretended to agree, but actually sent Antigone (whom he had already married, and who was pregnant) to live with shepherds on Mount Kithairon. Antigone bore a son, and when he grew up he went to Thebes to take part in an athletics contest. Kreon recognised the serpent-birthmark which only Kadmos' descendants carried, and executed him – and Haimon, driven mad by grief, killed Antigone and committed suicide. (This stagy story may have been invented by Euripides for his play *Antigone*, now lost. He was fond of rewriting legends in unexpected ways: in his *Phoenicians*, for example, Oedipus and Jokasta are still alive, and living in Thebes, at the time of the attack by the seven champions.)

ALKMAION (*page 165*)

The story of the bribing of Eriphyle (see page 255) was repeated in the legend of Amphiaraos' son Alkmaion. Like his father, he was reluctant to join the other Argives in an expedition against Thebes, but left the decision to his mother Eriphyle. Polyneikes' son Thesandros bribed her, this time with Harmonia's golden dress, and she chose war. So Alkmaion led the Epigonoi in their attack on Thebes.

Alkmaion knew nothing of the bribery until Thesandros boasted about it after the fall of Thebes. He asked the Delphic oracle what the punishment was for a woman who took gold to send her husband and son to war, and the oracle answered 'Death'. Alkmaion murdered his mother, and the Furies drove him mad for it (as they later did Orestes: see page 205). He wandered all over Greece in search of purification. King Phegeus of Psophis helped him, and in gratitude he married Phegeus' daughter Arsinoë and gave her Harmonia's golden dress and necklace. But then the Furies returned, and he forgot Arsinoë and began his wanderings again. Before she died Eriphyle had cursed him, saying that he would never find purification on any land then existing. The gods guided him to a patch of new land, sand washed down since Eriphyle's death by the river Acheloös; Alkmaion was purified from madness, and married the river-god's daughter Kallirhoë.

Alkmaion and Kallirhoë had two baby sons. But then, like Eriphyle before her, Kallirhoë began to fear that she would grow ugly as she grew older. She refused to sleep with Alkmaion unless he gave her Harmonia's dress and necklace. Alkmaion had to go to Psophis and steal them from Arsinoë, the wife he had long ago abandoned – and on the way home he was ambushed by Phegeus' sons and killed. Arsinoë, now truly a widow, cursed Phegeus and her brothers, and prayed to the gods to kill them before the next moon waned. Phegeus locked her in a box and sold her into slavery.

Meanwhile, word reached Kallirhoë of Alkmaion's death, and she prayed to Zeus that her baby sons might grow to manhood in a single day and avenge him. Zeus granted her prayer: the babies jumped out of their cradle, turned into grown men before they touched the ground, went to Psophis and killed Phegeus and his sons. Harmonia's golden dress and necklace were given for safety to the priests of Apollo, and lay for centuries in one of the treasuries at Delphi.

PRIAM'S CHILDREN (page 168)

Priam's only child by his wife Arisbe was Aisakos. He fell in love with Asterope, daughter of the river-god Kebrenos. But she died, and in his grief he tried time and time again to commit suicide by throwing himself from a high cliff into the sea. Each time, however, his river father-in-law Kebrenos caught him and saved his life. Finally the gods turned Aisakos into a gannet: to this day his descendants gather on high cliffs and plummet ceaselessly into the sea below.

Priam's daughters by his wife Hekabe included Kreousa, Laodike, Polyxena and Kassandra. Apollo fell in love with Kassandra, and offered her the gift of prophecy if she slept with him. Kassandra agreed, but as soon as he gave her prophecy refused to keep her part of the bargain. Apollo cursed her with a second gift: although all her prophecies were fated to be true, no one would ever believe a word of them. From then on until her death in Mycenae (see page 271), Kassandra continually forecast the fall of Troy and the death of many heroes, and for her pains everyone ignored her or called her mad.

Priam's and Hekabe's fifty sons included the prophets Helenos (Kassandra's twin) and Laokoön, the heroes Antiphos, Deiphobos, Hektor, Pammon, Paris and Polites, all of whom fought at Troy, Antenor who betrayed Troy to the Greeks (see page 177), and Polydoros (whose story is told on page 265).

ANCHISES AND APHRODITE
(page 168)

Prince Anchises of Troy was one of the handsomest of mortal men, a rival even to Paris. One night, when he was sleeping in a cave on Mount Ida after a hunting expedition, Aphrodite visited him and made love to him. She made him promise to tell no one; but Anchises could not resist boasting, and Zeus threw a thunderbolt and crippled him. Aphrodite's and Anchises' son Aeneas grew up to be as handsome and princely as his father. After the fall of Troy, Aphrodite guided Aeneas and his followers south, and after many adventures they landed in Italy and founded the settlement which later gave birth to Rome.

PARIS (*page 168*)

On the night before Paris was born, his mother Hekabe dreamed that she gave birth not to a human child but to a blazing torch whose flames engulfed all Troy. The prophets advised Priam to have the baby killed at birth, and Priam gave the job to his herdsman Agelaos, and told him to bring back the child's tongue as proof that he was dead. Agelaos left baby Paris to die on Mount Ida, but when he came back next day found him alive and well, being suckled by a she-bear. Impressed by this sign of the gods' favour, he took Priam a dog's tongue to make him think the baby was dead, and brought Paris up as his own son.

When Paris grew up he married the mountain-nymph Oinone, and together they herded Agelaos' cattle on the mountainside. On one occasion, Ares disguised himself as a bull and fought a locked-horns contest with Paris' prize bull. Paris awarded bull-Ares the prize, and it was this proof of his good judgement that made Zeus choose him to decide the contest of beauty between the goddesses.

Soon after the Judgement of Paris, his father Priam sent for a choice bull for sacrifice at a lavish funeral games. Paris himself drove his bull into Troy, competed in the games and won. Priam's sons attacked him and would have killed him; but Agelaos ran to Priam and told him who Paris really was. Priam was so delighted with his new-found son that he welcomed him back to Troy, and ignored the prophets who warned him that if Paris lived Troy must die.

PARIS AND HELEN (*page 168*)

One reason why Paris found it so easy to steal Helen from Sparta was that King Menelaos was away from the city when he arrived (at the funeral of his grandfather Katreus, in Crete). As well as Helen, Paris stole half the treasure in Sparta, including gold from Apollo's temple – and so hardened the hatred for Troy already in most gods' hearts.

When Hera saw Paris and Helen far out to sea, her anger at Paris (whom she had never forgiven for not judging her the most beautiful of the three goddesses) overflowed and she sent a storm to drown him. As his death would have prevented the Trojan war before it started, Aphrodite snatched his ship from danger and beached it on her sacred island, Cyprus. From Cyprus Paris and Helen sailed to Egypt and Phoenicia, and from there to Troy.

In one version of the myth, King Proteus of Egypt arrested them there, sent Paris packing and kept Helen safe until his friend King Menelaos could come and fetch her. At this the gods, fearing once again that there would be no Trojan war, made a phantom Helen out of cloud and sent it to Troy at Paris' side. (Thus, when the Greeks attacked Troy, they were fighting not for a real woman but for a shadow.) Helen stayed in Egypt for the entire ten years of the war, and then Menelaos went there and rescued her. (Euripides used this version of the story in his play *Helen*.)

ACHILLES' CHILDHOOD (*page 169*)

Achilles was the son of Peleus and Thetis. He was brought up, like many other heroes, by the centaur Cheiron, who taught him to ride, shoot and hunt, as well as the arts of music and medicine. He was nine years old when Thetis heard an oracle that he would either die young and gloriously at Troy or would live at home to an inglorious but ripe old age. She chose the second alternative, disguised Achilles as a girl and hid him on Skyros. Achilles (whose girl's name was Pyrrha – Fiery – after his red hair) lived on Skyros for ten years; he even married Princess Deidamia and had a son, Neoptolemos. But every time visitors arrived, he had to put on a dress and hide in the women's quarters. It was hardly a hero's life; no wonder that when the chance came Achilles preferred the oracle's first alternative, an early but noble death, and chose to reveal who he was and go to Troy.

The men Achilles led at Troy were Myrmidons, sons of the ant-soldiers Zeus made for his father Peleus (see page 226). His closest companion was Patroklos, son of King Menoitios of Opos: Patroklos killed a man in an argument, took refuge with Achilles' father, and he and Achilles became inseparable friends. (Later in the war, it was Patroklos' death which ended Achilles' quarrel with Agamemnon and brought him back into the fighting: see page 174.)

THE SIZE OF THE GREEK FLEET (*page 169*)

Ever since Greek times there has been argument about how many ships sailed for Troy. In Book 2 of Homer's *Iliad* a precise number is given (1,186), with details of how many ships each Greek state

sent; later writers fixed the number as between 1,000 and 1,200. But this is an enormous force (involving at least 100,000 men), quite unlike any of the other armies or expeditions of heroic times.

The various accounts of kings being reluctant to sail to Troy at all, and especially stories like that of Kinyras' model boats (see page 169), suggest a different explanation: that there were far more promises than actual ships, and that the fleet which finally sailed was only a fraction of the numbers originally planned. Not only that, but some accounts tell of two separate voyages. The first expedition ran into storms and was driven off course to Mysia (where the battle with King Telephos was fought: see page 260). After this, many Greek kings went home in disgust, and Agamemnon and Menelaos had to go round Greece again trying to raise a second expedition. It was this second fleet – probably much smaller than the first – which set out after the sacrifice of Iphigeneia, and after a ten-year siege finally conquered Troy. (How many ships and men did it contain? No one knows. Homer mentions by name over 70 individual princes and heroes, and if each of them had an average of 20 followers, this suggests an army of no more than 1,400 and a fleet of some 50 ships. But these figures, like all others from the Trojan war, are guesswork.)

AUGE AND TELEPHOS (*page 169*)

The Delphic oracle told King Aleus of Tegea that his daughter Auge would bear a son who would one day murder two of his own relatives. To prevent this, he made Auge a priestess of Athene, forbidden to sleep with men. But one day the god Herakles visited Tegea, drank too much and raped Auge. Athene sent plague on the city, and refused to lift it until Auge was sent away. So Auge was locked in a wooden chest and floated out to sea. Athene guided the chest to Mysia in Asia Minor, where King Teuthras opened it, found Auge and her newborn son and gave them refuge.

In another version, Auge was taken from Tegea to be sold into slavery. On the way she gave birth, and left the baby to die on Mount Parthenios. He was suckled by a doe and survived. (The name Telephos means 'Doe's nursling'.) He grew up to be the foster-son of King Korythos, and later rescued his mother from slavery (in Mysia, to King Teuthras), and went for vengeance to Tegea, where he fulfilled the oracle by killing not his grandfather Aleus, but Aleus' brothers Hippothoös and Neleos.

Later, when the Greeks passed through Mysia on their way to Troy, Telephos (now its king) fought them and was wounded by Achilles. An oracle told him that only what had wounded him would heal him, so he limped all the way to Troy and came before Achilles dressed as a lame beggar. He snatched Orestes, Agamemnon's baby son, and threatened to kill him unless he was cured. (This part of the story was made into a play, *Telephos*, by Euripides, and made fun of in Aristophanes' comedy *The Acharnians*.) Achilles agreed to help, and (on Odysseus' advice) took filings from his spear and made a poultice from them to bandage Telephos' leg. So what wounded Telephos also cured him, and the second oracle was fulfilled.

PHILOKTETES (*page 170*)

In another version of the myth, Philoktetes' foot was poisoned not by a snake but by one of Herakles' arrows. Herakles gave Philoktetes his bow and arrows as a reward for lighting his funeral pyre (see page 140), but on condition that he kept them secret and told no one how he had become such a skilful archer. The Greeks thought that the arrows had been buried with Herakles – and when they heard that unless they found them they would never take Troy, they asked Philoktetes to show them Herakles' grave. At first he refused, but finally gave way and stamped his foot on the ground over the place where Herakles' ashes lay. The stamping dislodged an arrow from his quiver, and it stabbed his foot and poisoned it. Even so, despite his agony, he refused to part with the arrows or the bow – and the Greeks were too afraid of Herakles' divine anger to take them by force. So they left Philoktetes on Lemnos to survive as best he could.

PROTESILAOS AND LAODAMIA
(*page 170*)

Protesilaos, the first Greek killed in the Trojan war, was a prince of Thessaly. The call to join the expedition came on the very day of his marriage, and he was forced to leave his young wife Laodamia and sail at once for Troy. After he left she was so lonely, and so much in love, that she had a wax statue made of him and held it in her arms every night until she fell asleep. When news came of Protesilaos' death she begged the gods to let her see him just once more, if only for a moment, and Hades released Protesilaos' ghost from the Underworld for just three hours. It crept into the statue, and shared with Laodamia three hours of love. Then it asked her to hurry after it to the Underworld, and disappeared. Laodamia built a funeral pyre and laid the wax statue on it; when the pyre was alight she stabbed herself, threw herself into the flames, and so went to join her beloved husband in the Underworld.

ACHILLES, TENES AND KYKNOS
(*page 170*)

Achilles' mother Thetis warned him never to fight any of Apollo's children, in case he killed them and roused Apollo's rage. Whenever Achilles went into battle, his servant Mnemon (Reminder) stood beside him to make sure he remembered this advice. But when Achilles swam ashore at Tenedos (see page 170), Mnemon lagged behind, and before he could shout a warning Achilles killed Tenes, Apollo's rock-throwing son. To pacify Apollo, Achilles built a temple in Tenes' honour and executed Mnemon. But Apollo was not satisfied, and throughout the war looked for every possible way to bring about Achilles' death.

Kyknos was Poseidon's son, and no mortal weapon could pierce or bruise his skin. He was famous for his cruelty. When his second wife Phylonome accused her stepson Tenes (who was Apollo's son by Kyknos' first wife, brought up as Kyknos' child) of rape, he floated Tenes in a leaky boat out to sea, where it drifted safely to Tenedos. Then, when Kyknos discovered that his wife's accusation was actually a lie (her revenge when Tenes refused to sleep with her), Kyknos buried her alive and went to Tenedos to ask Tenes' pardon. Tenes drove him away with a shower of stones. Kyknos went to defend Troy; Tenes stayed at Tenedos, hurling rocks at anyone who tried to land, until Achilles killed him (see paragraph above).

When the Greeks reached Troy, Kyk-nos was one of the leaders of the Trojans who tried to drive them off (see page 170). Achilles fought him with spear and sword: in vain, thanks to Tenes' invulnerable skin. In the end Achilles tripped him up and strangled him with his own helmet-straps. Poseidon changed Kyknos into a swan (*kyknos* is Greek for swan – and swans still have difficulty uttering sounds, because of Achilles' squeezing of Kyknos' throat), and thereafter joined with Apollo in plotting Achilles' death.

ACHILLES, PENTHESILEIA AND THERSITES (*page 170*)

One of the fiercest Trojan allies was Penthesileia, queen of the Amazons (sister of Hippolyte, whom Herakles killed: see page 132). She was Ares' daughter, and killed every Greek she fought. At last she came up against Achilles: the all-conquering daughter of a god was matched against the goddess' son no mortal weapons could harm. The duel was hard and long, but in the end Penthesileia's skill exhausted even Achilles. He dropped his guard for a moment; she stabbed him and he fell dying. Quickly Achilles' mother Thetis ran to Zeus and begged for Achilles' life, and Zeus made Achilles recover from his wound so fast that before Penthesileia could straighten up or defend herself he jumped to his feet and stabbed her.

Achilles fell on his knees and took dying Penthesileia in his arms: enemy or not, she had fought bravely and deserved respect. At this Thersites (an ugly, jeering man despised by most of the Greek army) said 'Why don't you rape her while you're at it?', and gouged out Penthesileia's eyes with his spear-point. Achilles punched him so hard that he broke all his teeth, smashed his jaw-bone and sent his soul whining down to the Underworld. The other Greeks, horrified that Achilles should kill even one of his most despised countrymen for the sake of an enemy, threw Penthesileia's body into the river Scamander; but Achilles dived in, rescued it and gave it honourable burial on the river-bank.

HEKTOR AND AIAS (*page 172*)

After the gods prevented single-handed combat between Paris and Menelaos, and massed fighting began, Hektor and Aias fought a day-long duel. In the evening, when it was too dark to see, they politely agreed that neither should be counted the winner, exchanged presents and retreated to their own camp-fires. Hektor gave Aias a sword; Aias gave Hektor a sword-belt of purple leather. The Fates were watching, and later saw to it that these presents were involved in each hero's death. (See pages 174 and 263.)

RHESOS' HORSES (*page 172*)

The hero Rhesos was a Trojan ally, a Thracian, the son of Ares and the Muse Kalliope. He owned a team of white horses, swift as the wind; the oracle said that if they once ate Trojan hay and drank water from the river Scamander, neither gods nor men would ever capture Troy. Odysseus and Diomedes knew of this oracle, and had heard rumours that Rhesos and his Thracians had just arrived and were camped not far from Troy. When they left Achilles after trying to persuade him to take Briseis back, they found out where Rhesos' camp was from a Trojan spy,

Dolon. They crept there in the darkness, killed Rhesos and set his horses free to gallop wherever they chose. So Rhesos never reached Troy, the horses never ate Trojan hay and the oracle was not fulfilled.

ACHILLES' SHIELD (*page 174*)

Book 18 of Homer's *Iliad* contains a description of Hephaistos making Achilles' armour, and of the scenes he engraved on the shield. Around its rim he pictured the river of Ocean, and inside that the circle of the universe, the sun, moon, earth, stars and constellations. The inner rings of the decoration showed scenes from mortal life: a wedding, a lawsuit, a battle, animals grazing, men ploughing, sowing and harvesting, a sacrifice and a village dance complete with minstrel and acrobats.

ACHILLES AND POLYXENA
(*page 174*)

One of Priam's daughters, Polyxena, often went up on to the Trojan battlements to watch the fighting, and Achilles saw her and fell in love. When the Trojans were ransoming Hektor's body, all Priam's treasure was exhausted before the scales balanced, and Polyxena gave Achilles her golden ear-rings to make up the weight. At this, Achilles admiringly offered Priam Hektor's body and all the treasure back, in exchange for Polyxena's hand in marriage – and as a result of this remark, the story spread that Priam had offered him Polyxena if he deserted the Greeks and fought for Troy. Many Greeks regarded Achilles from then on as a traitor, and when he was finally killed rejoiced at his death.

262

Another version of the myth says that Polyxena hated Achilles for killing her brother Troilos (see page 171), and pretended to admire him in order to trap him and kill him. She took him into Troy at night, slept with him – and wheedled out of him the secret of his immortal skin and its one vulnerable place, his heel. Then she arranged for Priam to invite Achilles to marry her; Paris was hiding behind the altar, and when Achilles came to the wedding stabbed him in the heel and killed him.

The Greeks did not forget Polyxena's treachery. After Troy was captured, they gave her as prisoner-of-war to Achilles' son Neoptolemos, and he sacrificed her and poured her blood as an offering on his father's grave.

MEMNON (page 175)

Memnon was the son of Tithonos, the mortal prince whom Eos loved (see page 218). His father had long ago emigrated to Assyria in Asia, and it was from there that Memnon was sent to Troy. He took an army of 2,000 men and 200 war-chariots. On the march westwards to Troy, he conquered every nation he pass-ed through, and built a straight, paved road with a fort every 20 kilometres. His arrival at Troy would have been catas-trophic for the Greeks if Achilles had not been there; but as soon as Achilles killed him (see page 175) his army gathered his body, burned it and marched home with his ashes. His many wives and mistress-es wept so bitterly over his grave that the gods turned them into hens (of the kind the Greeks called *Memnonides*, 'Memnon's little ones'); the goddess Eos still weeps for him, and her tears form dew on the morning grass.

AIAS' MADNESS (page 175)

After Achilles' death, his son Neop-tolemos was too young to wear the armour made by Hephaistos, and so Thetis offered it to the bravest Greek hero still alive. Everyone agreed that the choice was between Aias (who carried Achilles' body back from the walls of Troy) and Odysseus (who protected him against the Trojans while he did so). Agamemnon chose Odysseus – and the humiliation of being rejected sent Aias mad. He buckled on his own armour, snatched up the sword Hektor had given him (see page 262) and went to butcher the Greek leaders in their beds. But all he attacked, in his madness, was a flock of sheep; when his wits came back and he found himself surrounded by their blood-soaked carcasses, he stuck Hek-tor's sword point-upwards in the ground and fell on it, trying to commit suicide. At first the point would not pierce his skin (which Herakles had long ago made immortal: see page 249). But his repeated efforts bent the sword into a bow-shape, and its point slipped upwards into his one vulnerable part (his armpit) and pierced his heart. Years later, when Odysseus visited the Underworld and met all his dead companions from the Trojan war (see page 186), Aias' ghost, still blazing with rage because of Achil-les' armour, refused to speak to him.

The story of Aias' madness is told in Sophocles' play *Aias*.

PHILOKTETES AND NEOPTOLEMOS (page 175)

In Sophocles' play *Philoktetes*, Odysseus goes to Lemnos to bring back Philoktetes not with Diomedes but with Achilles' son Neoptolemos. Neoptolemos is hot with anger because Odysseus has his father's armour, and refuses to help Odysseus persuade Philoktetes back to Troy. In the end the god Herakles appears, tells Philoktetes his destiny is to topple Troy, and persuades both him and Neoptolemos to go with Odysseus.

STEALING THE PALLADION
(*page 177*)

After the fall of Troy, Helen and Odysseus – two of the most cunning tricksters in Greece – concocted a different story from the usual one about stealing the Palladion. It left out Diomedes and gave them all the credit. They said that Odysseus dressed himself in beggar's rags and made Diomedes flog his back raw; then, unrecognisable, he tricked his way into Troy by pretending to be a runaway slave who had escaped the Greeks. Only Helen saw through his disguise. She had never wanted to go to Troy in the first place, but was kidnapped by Paris and kept there against her will. She was only too eager to escape, and now she showed Odysseus the Palladion, helped him steal it and saw him safely out of Troy. (Helen herself tells part of this self-flattering tale in Book 4 of Homer's *Odyssey*; in Euripides' play *Hekabe*, which is about what happened to Polyxena after the fall of Troy (see page 180), Odysseus refers to it as if it was fact.)

In still another version of the myth, Odysseus and Diomedes climbed over the walls instead of using the drain (see page 177). When they were walking back with the statue in the moonlight, Odysseus crept up behind Diomedes (who was carrying the Palladion) to kill him and take all the credit. But Diomedes disarmed him and forced him to carry the Palladion back to the Greek camp, kicking and beating him as if he was a

slave. (This version was told by the Romans, who also claimed that the Palladion Odysseus and Diomedes stole was a wooden replica: the real Palladion was kept safe in Troy until Aeneas took it to Italy, where it was one of the main sacred relics in the settlement which gave birth to Rome.)

HELEN AND THE
WOODEN HORSE (*page 179*)

Several myths tell of the anxious time spent by the Greek heroes inside the wooden horse. They could hear every word said outside, including the proposal to take the horse to the shore and burn it (see page 178). When Laokoön threw his spear (see page 178), the blade went straight through the wooden belly and stuck a hair's-breadth from Neoptolemos' head. As the horse was dragged into Troy they were jolted, rolled and bruised, and constantly threatened with discovery because of the whimpering of the coward Epeios. But their worst moment of all came when the horse was inside the city. Helen walked round it with her husband Deiphobos (see page 176), stroking it and patting it – and she began telling Deiphobos about the wives of each of the hidden heroes, imitating their voices and the way they talked. Several of the heroes thought their wives were really there, and groaned and sweated to think that they were prisoners in Troy. One man, Antielos, was even about to call out when Odysseus grabbed him by the throat to silence him (some say so fiercely that he broke his neck).

LITTLE AIAS AND KASSANDRA
(*page 180*)

There were two Greek heroes at Troy called Aias (or Ajax, in the alternative form of the name). One of them, Aias son of Telamon, went mad and committed suicide when he was not given Achilles' armour (see page 263). The other, Aias son of Oineus, was nicknamed 'Little Aias' to distinguish him from the first one, and also because of his size.

During the sack of Troy, Little Aias found Kassandra in Athene's temple, clinging for safety to the holy statue. He dragged her out by force, and pulled the statue from its pedestal; this brought down on him Athene's rage. Kassandra was allotted to Agamemnon as spoils-of-war, and Athene borrowed one of Zeus' thunderbolts and blasted Aias dead. His soldiers took his ashes home and buried them on the island of Mykonos.

Even then, Athene was not satisfied. She sent plague on Aias' home city, and only lifted it when the people agreed to send two girls to her temple in Troy – the new Troy, the village built from the ruins of the great city sacked by the Greeks – each year for a thousand years. The girls had to climb secretly into the village – often they used the same drain as Odysseus and Diomedes had when they stole the Palladion (see page 177) – make offerings in Athene's temple and then become temple slaves. If they were caught before they reached the temple, they were stoned to death.

MENELAOS AND HELEN (page 180)

There are several versions of what happened between Menelaos and Helen after the fall of Troy. Some say that he stormed with Odysseus through the burning city to find her and kill her. They burst into Deiphobos' house, killed Deiphobos and tracked Helen to her bedroom. Menelaos lifted his sword to stab her; but she bared her breasts and

smiled, and the sight of her beauty filled him with such love that he threw down his sword, forgave her everything and took her back to Sparta to live happily ever afterwards as his queen.

In another account (the one which says that Helen never went to Troy at all, but stayed in Egypt while the gods sent a spirit-Helen with Paris in her place: see page 258), Menelaos searched the ruins of Troy for Helen, in vain. He set sail broken-hearted, deprived both of revenge and of his wife, and was blown off-course by storms. He wandered for eight years, and finally arrived in Egypt after advice from the Old Man of the Sea (see page 64). He found Helen waiting, forgave her and took her back to Sparta.

What was the end of Helen's life? Some accounts say that after a long, contented reign she and Menelaos died at the same moment and still enjoy harmonious marriage in the Underworld. Others link her death with the story of Orestes. Either she went with Menelaos to the country of the Taurians (see page 270) and Iphigeneia killed them there, or else Orestes was ordered, at his trial in Athens, to kill Helen and so end the chain of destruction and death she had caused in Greece. He fought a fierce battle with Menelaos; Apollo ended it by saying that Helen had been taken from earth to Olympos, and given the task of helping her brothers Kastor and Polydeukes (see page 230) protect sailors lost at sea.

POLYDOROS (page 180)

Polydoros, the youngest of Priam's and Hekabe's fifty sons, was a tiny child when the Trojan war began. To ensure his safety, Hekabe sent him away to be brought up by her sister Ilione, whose husband Polymnestor was king of a small but distant kingdom. Some accounts say that the Greeks found out where Polydoros was, kidnapped him, offered to exchange him for Helen, and when Priam refused butchered the baby before his eyes. Another version of the myth says that Polydoros grew up happily until the fall of Troy. Then the Greeks ordered his step-father Polymnestor to kill him (since oracles had foretold that if he lived he would avenge his father's death). Polymnestor, afraid to commit the crime of killing a child he had promised in the gods' names to protect, committed the even greater crime of murdering his own son instead and pretending he was Polydoros. When Polydoros grew up he punished Polymnestor for this murder by blinding him and then killing him. In still another account, Priam gave Polymnestor half his treasure to look after the child; but Polymnestor stole the treasure, killed the baby and threw his corpse into the sea. Its bones were washed up ten years later on the shore at Troy, and it was when Hekabe saw them that she went mad and began to rage at Odysseus (see page 180).

THE GREEKS RETURN HOME
(page 180)

The fall of Troy was not the end of the deaths caused by the war. The gods had suffering still in store for many of the victorious Greeks. Agamemnon, their leader, was murdered by his wife and her lover (see page 202); Menelaos spent eight years wandering the southern seas; Mopsos and Amphilochos fought for the same kingdom, killed each other and became joint voices in a prophetic oracle; Diomedes, Idomeneus, Philoktetes and many lesser kings found that their thrones had been taken by others while they were away, and were forced to

wander the world, strangers everywhere, until they died. Neoptolemos and his Trojan wife Andromache built a city near Zeus' oracle at Dodona, and lived there peaceably for a time. But then the heroic madness inherited from Achilles his father clouded Neoptolemos' mind and he attacked the Delphic oracle (at the same time as Orestes was there, trying to escape from the Furies: see page 206). The priestess shouted for help, and one of the temple priests killed Neoptolemos with the sacrificial knife.

The greatest ordeals of all were reserved for the greatest hero of all: Odysseus. The story of his return from Troy, and of what he found when he reached home at last, is told in Chapter 18.

ODYSSEUS, AUTOLYKOS AND PENELOPE (page 181)

Odysseus' real father was the arch-trickster Sisyphos, who raped the daughter of Autolykos on the day of her marriage to King Laertes of Ithaka (see page 238). Autolykos too was a clever trickster, and managed to persuade Laertes to bring Odysseus up as his own son, and to make him prince of Ithaka. When Odysseus was eighteen he went to visit Autolykos and thank him; they went hunting, and Odysseus was gored in the thigh by a boar. (The scar from this wound later helped his old nurse Eurykleia to recognise him despite Athene's disguise: see page 268.)

There are two stories of how Penelope got her name. Her original name was Arnaia (Lamb-like). One myth says that her father wanted a son, not a daughter, and when she was born he threw her into the sea to drown. But she was rescued by a flock of ducks, and her father was so impressed by the omen that he spared her life and changed her name to Penelope (after *Penelops*, the word for duck). The second myth fits the story of her weaving Laertes' shroud (see page 181): it connects her name with the word *pēnē*, which means the thread carried by the shuttle across a loom.

WINESKINS (*page 182*)

Most of the Greek commanders sailed south-west after the fall of Troy (see page 180), across the open sea towards the Greek mainland. But Odysseus sailed north, to Kikonia in Thrace. He sacked the city of Ismaros, and added its treasure to the booty already in his ships. The only place he left standing was Apollo's temple – and in gratitude its priest, Maro, gave him several skins of the darkest and strongest wine ever made on earth. (This was the wine which Odysseus later gave to Polyphemos: see page 183.) Odysseus and his men would have pressed further inland, sacking and looting; but the hill-tribesmen drove them back to the shore, killing many men. Hastily Odysseus embarked and sailed south – straight into the nine-day storm which drove him to the African coast and the country of the Lotos-eaters (see page 182).

POLYPHEMOS AND HIS RAM (*page 183*)

The story of the Cyclops is told in Book 9 of Homer's *Odyssey*, and in it Homer makes us feel more than just repulsion for Polyphemos: he may be a brainless, savage bully, but even so his plight is made pitiful as well as well-deserved. As the ram walks out of the cave, with Odysseus clinging for dear life underneath, Polyphemos speaks these ludicrous, touching words: 'What is it, ram, my pet? Why are you last out of the cave? I've never seen you lag behind before. You're always first to run out into the meadow and crop the soft grass, first to sip from the stream, first homeward-bound when evening comes. But today you're last. Are you crying for your master's eye, put out by that wicked man and his wicked crew, when he'd fuddled my wits with wine? Nobody, his name was, and he's not escaped me yet. If only you had a voice, you could tell me where he's hiding, and I'd show him my strength all right. I'd splatter his brains across the cave, till he'd eased my heart of all the pain he's caused me, that No-bloody-body that he is.'

MOLY (*page 185*)

No one knows exactly which plant moly was. Only the gods grew it or were allowed to pick it; mortals only ever saw it as a gift from heaven. It had white petals and a black stem and roots. Most herb-gardeners think that the nearest equivalents are wild cyclamen (which is very rare) or the kind of wild garlic called *allium moly*. (In the Middle Ages people thought garlic an excellent protection against witches, devils and other monstrous creatures: if you held out a clove of garlic to an approaching vampire, for example, there was a fair chance that he might turn and run.)

ODYSSEUS AND KIRKE (*page 185*)

Some accounts say that Odysseus stayed with Kirke not just for months but for several years, and that they even had three children together: Agrios, Latinos and Telegonos. But this clashes with the account that he later stayed with Kalypso for seven years (see page 188) – in ten years' wandering there was no time for both. It seems as if the myth-makers were as bemused by the gods' time-scale as Kirke's mortal guests. Even so, Telegonos is important in a later part of the myth, about Odysseus' death (see page 269).

ELPENOR (page 186)

In Book 11 of the *Odyssey*, Homer makes gentle fun of Elpenor, Odysseus' cabin-boy who died on Kirke's island. His sad end is touching, but also slightly ludicrous, and we smile even as we pity him. This is the sorrowful speech his ghost makes to Odysseus (see page 186): 'It was bad luck that finished me – that and too much wine. I'd been sleeping on Kirke's roof, and when I got up to come down I forgot to use the ladder. I fell off the roof and broke my neck, and my soul came down to the underworld. Oh please, in the name of all your dead companions, in the name of your wife, your father who looked after you when you were a little boy, your own son Telemachos whom you left alone at home, please don't forget me, please don't sail away and leave me here unburied and unwept. Don't risk the gods' anger. Bury me in my armour, such as it is, and pile a cairn of stones on the shore of the grey sea, so that future generations will all remember me. Set in it my oar, the one I pulled when I was alive beside my friends.'

EATING THE SUN'S CATTLE (page 188)

In Book 12 of the *Odyssey* Homer makes Odysseus' crewmen feed on the Sun's cattle for six whole days. The Sun knows nothing of it because his view is blotted out by a storm; but as soon as Zeus clears the sky the Sun sees that his cattle are dead, and attacks. Odysseus does nothing to help his men, and makes no offerings to appease the Sun: it is as if he resigns himself to the Fates' will, and accepts that Teiresias' prophecy in the Underworld (see page 186) must be exactly carried out.

POSEIDON AND THE PHAIAKIANS (page 189)

Although Poseidon could not prevent Odysseus' return to Ithaka, since it was the will of the Fates and of Zeus, he was in no mood to approve of anyone who gave Odysseus shelter or helped him on his way. When, therefore, the Phaiakian ship had landed Odysseus in Ithaka and turned for home, Poseidon struck it and its crew to stone: they can still be seen, like a small island just off the Ithakan coast. Poseidon then lifted a mountain-side to drop on King Alkinoös' Phaiakian city and smash the harbour; in the nick of time Alkinoös sacrificed a dozen white bulls (the most expensive sacrifice a mortal man could make) and soothed his rage.

ARGOS (page 190)

Disguised Odysseus was recognised only twice without the gods' help: once by his old nurse Eurykleia (who knew him by a hunting-scar on his thigh) and once by his faithful dog Argos. In Book 17 of the *Odyssey*, this is how Homer tells Argos' story: 'There was a dog lying there, and he pricked up his ears and lifted his head. He was Odysseus' own dog, Argos; he'd bred him long ago, but had to leave for Troy before he'd fully trained him. Other young men had taken Argos coursing hares and tracking wild goats. Now, with no master to care for him, he lay neglected on the dung-heap by the gate, where the dung from the farm animals was piled ready for Odysseus' farm-hands to spread on his wide fields. There the dog Argos lay, full of fleas. When he heard Odysseus near-by, he flattened his ears and wagged his tail. He lacked the strength, now, to get up and go to his master; and he had no sooner recognised Odysseus after twenty years than he gave himself up to death's dark hand.'

ODYSSEUS' DEATH (page 194)

Homer's *Odyssey* ends with the end of fighting in Ithaka. Other myth-tellers tidied up loose ends, in particular the ending of Poseidon's anger and the fulfilling of two prophecies: that Odysseus would be killed by his own son, and that his death would come from the sea.

To soothe Poseidon's anger, Odysseus had to leave Ithaka and wander the world until he found a people who had never seen or heard of the sea. If he sacrificed to Poseidon there, he would be set free from Poseidon's rage at last. He made Telemachos king of Ithaka and set off on his journey, carrying an oar across one shoulder. Everywhere he went, for ten years, people jeeringly asked 'Stranger, why are you carrying an oar so far inland?' At last he came to Thesprotia, deep in the countryside, and the people asked 'Stranger, why are you carrying that flail, so long before harvest-time?' He knew that this was the place where the sea was unknown, built an altar and sacrificed to Poseidon. (This part of Odysseus' wanderings is retold in a modern epic poem, *The Odyssey* by Nikos Kazantzakis, Secker & Warburg, Ltd, which begins where Homer ends.)

Safe at last from Poseidon's anger, Odysseus went back to Ithaka. Now he remembered the prophecy that his own son would kill him, and to prevent it sent Telemachos into exile. The death-dealing son, however, was not Telemachos at all, but Telegonos. He had been born to Kirke on Aiaia some months after Odysseus left the island; Odysseus had no idea of his existence, and Telegonos knew nothing of his father or where he lived. Telegonos set sail from Aiaia to find Odysseus, and landed with his sailors in Ithaka. Odysseus took them for pirates and ran to the shore to drive them off – and Telegonos fought him and killed him with a spear made from a sting-ray's spine. So the prophecies came true: Odysseus' death did come from the sea, and his own son did kill him. Telegonos married Penelope and became king of Ithaka; Telemachos went to find Kirke, married her and became king of Aiaia – and so every loose end was tied at last.

TANTALOS' CRIMES AND THEIR PUNISHMENT (page 195)

Feeding his son Pelops to the gods was Tantalos' greatest crime. But there were others too. He was a son of Zeus, welcome at feasts and banquets in Olympos – until he stole nectar and ambrosia and shared them with his mortal friends on earth. On another occasion he stole Zeus' golden guard-dog. This was made to guard baby Zeus in Crete (see page 6), and when Zeus grew up he placed it on guard in his temple in Dikte. Tantalos' friend Pandareos stole it and gave it to Tantalos to hide while the gods searched. (He rightly thought that they would never suspect a son of Zeus.) But when he tried to get the dog back from Tantalos, Tantalos swore by Zeus that he

269

had seen no such dog. The oath made Zeus suspicious; the dog was found and Tantalos and Pandareos were punished. Pandareos was turned to stone, and Zeus crushed Tantalos with a rock and hurled him headlong through the earth's crust to the Underworld.

In Tartaros, Tantalos was tied fast, and surrounded by luscious fruit and a pool of clear water; but whenever he tried to eat or drink they slipped out of reach, and he was left forever tantalized. The rock which had dashed him to the Underworld hung precariously overhead, perpetually half-slipping and threatening to crush him to even lower depths.

MYRTILOS (*page 196*)

Myrtilos was Hermes' son by Phaiethousa (one of the fifty daughters of Danaos: see page 92). After his death Hermes placed a constellation in the sky (Auriga, the Charioteer) in his memory.

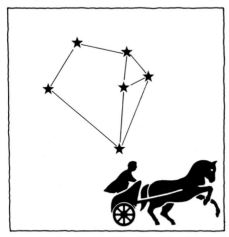

Constellation Auriga (The Charioteer)

Even though Myrtilos was remembered in this way, his body was lost at sea and was therefore never buried. His soul, de-nied rest in the Underworld, used to haunt the stadium at Olympia, and often caused chariot-accidents at the Olympic Games by looming out of the ground at the horses' feet.

IPHIGENEIA AMONG THE TAURIANS (*page 201*)

In one version of the legend (followed by Euripides in his play *Iphigeneia Among the Taurians*), Artemis relented at the last moment, and just as Kalchas' knife stabbed down to sacrifice Iphigeneia (see page 201), replaced her with a goat and hid her in a cloud. The Greeks sacrificed the goat, thinking it was Iphigeneia; the cloud carried Iphigeneia herself far away, to the country of the Taurians on the northern coast of the Black Sea. These savages sacrificed strangers to Artemis, and now Artemis made Iphigeneia her chief priestess, in charge of this bloodthirsty custom.

Years later, when Orestes was wandering the world in punishment for killing his mother, the Delphic oracle sent him, with Pylades, to steal the statue of Artemis from the Taurians' temple: if they brought it safely back, the oracle said, Orestes would be freed from his madness. They landed in the Taurians' country, and King Thoas ordered Iphigeneia to follow the custom and sacrifice them. But she heard them speaking Greek, and realised from what they said that Orestes was her baby brother, now grown-up. Instead of sacrificing them, she helped them to kill Thoas, steal the statue and sail away. They were driven far and wide by storms, and finally landed at Brauron, near Athens. Here Athene ordered them to build a temple to house the statue; Iphigeneia was to be its priestess, but was to give up the barbarous custom of human sacrifice.

In another version of the end of this story, the statue was taken not to Brauron but to Sparta. Here it was the centre of a bloodthirsty annual festival: instead of human sacrifice, Spartan boys volunteered to be flogged beside it each year, and to drench it with their blood. The contest was one of bravery and endurance, and the boys vied with each other to see who could bear most blows.

KLYTEMNESTRA AND AIGISTHOS
(*page 202*)

In some accounts, Klytemnestra hated Agamemnon long before the sacrifice of Iphigeneia (see page 201). She was originally the wife of King Tantalos of Pisa (Agamemnon's cousin, great-grandson of the Tantalos who outraged the gods). When Agamemnon became king of Mycenae he made war on Pisa, killed Tantalos and forcibly married his widow Klytemnestra. For years afterwards Klytemnestra nursed revenge.

It would never have occurred to Aigisthos that Klytemnestra hated Agamemnon and planned to kill him; but another Greek king, Nauplios, suggested to him that he should make himself Klytemnestra's lover and steal Agamemnon's throne. (Nauplios had a grudge against the Greek commanders at Troy, because of the execution of his son Palamedes: see page 171. He repaid them by visiting all the queens of Greece, telling them that the Trojan war was lost and their husbands dead, encouraging them to make new marriages, and then gleefully waiting for the war to end and the real husbands to come

home.) The gods tried to warn Aigisthos that if he became Klytemnestra's lover he would one day die for it; but Aigisthos had inherited the love of money and power from his father Thyestes and uncle Atreus, and took no notice.

KASSANDRA (*page 202*)

In the version of the story used by Aeschylus in his play *Agamemnon*, one of the captives Agamemnon brought from Troy was the prophetess Kassandra (see page 33). She refused to enter the palace, and warned Agamemnon that he would walk the crimson pathway to his death. But Agamemnon ignored her – it was Kassandra's fate always to speak the truth and never to be believed – and after he was murdered Klytemnestra butchered Kassandra with the other prisoners.

ORESTES' BONES (*page 207*)

Orestes' burial-place (like the grave of King Arthur in the myths of another country and a later time) was unknown. Some said that he left Mycenae, ruled for a time in Arcadia, and then went to found colonies on the islands of Lesbos and Tenedos: the people there certainly honoured him as the founder of their race. Another account says that he was buried at Tegeia, and the Delphic oracle later ordered the removal of his bones from there to Sparta. (Nevertheless, although the bones buried in Sparta were impressive – the skeleton of a warrior 2.5 metres tall – there was never any proof that they belonged to Orestes.)

SOME · BOOKS
TO · READ

This is a selection of particularly enjoyable books and plays, both ancient and modern, which use Greek myths. Most libraries should have copies – and browsing through the Classics and Mythology shelves will lead to many discoveries not mentioned here. (For classical writers, we recommend the translations in the *Penguin Classics* series or the *Loeb Classical Library* published by Heinemann). Dates and publishers are given for modern writers' works: these should be enough to help librarians or booksellers locate them in reference books such as *British Books in Print*.

GENERAL

For clear maps, beautiful photographs and well-written information about Greece, one of the best books is *Atlas of the Greek World* by Peter Levi (Phaidon 1980). A plain account of Greek mythology, set against the myths of other nations (eg India, China, Scandinavia), and magnificently illustrated, is *The world's mythology in colour* by Virginia Ions (Hamlyn 1974). *The Greek myths* by Robert Graves (Penguin 1955) tells the stories in full detail, and also gives many pages of explanation and comment, showing how the myths came into exist-

ence and what they meant to the ancient Greeks themselves. Some scholars have complained about parts of Graves' book, but nevertheless, for anyone who enjoys Greek myths, it is an essential, exciting read.

CHAPTERS 1–8

Hesiod's *Theogony* (c 8th century B.C., one of the oldest of all surviving books) gives a complex but fascinating account in verse of the birth of the universe, and tells many myths about the gods. The *Homeric hymns* (c 8th century B.C.) are shorter poems (in a similar, rather old-fashioned style – they are to Greek literature what Anglo-Saxon poems are to English), each telling the myths about one particular god: Apollo, Demeter, Dionysos, etc. Aeschylus' play *Prometheus bound* (5th century B.C.), set on Mount Caucasus during Prometheus' punishment, uses the myths of Prometheus and of Io. (The English poet Shelley, 24 centuries later, wrote a sequel, *Prometheus unbound*.) Euripides' play *The Bacchae* (5th century B.C.) tells of the coming of Dionysos-worship to Thebes, and the fate of those like Pentheus who opposed it.

CHAPTERS 9–12

Metamorphoses (1st century B.C.), by the Roman writer Ovid, is a witty, readable retelling of dozens of myths about mortals who met the gods and were changed by them into something else (usually animals or plants). Pausanias' *Guide to Greece* (2nd century A.D.) painstakingly describes each place he visited, and recounts the local myths. It is long (and long-winded), ideal for browsing in, or for taking along, together with a modern guide-book, when you travel in Greece yourself. Aeschylus' play *The Suppliants* (5th century B.C.) uses the myth of Danaos and his daughters.

CHAPTER 13

Apollonius' *The Argonauts* (3rd century B.C.) tells the story of Jason's quest for the golden fleece, and the same story is told from a modern point of view in Robert Graves' novel *The golden fleece* (Cassell Ltd, 1944). Euripides' play *Medea* (5th century B.C.) is about Medea's vengeance in Corinth when Jason deserts her to marry Glauke; Henry Treece's novel *Jason* (Bodley Head, 1961) deals with many of the same events.

CHAPTER 14

The story of Herakles has attracted surprisingly few great writers: a pity, as the events of his life would make a magnificent saga, along the lines of Homer's *Odyssey* or Apollonius' *The Argonauts*. Hesiod's poem *The shield of Herakles* (c 8th century B.C.) deals with his birth and early life; Euripides' play *Herakles the madman* (5th century B.C.) is about his first bout of madness when he attacked his children; Sophocles' play *The women of Trachis* (5th century B.C.) concerns his marriage to Deianeira and his death. Herakles is a larger-than-life character in Euripides' tragi-comedy *Alcestis* (see page 214), and two lively comedies, Plautus' *Amphitryon* (3rd century B.C.) and Giraudoux' *Amphitryon 38* (1929), tell of Zeus' attempt to seduce Alkmena by disguising himself as her husband Amphitryon – the event which led to Herakles' birth.

CHAPTER 15

Mary Renault's novels *The king must die* (Longman 1958) and *The bull from the sea* (Longman 1962) tell Theseus' story in absorbing detail. Euripides' play *Hippolytos* (5th century B.C.) is about Phaidra's tragic love for Hippolytos. The story of Daidalos has inspired many books and works of art: the 20th-century British artist Michael Ayrton, for example, made a golden honeycomb and several sculptures of Minotaurs and bull-leapers, as well as writing a complex novel called *The maze-maker* (Longman 1967).

CHAPTER 16

The story of Thebes has been told in more forms than almost any other. Some of the best are Sophocles' plays *King Oedipus* and *Antigone* (both 5th century B.C), Aeschylus' play *Seven against Thebes* (5th century B.C), Cocteau's modern play *The infernal machine* (1934), Henry Treece's novel *Oedipus* (Bodley Head 1964), and Anouilh's modern version of *Antigone* (1944).

CHAPTER 17

Homer's *Iliad* (c 8th century B.C.) thrillingly recounts the parts of the Trojan

274

myth concerned with Achilles, from his quarrel with Agamemnon to his death. Virgil's *Aeneid* (1st century A.D.) tells of the wooden horse, the fall of Troy and the later adventures of Aeneas and his followers as they escape to new homes in Italy. An amusing modern play, Giraudoux' *Tiger at the gates* (or *The Trojan war won't happen*) (1935) is set among the bickering Trojan leaders during the battle, just as Shakespeare's play *Troilus and Cressida* (1603) is set among the squabbling Greeks. Several episodes from the story are treated separately: for example, Sophocles' plays *Philoktetes* and *Aias* (both 5th century B.C.) tell the stories of those heroes; Euripides' play *The Trojan women* (5th century B.C.) is about what happened to the prisoners after the city fell.

CHAPTER 18

One of the most enjoyable of all Greek books, Homer's *Odyssey* (c 8th century B.C.) tells the full story of Odysseus' wanderings and of his battle against the suitors. Robert Graves' novel *Homer's daughter* (Cassell Ltd 1955) is about how the *Odyssey* came to be written – and contains some surprising ideas, for example that 'Homer' was a woman. The modern Greek writer Nikos Kazantzakis also wrote an *Odyssey* (Secker & Warburg Ltd 1959), relating Odysseus' adventures after his homecoming in Ithaka.

CHAPTER 19

Most writers about Tantalos and his descendants have concentrated on the events at Mycenae surrounding Klytemnestra's murder of Agamemnon and her own murder by Orestes. Aeschylus' set of three plays *The Oresteia* (5th century B.C.) tells this story magnificently, and both Sophocles and Euripides wrote plays called *Electra* (both 5th century B.C.) centred on Elektra's and Orestes' revenge. Sartre's modern play *The flies* (1943) and Henry Treece's novel *Electra* (Bodley Head 1963) deal in quite different ways with these same events.

275

FAMILY · CHARTS

THE COMING OF THE GODS

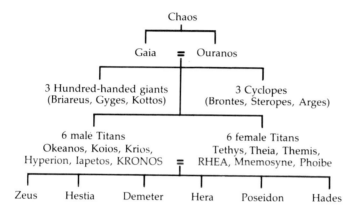

THE FAMILY OF AIAKOS

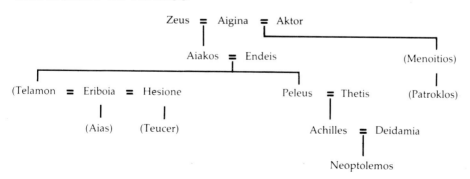

PERSEUS' FAMILY TREE

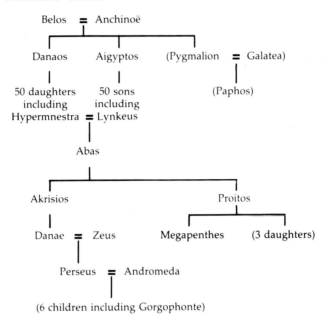

SISYPHOS' FAMILY TREE

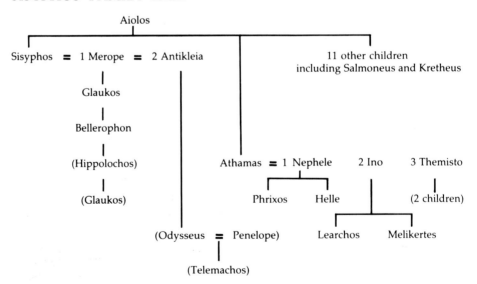

JASON'S FAMILY TREE

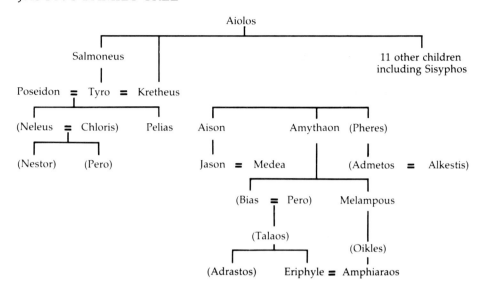

HERAKLES' FAMILY TREE

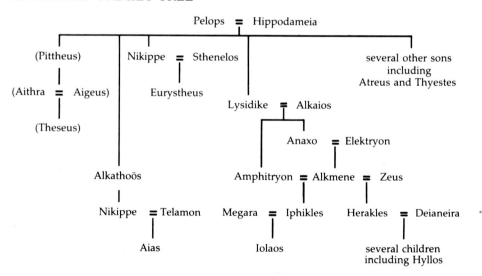

THESEUS' FAMILY TREE

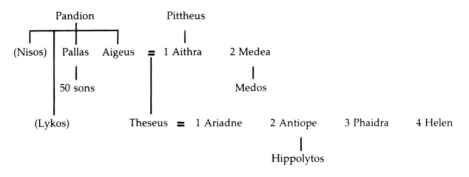

THEBAN FAMILY TREES

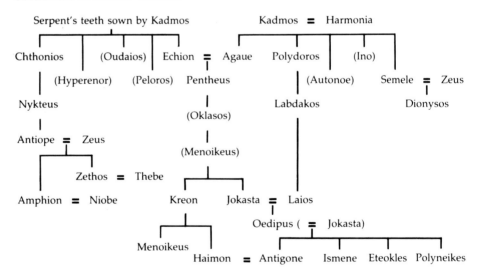

ODYSSEUS' FAMILY TREE

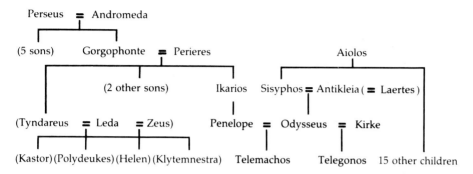

Note: Some versions of the myth, including Homer's *Odyssey*, say that Odysseus' father was not Sisyphos, but King Laertes of Ithaka, who married Antikleia at about the same time as she was raped by Sisyphos

TANTALOS AND HIS DESCENDANTS

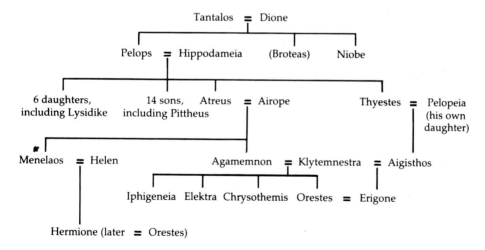

281

INDEX

Names in brackets are alternative spellings.
Numbers in bold type indicate
the main myths about the characters.